L. S. L. No 470

A STEP

FROM

THE NEW WORLD TO THE OLD,

AND

BACK AGAIN:

WITH

THOUGHTS ON THE GOOD AND EVIL IN BOTH.

BY

HENRY P. TAPPAN.

VOL. II.

NEW-YORK:
D. APPLETON AND COMPANY,
200 BROADWAY, & 16 LITTLE BRITAIN, LONDON.
M.DCCC.LII.

Entered, according to Act of Congress, in the year 1852, by
HENRY P. TAPPAN,
In the Clerk's Office of the District Court for the Southern District of New-York.

ERRATA.

Vol. I. p. 48, line 4 from the top, for *reputation* read *repetition.*
" p. 267, line 8 from the bottom, for *bespeak* read *bespoke.*
Vol. II. p. 34, line 10 from the bottom, dele *much* before *dazzling.*
" p. 51, line 15 from the bottom, for *then* read *there.*
" p. 52, line 2 from the bottom, for *breaks* read *break.*
" p. 74, line 1 at top, for *view* read *vine.*
" p. 76, line 3 from top, for *arrayed* read *arranged.*
" p. 82, line 5 from bottom, for *their* read *these.*
" p. 99, line 8 from top, for *toon* read *tour.*
" p. 133, line 3 from top, for *western* read *water.*
" p. 158, line 15 from bottom, for *begun* read *began.*

VOL. II.

THE RHINE, SWITZERLAND, BELGIUM, AND FRANCE.

CONTENTS OF VOL. II.

I.

The Lower Rhine.

THE Maase or Meuse at Rotterdam, the Waal—so called above the junction with the Meuse as far as Pannerden—the Ligne, the Leck, the Old Rhine at Leyden, the Vecht at Utrecht, the Yssel that flows past Zutphen and thence to the Zuyder Zee, what are these but the Rhine itself, which having received the waters of a multitude of tributaries, finds the ocean through the mud and sand of Holland—mud and sand which it has itself there deposited? Its sources are in the Alps. The avalanches and the glaciers feed the lakes and streams of Switzerland. These find their outlet in the mighty Rhine—the king of rivers—holding its course nearly a thousand miles through the fairest and richest fields of Europe, its banks crowded with cities and towns, or rising into vineclad hills—an historic and a "wizard stream" beyond all others—navigable for six hundred miles from Basil to the sea, it quietly loses itself in the ocean in sluggish and meandering streams. The river is called the Lower Rhine from Cologne or Köln to its mouths, a distance of three hundred miles. The country on either side is low, and in many cases the dykes which protect it from inundations are so elevated that but little prospect can be gained from the low steamers which ply upon this river.

At Amsterdam we took the train for Arnheim, passing through Utrecht. The same rich cultivation prevailed, and many villas embowered in trees came into view. As we approached Utrecht, the country became somewhat more elevated and the flat lands were left behind. The morning had been hazy, but when we reached Arnheim, we had a glorious sunshine, and the temperature was delightful. The country about Arnheim is very pleasing. In full view of the Station House, Hartzerberg, the seat of a Baron, spreads out its lawn of brilliant verdure tastefully diversified with trees. The mansion is not exceedingly large, and is quite simple in its effect. The whole attracted my fancy by the quiet good taste which seemed to predominate, and a cheerful homelike air. But every thing appeared cheerful this day: I had reached the Rhine, I was about to ascend it—the glories of the Rhine and of Switzerland were before me—the dreams of many years were about to be realized.

Above the Station House, in the second story, was an excellent Restaurant with a large and well-furnished saloon connected with a piazza. Here we ordered our dinner. In an adjoining room was a band of music playing many beautiful airs. The serene day, the presence of the Rhine, the river of story and of song, the sound of the German tongue on every side, the music, the exquisite exhilaration arising when expectation is about to grasp its object, all combined to produce a state of feeling which is too delicate and complex to admit of description, but which when once experienced can never be forgotten, and the moments are afterwards recalled as moments in which the very sense of life was luxury.

Imagination indeed made the sky brighter, the verdure fresher, the spot more romantic, the music sweeter, removed commonness from common men and common things; and, perhaps, from ordinary materials made a beautiful picture for herself by scattering profusely over every thing colors of her own. But do we not always half create the beauty which seems to surround us, and breathe from our own souls the melody which seems to enchant our ear?

The steamer, through some accident, was delayed several hours beyond the appointed time. Passengers were collected in the steamboat office, some seated on chairs, some on trunks, while others were pacing along the wharf chattering and smoking, and endeavoring to wear away the weary time. To me, however, as all was novelty, so nothing was wearisome. At length, over the land in front of us, a little wreath of smoke was seen in the distance; but so numerous are the turns of the river, that it was a considerable time before the pipe came into view, and still a good while ere the low, long, narrow and dark thing came puffing up to the wharf as if tired out with tugging against the current. And so we got aboard amid a promiscuous company, chiefly Hollanders and Germans. The bow of the boat was appropriated to a crowd of the peasantry who had probably descended the Rhine on rafts, and were now returning home to the Duchy of Nassau, where most of the rafts are launched. They were dressed in *blouses*, with wooden shoes on the feet, and little caps on the head, from under which straggled long locks, generally light colored, and many of a perfect flaxen hue. Each man, too, had his pipe. The pipe was evidently a matter of pride and ornament, as well as comfort, and appeared in every variety of fantastic form. Some were sitting some reclining, some collected in groups talking. There was little of frolicksomeness among them. They seemed rather to be enjoying the repose of the return voyage, and had a meditative air while sending forth clouds of smoke from the constantly employed pipe. I observed, too, now, as well as afterwards, that the German peasantry, both men and women, have a care-worn, anxious and depressed expression. They have strongly marked and intelligent faces, they are very civil and obliging in their manners; but they appear like beings who seldom know pleasure, whose lives are an unintermitted toil which yields them little, —a hard struggle for a bare subsistence—a life of stern experience without any hope of brighter days—an inexorable necessity. Can their thoughts find relief except in theories of socialism, dreams of revolution, or possibilities of emigration?

The stern of the boat was occupied by passengers of a widely different description. Here were well-dressed people of both sexes and all ages, full of sociability and hilarity. Many of them were ascending the Rhine on pleasure excursions to the watering-places and to Switzerland. Here, too, smoking was universal among the men; generally cigars, not fine

Havanas, but made of Dutch tobacco, and to me not very agreeable. I had some Havanas with me, and so I lighted one to make an atmosphere for myself: as the trappers on the prairies fight fire with fire, so I fought tobacco with tobacco. There were also bottles of bright Rhenish wine plentifully scattered about.

When I went below, I found the saloon filled with men and women taking coffee. Here also smoking was going on. There was no compunction whatever in smoking in the presence of the fair sex; and the fair sex seemed to experience no inconvenience from it. It was an established custom which the lords of creation had made. Whatever rebellion there may have been at its first institution, this rebellion had died away in past generations, and tobacco-smoke was now universally accepted as an essential element of the social atmosphere.

Steamboats on the Rhine are not "floating palaces" like those on the Hudson, and have no accommodations for sleeping. Hence at night the passengers go ashore at some of the towns. This is all the better, for there are some parts of the Rhine where it would be almost a sin to go to sleep; and to a stranger all the towns have something worth seeing. Our stopping-place for the night was Emmerich, the first Prussian town. We ought to have reached here at sunset, but owing to the delay above mentioned it was eleven o'clock at night before we were moored at the wharf. We however had lost nothing as to scenery. At Emmerich the Custom-house officers boarded us. How the others fared I did not pause to see, but for myself I began at once to unlock my trunks, when one of the officers, just glancing at the contents of a trunk, allowed me to proceed no farther, saying it was sufficient, expressing to another officer at the same time, in an under tone, his satisfaction at my readiness.

It was midnight ere our weary limbs were stretched out for repose. Scarcely had we sunk into that disturbed sleep which follows a day of excitement, when some one thundered at our door; it was four o'clock, and the steamer would be off at five. Oh, the agony of that getting up! The cathedrals of Cologne and Strasburg, the Drachenfels, Ehrenbreitstein—the glorious Rhine—the glorious Alps—all sunk into insignificance in the intense longing to lie still and sleep. With eyes half open, muttering dissatisfaction, quarrelling with fate, we dragged our reluctant steps on board. But when the steamer began again to stem the current of the Rhine, and the fresh morning air to play upon our faces, the mists of night, too, began to vanish from our spirits, and the sense of pleasurable existence to revive. Then as we wound our way through the rich verdant champagne, where villas and towns were rushing into view, attention grew fully awake, the charm of novelty again exerted its power, and we felt that indescribable emotion which every imaginative traveller must experience when he exclaims to himself for the first time, I am ascending the Rhine!

It was not long before the passengers were seen arranging themselves in groups, or sitting solitarily by little tables on the deck, where coffee and bread and butter, and, in some instances, other viands, were served according to each one's fancy. Coffee and bread and butter was the common breakfast. With the coffee, conversation revived. As each one took his cup of the delightful beverage, and stirred it with the spoon and sipped, the eye brightened, an air of comfort and satisfaction spread over the countenance, over the whole man; and the nervousness of slumber untimely broken, and the fretfulness of the hurry of getting on board which had been universal, and which the morning air and the Rhine had not dissipated in many who were not very sensitive to the one, and found no novelty in the other, now yielded to this nectar. The change was instantaneous and marvellous, and the currents of Low Dutch and German were pleasantly running together, until the conversation became like the babbling of brooks running over smooth stones and through green meadows. Those who did not fancy the morning air took to the saloon below; and thus above and below the same revivification was in progress.

After the coffee and bread and butter had been disposed of, smoking recommenced. Each one did his best. Was it the smoke of the steamer's pipe, or the smoke of our pipes and cigars that streamed behind through the air? I again in pure self-defence lighted my Havana; and getting into conversation with a group of Hollanders and Germans where Low Dutch and High Dutch seemed to be mutually intelligible, and which I intermingled in a strange jargon, I passed around my Havanas to enlarge the circumference of a more fragrant atmosphere. I was charmed with the universal sociability, and talked away, hit or miss. At first I was taken for an Englishman; but I found, both then and ever afterwards, that I gained a hundred per cent. in the good will and kind offices of my fellow-travellers by letting out that I was an American. America—the land of freedom, and the new home of so many thousands of their countrymen—is a theme of the liveliest interest to the German people. With the Hollanders I claimed a common nationality. "Ah! and what is your name?" said they. "My name," I replied; "oh, may-be you will not own that: my ancestor was a Belgian, or perhaps a French Huguenot who emigrated with the Dutch from Holland to America; but on my mother's side, at least, I am pure Dutch; her name was De Witt." "Oh yes," said they; "we still have that name in Holland." And thus we drew still more closely together.

As the day advanced, bottles of Rhenish wine were brought up. There was universal hilarity and good-fellowship. There was nothing drunk stronger than light Rhenish wine, and this was not taken to excess. No one that drinks the native unadulterated wine becomes intoxicated; at least, I never saw a drunken man in the whole Rhine country. The elderly Scotch gentleman who had kept us company since we landed at Rotterdam, seeing every body drinking Rhenish wine, said to me, "I believe I will get a bottle, and try what kind of stuff it is." After he had taken a glass or two with quite a dubious expression of countenance, he paused and meditated a few moments; "Och!" he then exclaimed, "there is mair virtue in ane glass o' Scotch whiskey than in a bottle o' this."

Our dinner was served on the deck, over which an awning was stretched. Here I had the first specimen of a German dinner, consisting of a multitude of courses—the pudding being served about midway. Some of the courses were simply vegetables. Judging from the number of courses, the eating was immense; but then it must be recollected that the same viands which we jumble into one course, were here kept distinct; and that the expectation of many courses had begotten a sort of habitual calculation as to the quantity to be taken of each course, so that none but a stranger would be in great danger of exceeding the bounds of temperance. As I had heard of German dinners, I hope I exercised a proper caution. One of the courses was *sour krout*, a friend of my early life, long neglected and almost forgotten. In renewing my acquaintance I cannot say that the old relish returned.

The scenery of the Lower Rhine presents no natural objects of striking interest. The guide-books, therefore, advise the traveller to avoid this part of the navigation, and to take the steamer at Bonn. Once, however, if not from Rotterdam, yet certainly from Arnheim, every one ought to ascend the Rhine, or ought to descend the same portion of it. One cannot form an adequate impression of the majestic river, without seeing it winding through the low countries as well as rushing through the mountain gorges above. I think the ascent is to be preferred to the descent, since it is the natural order to go from the plains to the mountains—from the beautiful to the sublime.

The Lower Rhine, too, is rich with historical associations. There are many localities of course which have a peculiar interest, such as Kaiserswerth—an island which was once the seat of the German emperors, and certain battle-fields and fortresses; but, to my mind, the plains of the Rhine had a solemn grandeur collectively, as the great scene over which the generations of the mightiest nations from the Romans downwards had swept and passed away like the inundations of the river. Here kingdoms and empires had been lost and won. What displays of human passion and strength had here been made! These fair fields, spread out by the hand of nature for peaceful cultivation and the abode of happy multitudes, had been trampled over innumerable times by armed hosts: was there a spot which had not been stained by human blood! And the great river ever flowing on was there the perpetual witness: the murmur of its waters touched my ear like the voice of centuries.

On the Lower Rhine we had an opportunity of contemplating a floating village—I mean a raft of logs some six or eight hundred feet long by two hundred and fifty broad, with eight or ten houses made of boards scattered over it. It was inhabited and navigated by some five hundred men, besides women and children. There were pigs and poultry and a butcher's stall also on board; and the women were engaged in spinning, sewing, and knitting. Many long sweeps were attached to it fore and aft, by which it was managed. A number of little boats fastened and floating behind showed that the island could at pleasure communicate with the shore. These logs had been collected from many distant hills and mountains; and, floated into the Rhine by different tributaries, were there united into one huge structure, and then brought down to be sold in Holland. The voyage sometimes occupies several weeks.

We at first thought of proceeding as far as Cologne with

the steamer; but reaching Düsseldorf only a little before sunset, we concluded to stop there. We put up at the Breidenbacker Hof, where, obtaining very pleasant accommodations, we remained several days.

The morning after our arrival we were attracted to the window by strains of very sweet but mournful music. It was a funeral procession following the bier of a youth, a member of the gymnasium, and the music was a funeral hymn sung by his companions. I never witnessed any thing more mournfully beautiful and affecting.

Düsseldorf is a good specimen of a German town. The Altstadt, which we entered from the Rhine, is unpleasant, consisting of narrow and rather filthy streets. But the other two quarters, Carlstadt and Neustadt, are handsomely built and exceedingly neat. The public gardens about Düsseldorf are beautiful. The *Hofgarten*, the principal one, is considered one of the finest in Germany. It is filled with dense groves, and is cut in every direction by charming drives and walks. It extends to the bank of the Rhine, where, from an elevation similar to a *bluff*, an extensive view is obtained up and down and beyond the river. The Düssel, a small river which here empties into the Rhine, skirts it, on whose farther bank are spread soft green meadows. These grounds are never invaded by the spirit of improvement. The town is quite large, containing between thirty and forty thousand inhabitants, and appears to be increasing: but the new buildings are erected without the garden. Here the people congregate after dinner, walking or sitting, or smoking, and drinking coffee at the restaurant situated on a mound in the centre of the garden.

The Germans live much in the open air, and appear to enjoy far more leisure than we do. Their pleasures are unexpensive, simple, and innocent.

Düsseldorf contains a large garrison. Military parades are frequent, and the military bands fill the town with music. In Prussia all the males, who are not exempted by ill health or personal defects, are compelled to serve in the army one year at their own charges, or three years at the public expense. Those who serve at the public expense are provided with soldier's clothing, and receive daily a ration of black bread and two and a half groschen, or about six cents of our money. In this case, they must in part support themselves, as it is hardly possible that they can live on the allowance of the government.

Düsseldorf has within a few years become a familiar name to us through the gallery of fine paintings collected in New York, and known as the Düsseldorf gallery. We have in this gallery some of the best paintings of the Düsseldorf school. The famous gallery of paintings now in Munich was removed from Düsseldorf in 1805. The Düsseldorf school was established long after this, in 1828, by Cornelius, a native of the town. In his studio the first artists of this school were formed. The artists who are now quite numerous, occupy a palace built by one of the electors. In historical and landscape painting this school has unquestionably attained eminence The annual exhibition which was open during our visit, contained many pieces of merit. There was here a series of drawings in crayon, by a Norwegian, so extremely beautiful that I cannot forbear giving a brief description of them.

They represent the course of human life. In the first a shepherd boy barefooted and bareheaded, with a hale rustic air, is playing on a pipe with all the earnestness of his soul. Beside him sits a gentle girl with downcast eyes. She is employed in knitting, but her soul seems absorbed by some inexpressible thought. They appear to be a mystery to themselves. A sentiment is working in them which they cannot explain, of which they dare not speak. He can only play upon his pipe, commanded by a delicious inspiration which comes he knows not how, only that the form beside him and the music seem to be one, and her name is the only song which his thoughts fit to the air. And she can only sit and knit, and hear in silence, while the soul of the musician is strangely entering her soul through the music, and she feels in mingled confusion and delight that he is reading a secret of her heart. This picture represents the first sense of love. In the second picture love has come to understand itself, and has found words in which to express itself. The boy and girl are ripened into early manhood and womanhood. The years of inexpressible and delightful torment melt into the exquisite pleasure of telling the tale of love. He speaks, she hears and replies by the yielding hand, and by looks of innocent and rapturous affection. This is the betrothment.

In the third picture is a rustic church, and a bridal procession is entering the portal. How beautiful and natural the expressions which beam in the faces of the happy pair! Hopes realized, joy overflowing, brighter hopes awakening, more tender joys in store, pure delight as of an opening heaven without a dream of sorrow!

In the fourth picture love has borne its first beautiful fruit, and father and mother are gazing upon the infant in a cradle.

In the fifth picture comes the first sad experience of life—the parents are hanging in speechless anxiety over the sick child.

In the sixth picture, is a quiet family scene—the mother is teaching two little girls to read and knit. In the seventh, the father is teaching his boy a trade—they are hammering out a bar of iron together upon an anvil. In the eighth picture, the strong and hopeful youth is leaving his home to seek his fortunes in the world. The parents are full of sorrow as they bid adieu, and give their parting blessing. The youth with staff and knapsack is eager to depart, and appears hardly to sympathize with the grief he leaves behind.

The last of the series is called The Last Consolation. The boy and girl of the first picture have now become an aged man and woman. Again they are alone, and most dear of all the world to each other. They sit together reading the Bible with resigned and heavenly expressions. Earthly hope and activity are gone. They are quietly awaiting the call to depart.

There is so much character, force, and truthfulness in the whole, and such an exquisite moral tone, that the eyes of the beholder become suffused with tears.

I could describe many pictures which interested me, but the description of pictures is not apt to be interesting to others. If any one visiting Düsseldorf should find there still remaining the crayon sketches I have above described, I know full well that my estimation of them will be sustained. And there are two other pictures before which he will pause with unmingled delight. One is the Eve of St. Nicholas, where a mock St. Nicholas enters among a group of children. Some of the children are quite terrified, and endeavor to hide themselves, overturning chairs and tables in their flight; others are partly terrified and partly pleased; while others again have quite a composed air of boldness: surprise, fright and pleasure are all expressed together; the cheat is half suspected, and yet credulity half prevails.

The other picture speaks still more to the child's heart which never wholly dies within us. Here the gifts of St. Nicholas are examined on the morning after his visitation. It is a scene in humble life. The mother is seated with a well-grown baby on her lap, whose eyes are filled with wonder and delight, noticing every thing with dawning intelligence. A girl stands by the mother's side all absorbed in a doll. A little way off is a chubby-faced boy blowing his trumpet with distended cheeks, and eyes starting out of his head, regardless of every thing around him. On the other side of the mother, and between her and the grandmother, stands the eldest boy, crying with the most perfectly disappointed and woe-begone countenance—he has received only a bundle of whips. The father stands behind the mother contemplating the scene with a half smile and a knowing expression. The mother looks grave, but it is an assumed gravity—something evidently is behind the scenes. The whole is explained by looking at the grandmother, who, stopping her wheel for a moment, is just beginning to pull the elbow of the blubbering boy, while a pair of new shoes peep from under her apron. I love these subjects taken from simple natural life; they carry us back to what we were; they make us feel what we are; and they restore to us some of our lost humanity.

Our table d'hôte at the Breidenbacker Hof was excellent. Here I became fully initiated into the peculiarities of the German *cuisine*. The courses were more numerous and elegant than on board the steamer, which was but a miniature of the hotel. If there were dishes not agreeable to every taste, there was ample room for selection. At every plate stood a small bottle of light Moselle wine. If wine of a finer quality was desired, it was called for.

The company at the table varied from day to day, and was always well-bred, and sometimes high-bred. There always reigned a charming ease, and pleasant sociability. There were no airs of pretension, no attempts to appear consequential, no studied looks of dignity, no fidgety anxiety to seem to be *somebody*. All Germans are remote from all this. Simplicity is an element of their character. All truly well-bred people of all nations have none of it. There is a certain class of English and Americans who are full of it. This class have no desire to pass for exactly what they are; they wish to surround themselves with a certain indefinite and mysterious greatness. If they have plenty of money to spend, they will, at least, succeed in impressing the weight of their purse upon minds who have little regard to any thing else.

The proprietor of our hotel, a well-dressed and young-looking man of modest and polite manners, sat at table with his guests like one of them, and paid no attention to the serving. This was managed by the waiters very methodically, neatly, and quietly. These German waiters perfectly understood their business. One of them also made up the accounts, and received the money ; so that the proprietor, although he really was at the bottom of every thing and had an eye to every thing, appeared to the guests to be a gentleman at large.

The breakfast is a light meal in Germany—a cup of coffee and a roll of bread with or without butter, taken in your room or in the dining hall. The dinner-hour is one o'clock. After dinner it is customary to take a cup of coffee in the public garden, where you are served with the very best. Düsseldorf is celebrated for its bread. It is not made into loaves, but into small oval rolls about the size of a large apple. It is the finest bread I ever ate. Paris does not furnish any equal to it.

In one corner of the dining-room stood a table where the German newspapers were laid daily for the use of the guests. They were very small in size, and contained summaries of general news and bits of literature, but did not indulge much in political discussion. Germany is the land of books, but not of newspapers, contrasting thus strongly with our own country. While looking over these papers from day to day, I was naturally led into speculations about newspapers in general. Nothing so marks the difference between despotic and free governments. The former must guard newspapers as they would firebrands: to allow them to say what they please, and to have free circulation among the people, would produce a revolution. In our country, any one who pleases may set up a newspaper and publish what he pleases. While this right is preserved, our country must remain free. The unrestricted newspaper is the palladium of civil and religious freedom. We may laugh at kingcraft and priestcraft while we have this. The abuse of newspapers with us is self-conceit and demagoguism. Could high talent and education, manly independence, and pure patriotism and morality, always be enlisted in conducting them, they would be pure streams of light and life. But how often do we see men, who have only capital and adroit management, acquire, by editing a paper, a consequence and influence to which they are wholly unentitled. It is amusing and often disgusting to see a man of small capacity, when seated in an editor's chair, assume the airs of a Sir Oracle in politics, religion, social questions, and criticism. The demagoguism is one of the worst features. Such a paper panders to the multitude to make gain out of them; it enlists in the cause of a party with the spirit and aims which characterize all demagogues. It is the worst of all demagogues, too, because it occupies a taller stump, and speaks to a greater multitude. We have not in our country a greater interest than the establishment of newspapers and reviews as the vehicles of sound principles and good taste, and removed from the domination of sects and parties. I can conceive of a no more exalted position for a great and gifted mind than the editorship of such a publication. I can conceive of no field so ample and momentous for the exercise of the highest and holiest gifts.

Dr. Robinson and his family were our fellow-passengers in the Washington. We separated at the Isle of Wight. By a happy chance, we met again at the Breidenbacker Hof. He had left his family at Berlin, and was now on his way back to America previous to his journey to the Holy Land. Last December he sailed again for Germany on his way to the scene of his researches. A ripe, exact, and indefatigable scholar, he is an ornament to our country. May God prosper him, and bring him back in safety. I perceived in Düsseldorf that he was taken for a German. An early education in that country gives untold advantages.

We went together on Sunday to the *Grosse-Kirche.* It is a large building, plain and neat. On the walls, and along the front of the gallery, passages of Scripture are painted in a distinct character. The floor was sprinkled with white sand. The men and women sat apart. In the German churches the numbers of the psalms and hymns for the day are exhibited to the whole congregation on a placard beside the pulpit. The whole congregation united in singing these beautiful compositions. The music was solemn, sweet, and grand. Here music is cultivated by all; hence, all are prepared to sing with taste. I never was more impressed with church music as an expression of sublime devotional feeling. There was no attempt at an operatic display; it was purely sacred music. I was deeply affected by the whole worship; my mind was filled with thoughts of Luther and the glorious scenes of the Reformation. I said to myself, Germany must be dear to all Protestants. I felt that this people was my people—I was at home among them. Although little accustomed to the German as a spoken language, the enunciation of the preacher was so distinct and clear that I followed him very well; and I felt assured that a few months' residence in Germany would make me quite familiar with the language.

The sermon was an excellent one, and what we would call evangelical—the old Lutheran doctrine. The German preachers generally speak with a great deal of animation and fervor; but they have a decidedly preaching tone which is stereotyped among them.

After dinner I walked for a short time in the Hofgarten to see what the people were about. I found them here as on other days, taking their coffee and playing at dominos. All was quiet and decent as usual, but nothing that indicated the Sabbath particularly. Sunday in Germany is considered a day of relaxation as well as of worship. Our strict observance of the day had its modern origin with the Puritans. I believe we are right in considering it as the Holy Day. If the Puritans Judæized it to some extent, the rest of the Protestant world have erred on the other hand in conforming to the lax notions introduced by the Romish church. A multitude of holy days of mere human institution, are a poor substitute for the one Holy Day which God has appointed; which is not so frequent as to interfere with our necessary labors, and yet, which regularly occurring every seventh day, makes a solemn and grateful pause in our earthly pursuits, and brings us to sit a while at the gates of heaven. A holy Sabbath will make a holy church and a happy state.

It is but justice to the Germans to remark, that while the Sabbath is not kept so strictly with them, neither is it made a day of dissolute amusement. I walked about Düsseldorf in the evening, and I saw no drunkenness, heard no profanity, and witnessed no rowdyism.

In the course of my walk, I chanced, about the time of sunset to come upon a large Catholic cathedral, where a curious scene presented itself. On the outside, in a deep angle of the wall and open to the street, a mound of rough stones was piled up: on its top was planted a granite cross about eight feet high. It was evidently intended to represent Calvary. The cross was hung with bouquets and garlands. All over the mound tallow candles were stuck, which they were beginning to light. A rude railing surrounded the whole: on the outside the worshippers were kneeling. A stone in front of the mound bore the inscription, "Mission MDCCCLI." So I concluded that this was a Roman mission church, designed to collect the passers-by. But few were assembled as yet. At nine o'clock I went again to see what was going on. Two or three hundred were now kneeling on the pavement. The forest of tallow candles was flaring and smoking. A priest inside of the railing was reading prayers with great volubility and in a sing-song tone, while the people without responded with the same volubility and in a similar tone. The crowd was increasing continually. Men and women would approach, drop on their knees, cross themselves, and join at once in the responses. I stepped in among the crowd, and took off my hat; but the night air being rather cool, after a while I put it on again, when a woman came softly behind me and tipped it off my head. Fearful of taking cold, and not wishing to give offence, I walked away. It was no place for a Quaker, at least, to worship.

My obliging host invited me one day to make an excursion with him by railway to Benrath, a few miles from

Düsseldorf. It is a chateau built by the electors of Cleve and Berg. Murat occupied it when Grand Duke. It is now occupied by the king of Prussia on occasional visits. The building contains some apartments approaching to magnificence, but its general air is that of elegance and comfort. There are some fine paintings and frescoes also. The grounds are laid out with great regularity, and are too much in the French style to suit the freedom and ease of an English taste. The general effect, however, is to be admired. There were no inhabitants but an old man, who might be an old soldier, who conducted us through the apartments. When we went out we dropped some coins into his hand. I, partly through carelessness, and partly through ignorance of the exact value of the coins, happened to make a donation quite below what he expected and I suppose ordinarily received. As I walked away I heard him muttering, and turning around saw him holding my donation in his extended palm, soliloquizing to himself with an expression so comic, that I understood him at once and burst into laughter. There was no impatience, and no movement to obtain redress; he seemed to be amused at his own disappointed expectations. I went back of course, and corrected my mistake to his satisfaction.

The grounds were equally solitary. I saw only a boy, who was feeding two patriarchal and venerable looking storks. And what was he feeding them? He had in his hand a covered basket, from which he took out live frogs and cast them before the long-beaked and voracious birds. The poor frogs seemed instinctively to apprehend their fate, and hopped as fast as they could to get out of the way, but the storks were sure to grab them and swallow them down whole as quick as thought—*grab*, *cluck*, and they were gone. Then I thought that the storks represented the despots who sit upon thrones, and the frogs the people, and the boy the ministers of state,

II.

Something about Politics.

IT would be unjust to represent despotic governments, universally, in point of fact, by the boy feeding the storks, for there have been despots with great virtues, and who have not devoured the people; and there have been good ministers of state under despots. The history of despotic governments, however, is generally very much like this; and it cannot be denied that the tendency of such governments is to give the many as food to the few: the despots have it in their power to become the storks, and then the people must become the frogs, and then, too, the boy will be found to keep the frogs in a basket, to be served out as may be required.

The theory of a despotic government is very beautiful; but it is always attended with the fallacy of assuming that the monarch is gifted with a divine wisdom, power and goodness, and that his ministers are angels. But since the monarch is always a fallible man, and may be a very bad man; and even when a good man, must necessarily intrust the details of government to a multitude of subordinates who are liable to be ambitious, selfish, and oppressive, the chances of a wise and happy administration are clearly very few. If it be granted that in a country like Russia, where the people are semi-barbarous, a despotism is the only practicable form of government, then it were just to demand of such a government that it should employ its functions for meliorating the condition of the people, and preparing them for more liberal institutions, and a form of government less liable to abuse. But despotic governments always assume that they are the true and just form of government; and not only check every attempt at change within themselves, but also look with jealous eyes upon free institutions wherever found, and would, if they had the power, reduce all nations to their own granitic stratum. Who can doubt that the Czar of Russia is sternly fixed in the idea of an autocracy; that his policy is to check all liberal movements in Europe, and that the overthrow of all free governments would appear to him like a political millennium? That the kings and princes of Germany entertain the same sentiments is plain from the fact that, although under solemn obligations arising from express stipulations made before the battle of Waterloo, to grant to their subjects constitutional governments, they have ever studiously evaded the fulfilment, and will probably continue to do so until compelled to adopt a different course by the resistless combination of the people. In despotisms there is no tendency to change. All their natural influences, as well as their professed policy, is to perpetuate themselves. Their leading axiom appears to be that the people are for the government, and not the government for the people: the frogs were made to be eaten, and the storks, having the instinct and power, have a right to eat them.

It is a sad thing that princes will be so stolid and miscalculating, and instead of gracefully bestowing, and thus making themselves the objects of a people's gratitude, will obstinately withstand, until compelled to yield, at the risk of popular execration, and perhaps of absolute expulsion from their thrones. Nor can the German princes plead, in self-justification, that their subjects are not prepared for a more liberal form of government; for if there ever was a people prepared for such a change by intelligence, general education, and fine social and moral sentiments, the Germans are that people. But if they be not yet prepared for freedom, how is that preparation to be gained under the nurture of despotism? Shall we refuse to open the eyes of the blind because, unaccustomed to the light, it may prove too much dazzling for them? Or is it the best preparation for a future, indefinite, hypothetical vision to pursue measures which can serve only to perpetuate blindness?

A people will gain intelligence and advance in civilization through the necessary progress of mankind, in spite of the direct tendencies of despotism. Despotism, as such, can lead to freedom only by creating a terrible reaction against itself. Then freedom comes through the storm and desolation of revolution. Alas! alas! that we cannot bring in peaceably what humanity will sooner or later demand. The good pastor whom I heard preach on Sunday, thanked God in his prayer, that the storms which had so lately threatened the country had passed away. True, so it appeared; there were no longer any visible signs of storms: there were many thousands of troops in the garrisons; and the people were at work in the fields; the vines were growing upon the hills, and the rafts were floating down the Rhine. But were not the hearts of men the same? Discontent, thoughts, dreams, hopes, determinations, have chambers to dwell in which no police can enter. The outward forms of power may often succeed in breaking up the combinations of the people, and crushing nascent revolutions, but the people still live and think. The struggle that has been still lives in memory and in history; it remains a fact that there was a struggle between the people and the government—a struggle that had some meaning. The people failed—the government triumphed. But why? These speculations respecting the causes of failure are dangerous, and yet who can repress them? And these men will say to themselves: The government had old political experience and discipline; it had thousands of trained and skilful subordinates, from the ministers of state to the policeman; it had the money and the soldiers; it had its leaders all ready; it had alliances with other governments organized in like manner; and the people—what had they but their rough, bare hands? They could gain the consciousness of strength only by rude, and it may be, ill-directed attempts. They had to grope about to find a leader, and perhaps they did not find one. Partial and unsuccessful insurrections may be the necessary discipline for the great revolution. Nay, a great movement may fail only to bring about a more mighty concentration of popular energy. The Elector of Saxony, the Landgrave of Hesse, and the hopes of Germany once seemed all to go down together before the great Emperor: and yet the man and the hour of deliverance were then just getting ready.

I have heard the remark made again and again, that the failure of the revolutionary movement of 1848 demonstrated that the people of Europe were not prepared for a change in their institutions. But, can it be denied that whatever stolidity, ignorance, want of capacity for self-direction, and imbecility of purpose and action may be affirmed of them, were characteristics which had grown and ripened under despotism? Shall we reproach them with the degradation which had been ground into their souls by centuries of oppression? There was, surely, some merit in making an attempt to deliver themselves; it indicated some sense of their degradation, some relish for freedom; a wish, a hope, a purpose, however feeble, to reach a better condition. There was, therefore, some preparation for a better condition; an aspiration after freedom is the first taste of freedom, as an aspiration after virtue is the first taste of virtue. But there were causes not difficult to discern for the failure of the revolutionary movement of 1848, independently of any presumed unfitness of the people for free institutions. France was a constitutional government aiming, in the first instance, merely at the correction of certain abuses, and not at a revolution. The revolution was an accident, and not a purpose. Suddenly thrown into an unlooked for position, she was led astray by the mere name of a glory which had departed; and that name has now forced her into a despotism. It is a singular drama: beginning with a sort of comedy, in its progress it has become tragic; the catastrophe is yet to come. The revolution in Italy was repressed by the French and Austrians, co-working with the incapacity, if not the treachery of Carlo Alberto. The Hungarian cause, cankered by treachery within its own bosom, fell by the crushing force of Russia, and the supineness of England. The dawning confederacy of Germany melted into air before the spells of diplomacy. Had there been a power to back the cause of freedom, as Russia backed the cause of despotism, we should now be looking upon regenerated nations, instead of listening to the laments and appeals of exiled patriotism upon our own shores, in one of the most eloquent voices that ever gave utterance to the thoughts of a great and true soul.

There was such a combination of untoward events to change the fair promise into darkness and horror, that it takes the form of a fatality to a superficial vision; but to a deeper insight it is so marked and singular, that one cannot help believing that it is the womb of something more momentous than has yet appeared—perhaps the weeping which endures for a night preceding a morning of brightness, of joy, of triumph. The common thought, emotion, or purpose which passed through so many peoples, tongues, and languages, indicates a force which has not spent itself. After the first burst of the hurricane, there has come a lull, which the simple may flatter themselves is the calm which the storm leaves behind it when it has swept far away; but the observer of storms knows full well that it is but the momentary repose of the terror, which returning with ten-fold violence, will hurry to destruction whatever lies within its path.

Much, too, is said at the present time of "socialism," and "red republicanism;" they have become the watchwords of terrorists. Those who do not clearly comprehend their meaning, are the more affected by them; since an indefinable evil gives full scope to the imagination. Nay, I know not but many, even in our own country, are inclined to look upon the compound tyranny of Jesuitism and Napoleonism, as better than the compound *madness* of socialism and red republicanism. Let us have, say they, some system of order, although it be held together by iron chains, and be protected by bayonets, rather than a state broken up into warring fragments: the luxurious and elegant tyranny of Louis XIV. is better than the "Reign of Terror." But shall we forget that the elegant and luxurious tyranny produced the "Reign of Terror?" And who can deny that socialism and red republicanism are a similar reaction of humanity maddened by oppression? Indeed we shall preserve order if we can make our tyranny heavy enough to compress the turbulent elements: but, suppose our tyranny be not heavy enough, is it not plain that when an explosion takes place, it will be destructive in proportion to the previous compression?

Those are the authors of the evil who drive the people to the madness of despair. We shall now have fearful theories of human rights; and in the first battle for liberty, the furies will seem to have been let loose. Let me quote from Macaulay one of his fine and apt illustrations: "Ariosto tells a pretty story of a fairy, who, by some mysterious law of her nature, was condemned to appear at certain seasons in the form of a foul and poisonous snake. Those who injured her during this period of her disguise, were for ever excluded from participation in the blessings she bestowed. But to those, who, in spite of her loathsome aspect, pitied and protected her, she afterwards revealed herself in the beautiful and celestial form which was natural to her; accompanied their footsteps, granted all their wishes, filled their houses with wealth, made them happy in love, and victorious in war. Such a spirit is liberty. At times she takes the form of a hateful reptile. She grovels, she hisses, she stings. But woe to those, who in disgust shall venture to crush her. And happy are those, who, having dared to receive her in her degraded and frightful shape, shall at length be rewarded by her in the time of her beauty and glory."

The government of a state, like the government of an individual, reaches its highest form and condition when it becomes a self-government, wherein the first implies a participation in the act of government by all the members of the state, as the second implies the free participation and activity of all the personal functions.

A republic presumes the intellectual and moral exaltation of the people; and what it presumes, it fosters and advances more and more. A republic honors humanity by committing to free men the power of choosing their own legislators, rulers, and judges. It affirms the principle that where the rights of opinion and conscience are conceded, and the means of education provided, there is a stronger probability that the majority of a whole people will elect proper representatives and rulers, than that a hereditary monarch will be found in the regular succession competent to unite in himself the functions of legislator and ruler.

A despotism, on the contrary, presumes the intellectual and moral degradation of the people, and their total incapacity to govern themselves. And then it elevates one man, whom it assumes to have divine rights, and well-nigh divine gifts to control and guide the childish, unthinking, and rude masses. Proceeding upon the theory of the wisdom, excellence, and glory of the One, and of the ignorance, weakness, and meanness of the many, all its influences must legitimately go to give power, exaltation, and splendor to the One, and humiliation and bondage to the many. It must make good its own cause. It is a strange thing this—the One governing the many. But how can the One govern the many? Legitimately, as we have said, only, when the One possesses attributes approximating to the divine. And if such a One could be found among mankind, he could not be surely found always in one house, in one unbroken succession. Philosophers, wise men, good men, statesmen, poets, heroes, are not such by descent in a particular line: neither can kings—kings fit to govern absolutely, be such by natural descent. But there is one thing, a particular House—a particular line can get,—they can get power—*de facto*, the supreme domination;—they can get possession of the revenue and the control of the army; they can surround themselves with a host of dependent and interested subordinates; they can surround themselves with the state and prestiges of majesty to awe and subdue the multitude. If they have not possessed themselves of divine attributes, they have succeeded in infusing into the popular mind the sentiment that "divinity doth hedge a king;" until it has gained all the force of an ancient superstition. And to make this sentiment the more effective, the hierarchy and the monarchy join hands—the priest and the king work together. The priest enters into the conscience—the stronghold of the human soul, he enslaves the inner man, and gives him over to the king. The king, with the outward array of power, enforces the decrees of the priest over the outward man. The one has his crown, his sceptre, his sword, his Bastile. The other has his mitre, his crosier, his purgatory. Poor humanity—what a helpless victim art thou now! The Lord's anointed has his foot upon thy neck; the vicegerent of God has his terrors in thy soul.

Where the church and the state are thus wedded together, a revolution in the state must involve a revolution in the church. It was so in the French revolution—church and state went down together. And in France now, the re-composition of despotism involves the re-composition of the hierarchy.

I will not deny the possibility of the existence of the Roman church separately from the state, and its existence under a free government. Many priests were engaged in the late struggle for liberty in Italy. Roman Catholics were engaged in the Hungarian revolution; Roman Catholics are becoming republicans in the United States. It may even be possible for the Pope to be acknowledged as the head of the Roman church while no longer the head of the Roman state. But if such a change take place in the temporal relations of this church, a corresponding change in its ecclesiastical vitality is inevitable. The history of many centuries cannot be made light of; and conclusions are forced upon us. Men whose consciences were held by the priest have been most easily held by the grasp of the despot; then the priest was the most powerful when the sword of the state was at his command. This is the great fact of history. Now break this alliance in the struggle for civil liberty, and the conscience must also soon regain its freedom. The Roman church which embraces men of free consciences will not be the Roman church of the past. This is our conclusion.

Again, break this alliance, and temporal power and rewards will no longer dazzle the ambition of the hierarchy. The priest now can no longer sell men with enslaved consciences to the state. When the market is closed, he will no longer have a motive for furnishing the commodity. There may indeed be some private trade between priests and demagogues; but in the presence of civil and religious liberty, it can never rise above the stealth and infamy of a contraband affair. The priest now will bear the same comparison to the priest of old, that the demagogue does to the tyrant of old. The inevitable change in the character of the priesthood is another conclusion. And then when the Roman church is brought to stand upon its real merits, to be determined by free and enlightened reason and the Word of God, it must, in a spiritual point of view, either become more powerful by vindicating its claims in a legitimate way, or sink away into the bosom of a universal, that is, a truly catholic Christianity.

Now in accounting for the failure of the movement in

1848, and in estimating the difficulties to be overcome in any new attempt, it is plain that the resistance of the Roman church in its grand and governing powers must be calculated. The present condition of France, taken in connection with the intervention of France in the affairs of Italy, shows the force of this resistance. Does not the hierarchy understand its own position in relation to the state?

The march of the people will be onward for civil liberty, regardless of consequences? This is our right, they will say; if the church be for us, it is well; but if the church be against us, then let it take care of itself as it best can; we must have our right. It is fortunate for the church just now that the ultraism into which the people have been driven enables it to array itself on the side of order. Now it does not appear to be in conflict with civil liberty, but with the excesses of Socialism and Red Republicanism. But what are these Orders of the people—if you please to call them so—compared with the Orders of Dominic and Loyola? The church has had enough of bloody fanaticism to justify some toleration of fanaticism on the part of the people.

While speculating about the modification of European governments, the inquiry arises, Are the people prepared for a republican form of goverment, or is a limited monarchy best adapted to their character?

It is easier to pursue principles than to experiment upon forms of government. Any people may more safely contend for their rights than pass through many changes of government in order to see which is best adapted to them.

A people, too, who perceive and appreciate their rights,

and are willing to die in their defence, may be assumed to be prepared to enjoy them. In the full enjoyment of what is genial to its noblest faculties and convictions, the soul of man repairs all its moral defects, and consequently improves all its outward conditions, more rapidly and securely than when good is measured out to it in a stinted way, and in the constant endeavor to give it only what it is deemed capable of bearing. It is true of nations as well as of individuals, that it is better to rush out of the chamber of the valetudinarian, and enjoy sunshine, fresh air, and free motion, than to sit pining away in the vain attempt to live by the scale and the thermometer. The examples of the Swiss and the Hollanders lead to favorable conclusions respecting the capacity of the European people for self-government. The people of Germany, to say nothing about other parts of Europe, are not less intelligent than the Swiss and Hollanders. The fact to be deplored in the history of all attempts to establish free institutions in the Old World, is the intervention of foreign powers unfriendly to those institutions. Switzerland has been saved only by her mountains; England by her insular position. Holland is the victim of intervention. Hungary, Germany and Italy, have not been suffered to develope their instinctive tendencies from the same cause. We cannot pronounce authoritatively against purely republican institutions, where a fair experiment has never been permitted by the watchful might of despotism. France, I know, is ever held up as an example of futile republican experiments. But the truth is, no fair experiment has ever been made in France. From extreme despotism she rushed by an inevitable reaction into the extreme and destructive fanaticism of freedom. Then her turbulent elements were gathered into a magnificent despotism, which still, in some sort, expressed the will of the people. By the determined resistance of legitimacy led on by England herself, this new despotism, in the vigor of its aroused might, was led to overleap its bounds, until an accumulated flood of nations rushed back upon it, carried it away, and restored the stale ancient despotism. This gave way to a constitutional monarchy. This in turn fell before a mock republic, which has grown into a despotism, putting on the forms of the Empire. No republic has really yet been established in France. Have not the party of the legitimates, and other parties of a kindred cast, served but to stimulate the excesses of the democratic parties? Nothing but the breath of a rational constitutional freedom will ever heal the torn members of the state.

It is unjust to charge all public disturbances upon the people, and to hold them up as the only objects of dread. The people ask for their rights, and the party in power denies that they have any rights. Who are the disturbers of the public peace, those who desire justice, or those who deny it? Those who say, Give us constitutional liberty, or those who are determined to support the old order of things? O trust the people, cherish the people—for they, after all, make up the mass of humanity—and then all the generous sympathies of human nature will be called into exercise to bind together, to heal, and to diffuse fresh life through the body politic.

The question between a pure republic and a limited monarchy, is chiefly one of expediency. It is not a question to be determined in respect to the supposed rights of royal houses; for they have no rights that can claim a sacrifice of the rights of the people. The people are not for them, but they for the people. The opposite doctrine is the great heresy of despotism. Where a limited monarchy already exists, like that of England, the people possess the cardinal rights of representation, freedom of conscience and opinion, and trial by jury. Whatever abuses exist, can be corrected constitutionally, and without the convulsion of a revolution. The monarch is a hereditary chief representing the sovereignty of the state, but through the Commons dependent upon the people. It is a form of government upheld by old custom, and use, and yet one under which the people are free. Why then disturb it? Where despotic monarchies now exist, it would be expedient to have them wisely and quietly slide into constitutional monarchies, to prevent the violence and uproar and confusion of civil war. It might be expedient to choose this form of government, even where it could be determined by simple choice when the exposed position of a country, or the mixed character of its inhabitants, as in Hungary, or other circumstances, might require at once a more concentrated executive power. In the present state of Europe, it is expedient to aim to establish popular freedom by constitutional guarantees, without making the form an essential question. It is infinitely to be desired that princes and people would unite in the wise and unbloody work of remodelling the governments upon the basis of rational liberty. The princes still have it in their power to do so, and thus to bind the people to themselves by everlasting ties of gratitude. But the day may come unexpectedly when it will be too late. Then there will be darkness, dismay, and scenes of woe. Conceive of the French Revolution falling upon the whole continent of Europe. But when the thrones are all overturned, the atmosphere will at length become clear again, the institutions of freedom will arise under a more glorious sunlight, and humanity will vindicate its capacity for self-government.

III.

Cologne and its Cathedral.

FROM Düsseldorf we proceeded to Cologne by the railroad. The Roman *Colonia* of the Emperor Claudius and his wife Agrippina is here still in the modern Cologne. You seem at once to plunge into the bosom of antiquity. The marks of the Roman survive in ancient walls, altars, inscriptions, and coins; in the names of the streets, and in the very features and complexions of the inhabitants.

From Deutz we crossed the bridge of boats in an omnibus, with the great cathedral in full view. And then we rattled along through the crooked and narrow streets, between tall houses, and ever and anon in front of some old time-worn church.

Every thing speaks of the past; even the air seems heavy and murky with the dust of ages. Coleridge has put every traveller upon the *scent*, in entering Cologne, by his lines:

"Ye nymphs who rule o'er sewers and sinks,
The river Rhine, it is well known,
Doth wash your city of Cologne:—
But tell me, nymphs, what power divine
Shall henceforth wash the river Rhine?"

I, however, was agreeably disappointed in this respect; partly because the city is admitted to have improved in cleanliness since Coleridge wrote his lines, and partly too, I am constrained to confess, because long accustomed to the streets of New-York. The streets of New-York are wider than those of Cologne, and are visited by the sea-breeze; but the latter city, independently of these circumstances, must yield the palm to the former. With water all around us, and washed almost by the ocean itself, with fountains in every street, so abundantly fed that we might well nigh turn our pavements into the beds of rivers, in wet weather we have black, nauseous compost mud to wade through, and in dry weather our houses, our shops, our clothes, our ears, noses, eyes, mouths and lungs are filled with the same compost triturated to a fine powder, and blown about in every direction. And then, oh happy city of Cologne! thou hast thy fragrant *Eau de Cologne* to hide thy smells and comfort thy inhabitants. Between twenty and thirty manufactories are constantly engaged in producing this article. We have our fountains of Croton which we do not use, but every man, woman, and child in Cologne may carry about a bottle of the *Eau* as a corrective of the evil which the poet celebrates. Nay, the very sight of the shops, all professing by huge signboards painted with large characters to be the genuine successors and heirs of the far-famed *Jean Marie Farina*, is refreshing. In truth, the manufacturers of the *Eau de Cologne* are engaged in the good work of creating an odoriferous atmosphere over a spot where sewers and charnel-houses have for many centuries taken the place of the virgin freshness of nature.

It would be very difficult, if not impossible, for a stranger to collate all the authorities, so as to determine satisfactorily who is the genuine successor of the great Farina. Our coachman drove us to a shop which in his judgment was the true fountain of excellence. But the ladies, upon consulting Murray, decided that it was a counterfeit; and so, turning our backs abruptly upon the plausible shopkeeper and his thousand and one arguments, and rebuking the coachman for deceiving us, off we drove for the establishment opposite Jülichs Platz. Here, the proprietor spoke in scornful indignation of the pretensions of his rivals, affirming that they bribed the coachmen to lead strangers astray; and produced, as a conclusive testimony that he alone possessed the mystic art by due inheritance, a biographical sketch of Jean Marie Farina, with a history of the invention and its transmission from generation to generation. The air of triumph with which he produced this document, together with a plentiful sprinkling of the cambric handkerchiefs of the ladies from a bottle kept ready for the purpose, was absolutely overpowering. The ladies have ever persisted in believing that this is the best *Eau de Cologne* they have ever met with. I for my part, while I am quite ready to grant that there is none better, am inclined to suspect that the supposed superiority is imaginary, and that the other shops furnished very much the same article. However, it is well to satisfy the imagination also, and therefore I would rcommend visitors to go to the Jülichs Platz.

But the reader will be ready to ask, Did you not go to see the great cathedral, and was all your time spent in searching for the genuine *Eau?* O yes, we went to see the great cathedral first of all; and our search for the *Eau* was an incident by the way on our return.

The great cathedral of Cologne—methinks I see it still—it rises before me in my "mind's eye." We stood before its ancient front, with its two unfinished towers covered with the most delicate carving, as if the artist's hand had touched every spot. But the finger of time, too, has touched every spot, and the edges are rounded, the lines of beauty confused, and the forms marred by the crumbling away of fragments. The original material was not hard enough. But then it rises in its majestic proportions, the survivor of ages—its veil of beauty torn and blackened. Certain portions of the exterior which had become very much dilapidated, have been restored by masonry and sculpture which rivals the old in delicacy of execution; but the contrast of the new and the old has an unpleasant effect. The choir is the only part finished. Within the last ten years vigorous efforts have been made to carry forward the building, and the nave, the aisles, and the transepts are now all thrown open, so that a conception can now be formed of the vastness and the splendor of the interior. The towers which, in the original plan, are intended to be five hundred feet high, remain as they were left centuries ago, not half completed. The estimated expense of completing the whole building is about four millions of dollars. But the age for building cathedrals is past, and it would not be surprising if the work should again stand still.

As we entered at the front a *commissionaire* stood ready to lay hold upon us. Wishing to indulge my contemplations without the disturbance of impertinent descriptions and stories, I could not help replying to him somewhat sharply, Have I not got eyes to see? One of the greatest vexations attending you while visiting works of art, is the multitude of people who are ever thrusting themselves in your way with books to sell, or the offer of their services. It were gain to pay them the franc to get rid of them, but your pockets would be empty ere you had found the end of them. Look at the grand and beautiful in solitude and silence. Or if there be any one with you, let it be some one who can feel with you and keep silence with you. I would gladly have bought an hour or two of solitude and silence in the cathedral of Cologne. We enter: What are these! petrified trees of the ancient world! long avenues of them—a forest of enormous majestic trees! how they spring up towards the heavens—how gracefully they stretch out and interlace their branches! We cannot see the heavens through the thick shade they make overhead; but a soft and beautiful light plays around us: does it struggle through variously colored leaves touched by the hand of autumn? We hear distant music, very sweet and solemn. We advance, and now we see a flood of glory pouring down as from the opening heavens. The choir, one hundred and sixty-one feet high, its pillars and arches, its chapels, its stained windows, through which the light streams in such effulgence, breaks upon the eye with an effect almost supernatural. The whole interior is like the work of magic. I walked about as one entranced. Ideas of art were mingled with a sort of superstitious awe. There were historical associations, too. There was something in the simple thought that I was standing in the old and far-famed cathedral of Cologne. While my eyes were roving over the splendors of art, and my ears were drinking in the solemn music without noticing from whence it came —strains that seemed born in the very atmosphere—and silent thought was busy, the rush of complex emotions was delicious—it was an intoxication of the pure sense.

But after a while I got engaged with other sights which dashed these high emotions—there was a descent from the sublime to the puerile and ridiculous. Several priests in the choir before the high altar were performing the daily service. The vestments of the priests, the tawdry embellishments of the altar, the images, the boys with candles, the genuflections, the various motions, the rapid and monotonous tones, affected me in a way that painfully contrasted with the impressions produced by the noble structure itself. Was it the prejudice of education—was it bigotry? I could not feel that it was either. Had this been the ritual of the temple at Jerusalem, it would have been inappropriate; but it was not even that: it surely was not a ritual ordered by the Divine Author of our religion, for when he abrogated both Mount Gerizim and Mount Sion, he proclaimed, "God is a spirit, and they that worship him must worship him in spirit and in truth." The temple at Jerusalem had no image of the Almighty: the worship there ordained was the worship of an invisible spirit. The Parthenon on the Acropolis had a beautiful and majestic image of Minerva. A Jew visiting the Parthenon might have admired that glorious temple as I admired the cathedral of Cologne; he might have experienced similar delicious emotions purely æsthetical: but had he witnessed the ceremonial of the Parthenon, he might have shrunk back as I did in the cathedral, in the irrepressible conviction that the worship before him was sensual and not spiritual: the sublime homage of the soul to the Invisible was wanting.

As we and some other visitors were perambulating the aisles, the sacristan approached us and offered to show us the shrine of the Three Kings of Cologne, or the Magi who presented the infant Christ with gold, frankincense, and myrrh. This privilege, of course, had to be purchased by a certain fee. A small chapel behind the high altar was unlocked and we were ushered in. The chapel was lighted by lamps. The shrine is of considerable magnitude, made of silver plates and gilt. The workmanship is very curious. It is adorned with figures of the prophets and apostles, and with precious stones, and elegant cameos, some of which are antiques. Although many of the gems were sold when it was removed for safety to Westphalia during the French Revolution, it is still valued at more than a million of dollars. After walking around the shrine and admiring its various curiosities, we came in front of it, when the sacristan touched a spring, and three grinning skulls with gilt crowns were suddenly presented to view. They had a very clean and polished appearance, and each one bore a name inscribed in rubies. These names were *Gasper*, *Melchior*, and *Balthazar*—names I suppose as signed by tradition. An elderly French priest—a portly man, with a shrewd good-humored face, of polished manners, and quite a man of the world, notwithstanding his gown and skull-cap, was one of our party. It was his first visit to the shrine. Well, how did he act? Like a very sensible man: he took it all quite indifferently, and appeared to be about as much affected as I was myself. The good sacristan, evidently, was familiar with the relics; and having got his fee, *made no bones* about showing them to heretical eyes.

And these three skulls were plundered from the city of Milan, and presented to the Archbishop of Cologne by the Emperor Frederic Barbarossa, nearly a century before the cathedral was begun; and now they constitute the great glory of this august temple. And is this splendid work of art dedicated to preserve these three miserable skulls!

What man in his senses believes they are the skulls of the Magi—and if they were, what are they worth? Bury the skulls, sell the shrine, and build up the towers. But the benighted multitude are imposed upon: they must believe what the church affirms.

Here is one of the evidences that Roman Catholics are undergoing a change in the free air of our country: bring these skulls to St. Patrick's cathedral in New-York, and they would become the objects of a public ridicule against which no votaries could defend them. The Catholics themselves would be ashamed of them.

If the Parthenon were still in a state of perfect preservation, it would probably be guarded as its ruins are now, merely as a monument of art. Perhaps it would be difficult to appropriate it to any useful purpose. It sprung into being in connection with a religion which no longer exists. The cathedrals of Europe had their origin in a peculiar religionism. Separate them from that religionism, and they become mere monuments of art. The leading idea of Grecian architecture is proportion, and the beauty which arises out of proportion. It is beautiful, therefore, independently of ornament. The idea of the ornaments which have been added is grace. But proportion and grace are immortal: therefore the elements of the Greek architecture are designed to be perpetuated. It is, also, the architecture of a free, enlightened, and polished people. It is a symbol of intellectual development—of human progress. The leading idea of Gothic architecture is solidity and strength. It is the architecture of fortification upon rocky and irregular heights, with angles accommodated to the nature of the site, and with buttresses, towers, and parapets for stern defence. A fair even space is required for the rectangular, symmetrical Grecian structure. Look along the castellated Rhine, and you see there is not a hill or rocky pinnacle where a Gothic fortress cannot be placed. A Gothic building is kingly, proud, stern, awful: it is the symbol of power and domination: it speaks of knightly robbers and a plundered peasantry; of throned monarchs, and subjugated multitudes. When this rigid and massive pile is ornamented, it is like the armor of a warrior—made for war and speaking of battle, but wrought all over with beautiful imagery and inlaid with gold and silver, as if to throw a charm and splendor over violence and terror.

When this architecture was introduced in the building of churches, its multifarious angles were reduced to order by giving the whole structure the form of a cross. Thus in its general form it was made a symbol of religion. Then the whole exterior was wrought into beautiful tracery work to veil the rugged features of massive stone, and covered with images of prophets, apostles, saints, angels, and heroes of the faith, until it appeared one vast and glorious monumental representation. And in the interior arose those branching columns; and pendent roofs were stretched above; and stained windows revealed sacred forms and shed their "dim religious light;" and holy chapels were multiplied along the walls; and graceful images and affecting paintings were scattered every where; and the solemn pealing organ was made to sound through the vaulted aisles; and the gorgeous monuments of the illustrious dead were erected in every nook and corner; and priests and a priestly worship filled the sacred places; and the people prostrated themselves in awe and veneration.

But the original idea still remained: it was still the architecture of power and subjugation. It had drawn around itself more beauty and fascination, it aimed to represent religious ideas and awaken devotional fervor; but, it contained a command more absolute and awful, it exercised a force more resistless and terrible through its mitred and stoled priests, than when in rude baronial halls it embraced helmed and spurred knights and men-at-arms.

If the Gothic castle represented the power of the monarch and barons, the Gothic cathedral represented no less the absolutism of the priest. There is in this architecture no type or symbol of freedom in church or state. It tells of wonderful art, but not of intellectual freedom and development. The frowns of the middle ages hang about its towers. The beautifully colored lights within fall upon the pages of old legends. Dreams of tyranny haunt its solemn aisles. Its buttresses seem reared to prevent the present and future from invading the past. Even now while walking in those old cathedrals, when the first fascination has passed away, and sober reflection again begins to assert its supremacy, you feel the presence of a dread power repressing thought, forbidding speech, limiting action, prescribing all things, and ready to fall upon you with a crushing weight, should you overstep its prescriptions.

The Gothic architecture, to reach its proper magnificent and striking development, requires vast magnitude, profuse and costly ornament, and ample time for its completion. A feeble attempt at it but reveals its ruggedness and defects without attaining its majesty and beauty. It cannot, therefore, be the architecture for a people like ourselves, who consult use and economy, and who aim to finish rapidly. Hence our Gothic churches, and other buildings in this style, are for the most part miserable abortions. It is one of our follies to be ever rushing after novelties; and since nothing is so *new* to us as the *old* of other nations, Gothic architecture is at present all the rage.

But besides its inappropriateness in respect to use, the fact that I have endeavored to set forth above, that it is the symbol of absolute power and the subjugation of the people, renders it unsuitable to the character of our institutions. Let us indulge a freedom of thought and a boldness of design in our architecture consonant with all our great enterprises and improvements. The naval architecture of the ancients does not govern us in our ship-building; why do we bow down before Gothic models in our civil and ecclesiastical architecture? If we are to gather ideas from any, let us rather go back to democratic Athens, where the spirit of a free people breathed through forms of art so cheerful and beautiful, that even now, when we gaze upon the ruins, we gain inspirations that make our free hearts leap within us.

There are several other churches of considerable note in Cologne besides the cathedral. It must have been once a city of churches, since it is said to have contained as many as there are days in the year. Once the seat of extensive commerce, it had one hundred and fifty thousand inhabitants, and was a city of great wealth and splendor. Then it experienced a mournful decline when priestly bigotry expelled the Protestants, who were its most industrious and enterprising citizens. At the time of the French Revolution, it contained little more than fifty thousand inhabitants; but it had two hundred churches, and a multitude of ecclesiastics. The French Revolution converted most of its churches to other uses, and only twenty-nine are retained for sacred purposes. Cologne is recovering her prosperity, and now numbers between eighty and ninety thousand inhabitants.

I was walking alone through the narrow streets remarking objects of antiquity, when I came opposite to what appeared to be, and undoubtedly had been, a very ancient church. A carriage was standing in front of an open gate on one side of the building. I entered the gate, and ascending a flight of rude stone steps, I encountered a man selling tickets of admission. It was the annual exhibition of the Art-Union of

Cologne. I found the collection quite extensive. There was a number of very fine portraits and landscapes. As I was sauntering about, I saw something that looked like the back of a large screen. Passing to the other side of it, I was startled by what met my eye, and uttered an exclamation of delight. It was Washington crossing the Delaware. I afterwards ascertained that this was the original painting of Leutze. The canvas had received some injury by fire before he had given it the finishing touches. He then painted the one which has been exhibited and sold in New-York. No damage was apparent on the one at Cologne. I was deeply affected by the painting. It seemed like a visitation from my beloved country. The grand and heroic character of Washington, the American Revolution, our national greatness and freedom, all rushed into my mind. I felt ennobled by my alliance to such a country and such a history. I said to myself: I am an American citizen—my father fought under Washington. Then I thought of the ancient city of Cologne, with its memorials of antiquity and its monuments of art; I thought of its magnificent cathedral; I thought of all I had seen and was about to see in Europe—I was ascending the Rhine to the Alps:—but, said I, they have nothing here so grand as our Washington, and he is all our own. Then I walked away musing. My mind has often since returned to the same thought: the character and example of Washington is the greatest possession a nation ever had. Let us prove ourselves worthy of the immortal trust.

IV.

Bonn and its University.

THE banks of the Rhine between Cologne and Bonn are flat like those below. We therefore proceeded by the railroad. At Bonn we put up at the Grand Hotel Royal, situated on the bank of the river, near the University, and overlooking the thickly wooded park which stretches in front of it. Our rooms commanded a view beyond the Rhine, up and down the river, and embraced the outline of the *Sieben-gebirge*—the seven mountains. It was a clear serene summer evening, and the temperature was delightful. Behind the hotel the grounds were tastefully laid out, and on the bank of the river seats were arranged for the guests. Here an admirable military band was performing delicious music. Travellers from all nations were collected, walking and chatting, or seated in groups; while here and there, some individual was lounging apart, quietly whiffing a cigar, resigned to pleasant meditations, and indulging to the full the *dolce far niente.* Among the company there was a plentiful sprinkling of English. Of Americans, besides ourselves, there were two very agreeable southern gentlemen, who had been our companions from Cologne. Every one was in a good humor. We appeared like beings who had left all care behind, and were making a voyage into enchanted regions. Life now was a holiday. Whatever had been, whatever hereafter might be of toil and sorrow, was not remembered or apprehended. The present was to us a pleasure boat upon a summer sea. It was an episode of beauty and joy on the weary way of human life. We were strangers to each other, and we cared not to know each other's names and occupations. We were to each other not like creatures of the common earth, but mysterious beings dropped from kindly skies—angels meeting angels, exchanging smiles and pleasant words, and then passing on, each to his own happy purpose, each full of his own enjoyments. We were on the banks of the legendary Rhine, under the soft twilight of a midsummer evening, "lapped in Elysian airs," and the morrow was full of promise. Is it not well thus sometimes to forget every thing but pleasure? Does not the breath of the beautiful recreate us, and renew our strength to return to the old reality of work?

In this happy mood we went to sleep. In the morning we arose to take a view of Bonn and its University. Bonn is not a large town; it contains only eighteen thousand inhabitants. But it is the more picturesque and agreeable in that it is not a large town. It leaves the hills and trees standing, and does not crowd upon the Rhine as if it were eager to drink up all the water. The Electors of Cologne once resided here. They removed their court from the dense noisy commercial city to this quiet town, reposing in the lap of nature. Here no restless improvements are going on; improvement seems to have been accomplished, and to be simply enjoyed. But, nevertheless, improvement is going on here, improvement that never can slumber or pause—the eternal improvement of mind. The palace of the Electors, a quarter of a mile in length, contains the University. Here are the lecture rooms, and the library of 150,000 volumes. It has at present forty professors, and one thousand and fifty students. It enjoys a high reputation. Niebuhr and A. W. Schlegel were professors here. The king of Prussia founded it in 1818, and bestowed upon it the palace of the Old Electors. The University, indeed, constitutes the importance of Bonn. The beauty of the situation, and the literary advantages make it a most desirable place of residence. I walked through the library in mute admiration. It is a noble collection of books. And yet this great and justly celebrated University has been established only thirty-four years. It is therefore a young institution. The idea that Universities must be of slow growth is not justified by the history of Prussia. The University of Berlin was established in 1810. In 1826, the number of matriculated students amounted to sixteen hundred and forty-two, four hundred of whom were foreigners. And yet Prussia has several other flourishing Universities. The whole monarchy equals in square miles only some two of our states, and contains fifteen and a half millions of inhabitants. But Prussia is no less distinguished for common schools and seminaries of every grade. In 1835, there were 21,790 elementary schools, in which two millions of children of both sexes received instruction. About the same time there were one hundred and twenty-four gymnasia, where 24,641 scholars were educated. Let it be remembered that the gymnasia are superior to our colleges. There are many schools, too, in Prussia, specially adapted to mechanics and to various kinds of manufacture and business. Probably no country in the world has an educational system so comprehensive and thorough.

The Universities nourish and bring together men eminent for genius and learning. The kings of Prussia, from Frederick the Great down to the present time, have been the enlightened patrons of learning and learned men. At Berlin, in the immediate vicinity of the Court, are found such men as Humboldt, Savigny, Ranke, Raumer, Ehrenberg, Ritter, Grimm, and Schelling. Here, too, lived Schleiermacher and Neander.

And now this Prussia is an unlimited monarchy: these kings are despots. I have said, in a previous chapter, that despotic governments are beautiful in theory; and I there intimated quite plainly that I deem them such, generally, only in theory. But we must be just. In the educational system of Prussia we have something more than theory. Here is a glorious achievement of an enlightened and energetic despotism. I admit that there are many evils in Prussia, and that the kings are both unwise, and in the wrong, for not granting a constitutional government. But here is a sublime work which they have accomplished for the public good. But, it may be asked, Do you allow this to be an argument in favor of unlimited monarchies? I answer that the government of Prussia is justly entitled to all the argument that can be made out of it. So far, the government may proudly say, Judge us by our fruits. And the only way in which we can nullify the force of the argument is by proving by our works that a republic, too, can create and foster the noblest institutions of learning, can patronize the arts and artists, and learning and learned men.

The immense and peculiar blessings which are enjoyed under a Republic are obvious to all; but it is required, too, that it should be favorable to the highest forms of culture. In order to prove that we are under the most elevated and the happiest conditions of human existence, it is not enough to show that men can be better fed and clothed here than in other lands, and that we enjoy the fairest opportunities for material accumulation; it must be shown, also, that we can develope the grandest forms of humanity itself. We cannot stand still; we must be advancing or deteriorating in national character: we cannot advance without culture; and we cannot have culture without great men as standards of excellence, and as lights to guide us. Now, we have not been without great men,—we have had our governing standards and our guiding lights,—whether in sufficient degree and number I shall not stop to inquire; but we have had them, and, perhaps, we have them now. But it is certain that in a country so vast as ours, and with destinies so momentous at stake, we want more great men than any other people, for we have a greater work for them to do here than elsewhere--to make a whole people great. It is not only demanded of us as a justification of our institutions that we show ourselves equal to every thing that advances and adorns humanity, but it is the very condition of the perpetuation of these institutions. A Republic like ours must be filled with the light of knowledge, must be permeated by principles of truth and integrity, must be guided by great men, must be filled by a great people—great in character and worth—or it will go to pieces. We are not an inorganic aggregation sustained by a mechanical force, but an organic growth spreading out our branches, bearing fruit, and sustained by a vigorous and sound life within. We want, therefore, both a popular education, in the sense of giving a good degree of education to all, and the possibilities and means of the highest forms of education open to all who choose to avail themselves of them. In our country we must open the most auspicious race to man for every thing that meets his wants and destinies, and contributes to his perfection.

In popular education we have done much; here we can point to our works with satisfaction: but, in the higher institutions, it must be confessed, we are sadly deficient. We have not got in our country one University. One fruitful cause of this deficiency is a current opinion that we are yet too young a country to develope a University system like that which has obtained in Europe, that it must be the slow growth of time, and that when we are prepared for it, we shall have it. But the early youth of our nation is the very season to plant those institutions which shall determine our growth and maturity. Nor is it true that they are necessarily of slow growth. Look at the Universities of Bonn, and of Berlin. We can create universities at once, if we will. Let us show that the spirit of a free people is no less enlightened and mighty than the unlimited monarchy of Prussia.

V.

The Middle Rhine. From Bonn to Biberich.

THE Middle Rhine extends from Cologne to Basil, a distance of three hundred and fifty miles. From Bonn to Biberich is the most beautiful portion of the Rhine. It has often been described. Will it not prove a commonplace affair to attempt to describe it again? The guide-books are full of it: read the guide-books, and have you not got the whole of it by heart? But who ever tires of the Rhine because it has been so often described? Who on this account will forbear to go and see it for himself? After we have seen it, do we not dream about it, and ever delight to talk about it? No, we never tire of the beautiful. Beautiful works of art, beautiful works of nature never satiate us. We read over sweet poems again and again. I have been up the Rhine and down the Rhine, and I wish to sail up and down again, to wander along its banks, to ascend its heights, to loiter in its old towns, to pass summer days among its old ruins. How could I grow weary of the Rhine! A fellow-traveller was ascending the Rhine for the nineteenth time, and he was gazing at and admiring its beauties. I can only speak as I feel; I can only tell my own story. If you have been there, you will sympathize with me; if you have not, perhaps you will feel a stronger desire to go.

There are four things which, taken together, make this part of the Rhine more interesting than any other river: its natural features are rare and striking; it is a record of romantic legends; it is a stirring history; it is an endless theme of poetry—nay, it is a poem in itself.

———"True Wisdom's world will be
Within its own creation, or in thine,
Maternal Nature! for who teems like thee,
Thus on the banks of thy majestic Rhine?
There Harold gazes on a work divine,
A blending of all beauties; streams and dells,
Fruit, foliage, crag, wood, cornfield, mountain, vine,
And chiefless castles breathing stern farewells,
From gray but leafy walls, where Ruin greenly dwells."

We are indeed much indebted to the poet—far more than to the guide-books. The poet has seen with clear and truthful eyes. The beautiful without has found an answering beauty within. He is the true painter; he does not give sketches here and there upon the canvas—a dim imitation—a glimpse at parts of objects; but he quickens our imagination by infusing his own spirit, and his words are symbols upon which our thoughts work, until within us there grows a full and lively representation. And then when we go to behold what he has gathered into his verse, we see with his eyes, we feel with his heart; he has thrown a purple light over every thing; or, rather, he has put us into a genuine communication with nature, by dissipating the mists of a gross common life, and opening those fountains of beauty which are somewhere to be found in every human soul.

From Bonn to Coblentz, is thirty miles or more, and thence to Biberich, between fifty and sixty miles. We went on board the steamer at midday; we were again stemming the current of the joyous Rhine. The change from the flat banks of the Lower Rhine to the noble scenery which begins with the Drachenfels, is most inspiriting. This steep hill rises more than a thousand feet above the river, terminating in almost perpendicular basaltic rocks, and crowned with those marvellous walls, the remnants of an ancient castle, which appear as imperishable as the rock itself. The vine is cultivated to the very foot of the rock. As we ascended the stream, the Siebengebirge came all clearly into view, crowned with ruins. The lowest is one thousand and fifty-three feet high, the highest fourteen hundred and fifty-three feet. They are the highest hills on the banks of the Middle Rhine. Between the Siebengebirge and around lie smaller hills covered with forests and vineyards. Köningswinter, a beautiful little town, lies nearly at the foot of the Drachenfels. Those who have time would do well to stop here, and make the ascent of the Drachenfels and other hills. The heights covered with the ruins of old castles, the level spaces on the banks making angles in the hills, covered with towns filled with antiquities; the steep hills around the towns, or where they rise abruptly from the water's edge, planted with vines; and wherever the banks are depressed, a beautiful undulating country in a high state of cultivation opening to view, with towns and villages—such is a general description of this scenery.

"The castled crag of Drachenfels
Frowns o'er the wide and winding Rhine,
Whose breast of waters broadly swells
Between the banks which bear the vine,
And hills all rich with blossomed trees,
And fields which promise corn and wine,
And scattered cities crowning these
Whose far white walls along them shine.
And peasant girls, with deep blue eyes,
And hands which gather early flowers,
Walk smiling o'er this paradise;
Above, the frequent feudal towers
Through green leaves lift their walls of gray,
And many a rock which steeply towers,
And noble arch in proud decay,
Look o'er this vale of vintage bowers;
The river nobly foams and flows,
The charm of this enchanted ground,
And all its thousand turns disclose
Some fresher beauty varying round;
The haughtiest breast its wish might bound
Through life to dwell delighted here,
Nor could on earth a spot be found
To nature and to me so dear."

Opposite the Drachenfels on the other side of the Rhine,

there is a precipitous rock jutting out so near the brink of the river as scarcely to leave space enough for a carriage track. On this rock stands a ruined arch, the last remains of the castle and tower of *Rolandsech.* Directly opposite in the middle of the river is the island of *Nonnenwerth,* where in a beautiful grove of trees, stands the Ursuline nunnery, built in the seventeenth century. This nunnery occupies the site of one more ancient, and coeval with the castle of Rolandsech. One of the most beautiful and affecting traditions of the Rhine, is connected with these ruins, and is rendered still more so by Schiller's ballad of the "Ritter Toggenburgh," which, indeed, is but a reproduction of it.

Roland, the gallant nephew of Charlemagne, was betrothed to a damsel of rare beauty. News came after the battle of Roncesvalles that he was among the slain. His betrothed bride retired to the convent of Nonnenwerth. The report of his death turned out false, and Roland returned to find his beloved pledged as the bride of heaven. The ballad of Schiller commences at this point. The knight has one meeting with his betrothed. She tells him her heart will be devoted to him with a true sisterly love, that she can give him no more, that they must calmly meet, and calmly separate. Stunned with grief, he gives her one embrace, leaps upon his horse and departs. Then he collects an armed band and joins a crusade to the Holy Land. Here he performs brave and knightly deeds—his banner is ever foremost in the fight. But the din and glory of battle cannot drive away the sorrow from his heart. After a year of secret pining and longing, he leaves the armed hosts, takes ship at Joppa, and sails for his native land. Now he again stands at the convent gate, a lonely pilgrim, and claims to see the one object upon whom his heart is fixed. He is told that he can never meet her more, that she had just taken the veil and was now irrevocably devoted to God. Then he builds himself a hermit's hut opposite her window, and there, with his eyes ever turned in that direction to catch a glimpse of the holy maiden, passes the remainder of his days. Whenever she opened the casement she bowed to the hermit and gently smiled. The vision as of an angel, charmed his soul to repose. At night he lay down in the hope of the morning. Every morning found him there seated with calm and tender eyes to see her bending towards him with that angelic smile. And so years wore away, until one morn he sat there, his face still in death.

From Rolandsech to Remagen the road on the banks of the Rhine winds along the edge of the water and appears to be cut into the rock. Near Remagen the beautiful Gothic Church of Apollinarisberg comes into view upon making a sharp turn in the river. The effect of these sudden apparitions of towns, churches and old ruins, is like the shifting scenes of a panorama, where the mind loses the enchantment of a present view, only, as it gives place to something new and perhaps still more enchanting.

Beyond Remagen, on the opposite bank, there are basaltic precipices seven hundred feet high, which are planted with vines in a most curious manner. Baskets filled with mould are fastened in the crevices of the rocks; and here the vines are planted, and grow luxuriantly. It is a warm, sunny exposure, and grateful to the view. Thus in these old and populous countries is every thing turned to account, and cultivation is made to invade what at first sight would seem inaccessible.

The scenery of the Rhine is very bold until at Andernach the river appears to rush through a gorge of the mountains. Thence to Coblentz the banks settle away into a plain, through which the Moselle pours its waters into the kingly river. The most interesting ruins, after the Drachenfels and Rolandsech, which meet the eye here, are those of the Castle of Hammerstein, over which more than seven centuries have swept their wings. Once a refuge of the Emperor Henry IV., there let it stand, a memorial of his sufferings and his vain struggles against the implacable Gregory. I have often wondered that a history so tragic has not been wrought into a drama or a romance. What a thrilling subject it would be in the hands of a historian like Macaulay.

A plain but intelligent and affable man with whom I chanced to get into conversation, and who pointed out to me many interesting objects, as we approached Neuwied told me he belonged to the Moravian Brethren, who occupy a distinct quarter of the town. The account he gave me of Neuwied led me to observe it more closely than perhaps I otherwise would have done. I remarked about it an unusual air of comfort, cleanliness, and prosperity. The streets are wide, and it is substantially built. This town was founded not much more than a century since, on the principle of entire religious freedom and equality. Catholics, Protestants, Moravians and Jews live together in perfect harmony, and cooperate in enterprise and industry for the common good. This liberal and rational policy is the source of all its prosperity. The heavens seemed brighter over this spot, the air more invigorating which breathed through it, and the people wore more open and happy faces. I thought some secret sympathy had drawn me into an acquaintance with the good Moravian brother, and we parted with mutual and cordial good wishes.

We reached Coblentz about six o'clock. The view of Ehrenbreitstein on one side of the river, and the town on the other side, lying at the junction of the Moselle and the Rhine, was very striking as we approached. We put up at the Giant, near the steamboat landing. The windows of our apartments were directly opposite Ehrenbreitstein, and commanded a view up and down the river. The traveller who does not get apartments which afford him a fine view where there is something to be seen, loses time while in doors. Ehrenbreitstein was an object of interest whenever we looked out of our windows; and I shall never forget a sunset when after a cloudy day the sun suddenly broke out and changed those frowning battlements into massive gold.

After tea, I took a walk through the city. I went through many narrow and dark streets, stood and gazed at old churches, and wandered about hither and thither, until the night fell upon me. While making my way back to the Giant, I approached a part of the city which appeared to be illuminated. When I came nearer, I found the illumination to proceed from a multitude of little lamps suspended about and within what appeared to be a public garden. Over the entrance was painted, in large characters, TEXAS. Upon going in, I found a band of musicians seated upon a platform in the centre; and all around were arrayed tables and benches, where men and women were seated drinking beer, and chatting with the greatest glee. They were apparently mechanics and common tradesmen who were taking their evening recreation. The name of the garden was rather ominous, and betokened considerable license. But I walked about freely and undisturbed, and observed neither intoxication nor indecency. It was a garden which the common people had all to themselves; and Texas, I suppose, was a name to them which symbolized freedom and plenty. Frequent conversations with the people of the middling and lower classes in Germany and Switzerland made it clear to me how strong were their aspirations after the boundless and glorious West. With political questions I did not intermeddle—a point of honor, I think, in a foreign country: I generally listened to what they had to say, and answered questions only to give them proper information.

I ascended Ehrenbreitstein. It is an extraordinary specimen of fortification; to me it was a great curiosity. All the heights in the neighborhood are fortified likewise. On the opposite side of the river are extensive fortifications overlooked by Ehrenbreitstein. Every point of defence is occupied. The beauty and strength of the masonry are admirable. All the fortifications together are capable of containing a hundred thousand men, and yet might be held by five thousand. From Ehrenbreitstein alone four hundred cannon stand ready to pour their fiery storm upon an invader. It is inconceivable how these defences could ever be overcome, unless by starvation; and this is quite improbable, since the magazines are large enough to contain provisions for eight thousand men for ten years. It is the Gibraltar of the Rhine. It absolutely commands the river. From the summit the view is magnificent. In front, the old city and the bridge of boats, the Moselle with its stone bridge, and the country stretching far away; below, the Rhine with its picturesque banks; above, the Rhine winding from out the gorges of the mountains which shut in the prospect.

It was ten o'clock in the morning when passing through the drawbridge we left Coblentz behind, and made our way to these gorges, from whence the breeze came rushing down with the swift current of the Rhine. The steamer buffeted the force of the current like a strong swimmer. And to us, who are now for the first time on the "Castellated Rhine," what can it be but a scene of wonder and romance? Are we not like children reading a book of fairy tales? Let us not be ashamed to be children—let us yield to wonder and romance. There is *Stolzenfels* standing high upon a rock, a proud feudal castle. But this is not a ruin; it has been restored, and looks too much like a modern ambitious Gothic structure. Here the King of Prussia received the young Queen of England. Now we are at the mouth of the Lahn, and just above is the old walled town of Oberlahnstein, and rising behind the town, a tall rock covered with the broken towers of *Lahneck*. And we scarcely lose sight of this when the stately towers of *Marxburg* come into sight—a castle of the middle ages in a perfect state of preservation. There is the old Donjon Keep overlooking hill and valley. Within are dungeons and chambers of torture. How grim its aspect! Were the secrets of its hoary centuries brought to light, what scenes of terror would be revealed!

And now sweeping past several villages in succession, and the white castle of *Liebenich*, we wind through a marvellous bend in the Rhine, and come up to that very ancient town of *Boppart*, whose narrow streets, and old houses, surrounded by an old crumbling wall, look as if antiquity were jealously brooding over it to save it from the polluting touch of repair.

Who has not read the story of the *Two Brothers* who occupied two neighboring castles; and who, falling in love with the same beautiful maiden, forgot the ties of brotherhood in the madness of a stronger passion, and fought for the possession of the beloved object, and pierced each other's bosom, and left her solitary to weep over their crime in the walls of a convent? And there rise before us the melancholy ruins of the *twin castles*—the castles of *Sternberg* and *Liebenstein.* A valley lies between them. Eternally separated, they frown upon each other.

And here is *Ehrenthal;* and, a little higher up, the village of *Welmich*, at the foot of a mountain; and on the top of the mountain stands the castle of *Thurnberg*, also called the *Mouse*, in allusion to another castle above, at St. Goarhausen, called the *Cat.* The Mouse and the Cat were deadly enemies, and ever watching each other. Both are now ruins; but the bare walls of the Mouse appear undecayed, and might easily be restored.

The beautiful town of St. Goar lies directly opposite the Cat on the other side of the river, and above it rise the vast and magnificent ruins of *Rheinfels*, built in the thirteenth century. Converted into a fortress by the Landgrave of Hesse, it was in perfect condition until taken and blown up by the French in 1794. All about here is wild and picturesque. But now St. Goar is passed by, and the river bends among black precipitous jagged rocks; and here is the dread whirlpool of the *Lurlei*—the mischievous water-spirit who, in days of old, when boatmen had to battle the whirlpool and rapids with their oars, lured them by her beauty and her songs, among the fatal rocks which lay beneath. But our steamer, which bears the name of the Water Spirit, is the more powerful Lurlei of the two. The beautiful syren is now unseen and unheard; the dash of our paddles, the hiss of our steam, our sparks and smoke have frightened her away to her caves in the bed of the river. Or, perhaps, she is sitting there invisible upon the pinnacles of those tall black rocks—the *Lurleifelsen*, lamenting with the shades of the robber-barons, that the river, which was once all their own, has now become a common and safe highway without drowning or toll-gathering. Suddenly we hear the blast of a bugle, and in an instant all the rocks are filled with answering bugles; and then a gun goes off, and every rock fires its gun in reply. We look around and we see a man stationed on the shore opposite the Lurleifelsen, with bugle and gun, prepared to wake the echoes as every steamer goes by—an attention to the entertainment of travellers characteristic of this region, where the love of the marvellous and the beautiful ever lives. It is said that there are fifteen distinct echoes. I could not count them: there seemed to me to be many more—the hills and rocks were full of them.

The Lurlei and her whirlpool are left behind, the echoes have died away, and we are now opposite *Oberwesel* with its turreted walls, its round tower, and its beautiful gothic church standing so light and airy upon a hill. And just above the town are the ruins of *Schönberg*, where lived the knight with his seven enchanting daughters, who were turned to stone for jilting all the noble young knights around. Who can doubt the story, when there just below Oberwesel we passed the seven rocks into which they were changed, and which lift their heads above water, a perpetual warning to all the fair who pass up and down the Rhine?

And then a little way above Schönberg, on the opposite side of the river, are the dismantled walls of *Gutenfels*, named after a fair lady whom an emperor loved. From this castle once thundered the cannon of Gustavus Adolphus, when he endeavored in vain to pass the Rhine in the face of the Spanish army. In the middle of the river stands the queer old castle of *Pfalz*, built at the beginning of the thirteenth century by the Emperor Lewis of Bavaria, as a toll-house. Here, or at the town of Caub, on the right bank, a toll is still collected by the Duke of Nassau, the only remaining toll of the thirty-two that were collected by the baronial oppressors of the middle ages. The toll of the Duke of Nassau, I suppose, is a right conceded by the German States. The toll system was broken up in the thirteenth century by the celebrated confederacy of sixty German towns, who sent powerful armies against these terrible strongholds on the Rhine, and reduced them to picturesque ruins, evermore to embellish where before they had wasted and destroyed.

And now we turn another abrupt bend of the river, and the ancient town of *Bacharach* is before us, with its ancient wall strengthened with twelve towers still standing. Nearly opposite the town is a small island; and adjoining the island is a rock, the *Bacchi ara*—the altar of Bacchus, which, when it appears above the surface of the water, denotes a dry season auspicious to the vine. There is another ruin on the lofty hill behind the town, and this is *Stahleck*, once the proud residence of the Electors Palatine. But what beautiful ruin is that, with pointed windows still perfect, and exhibiting the most exquisite tracery work—Melrose Abbey again!

> "Thou would'st have thought some fairy's hand
> 'Twixt poplars straight the ozier wand,
> In many a freakish knot had twined;
> Then framed a spell when the work was done,
> And changed the willow wreaths to stone."

It is but a fragment standing alone upon a rock, and so light, that you would almost expect it to wave gracefully in the breeze. It is all that is left of St. Werner's Church, built more than four hundred years ago, and is pronounced "the remains of the highest and most elegant lancet style existing."

And now we pass Lorchhausen, and here rises before us on those lofty rocks the ruins of *Nollengen*, and the height on which it stands is the *Devil's Ladder;* and then a short run brings us up to Lorch, lying at the mouth of the Wispenthal. O that I could stop here, and wander up that valley—but we are already past, and on the opposite shore is the village of Nieder Heimbech, and behind overlooking the houses, the ruined castle of *Heimburg.* We are now in the Rheingau, which begins at Lorch, and extends to Nieder Walluf, below Biberich. It is six leagues in length and two in breadth in the Duchy of Nassau, and is sheltered on the north by the Taunus mountains. Far famed is the Rheingau for its beauty and fertility, and for producing the richest and most delicate Rhenish wines. Here are produced the Johannisberg, the Steinburg, the Markobrunnen, the Rudesheim, the Rothenberg, and other kinds well known at least to travellers on the Rhine; and, indeed, well known nowhere else, for here they may be had unadulterated and with their delicate flavor preserved. Happy is that country in respect to temperance where the grape is cultivated, and light pure wines takes the place of strong drink. I believe the taste for these pure wines precludes the taste for strong drink. Are not the wine-growing countries the most temperate? that is the question. If so, then the cultivation of the vine would be the promotion of temperance.

But while I am writing this, or something like it in the leaves of my portfolio, we have reached *Sonneck*, once a robber castle, and destroyed when the vengeance of the people fell upon their strongholds of plunder, but now restored, and picturesque and peaceful where it clings to the rocks. Here all the heights seem to grow into turreted castles, for here follow in quick succession *Sonneck*, *Falkenburg*, *Clemenskirche*, and *Rheinstein*, the last restored also, and the knightly and imposing residence of Prince Frederick of Prussia. Scarcely have we passed these, when we sail between the broken walls of Ehrenfels on the right bank, and the *Mouse Tower* of Bishop Hatto, built on a rock near the left bank. The Legend of the Bishop may be found in verse among Southey's poems.

Just above the Mouse Tower the Nahe empties into the Rhine, and we are now running past Bingen. From Bingen to Biberich the Rhine widens and is filled with little islands, while the country opens, and the shores are less bold and jagged. The Rheingau presents an undulating surface over which the vineyards cluster. Rudesheim and Johannisberg resemble each other in situation, and in the form of the land. It would be natural to conclude that if Johannisberg produces fine wine, Rudesheim must do the same. But why one should be superior to the other, from a superficial view, it is hard to conceive. Perhaps the superiority of Johannisberg is owing to the nicer cultivation, and to the rejection of all but the perfect grapes in the vintage; the reputation which the wine has gained and the consequently high price warranting this particularity. The quantity of wine produced is so small, and is so generally bought by princes and nobles, that the traveller will act most prudently if he never calls for Johannisberg on steamboats or at hotels. Rudesheim of a fine quality he will sometimes meet with.

Well, we have left the Rheingau behind with its towns and villages, its beautiful hills and valleys, its vineyards and cornfields, its ruined towers and its princely seats, and we are now at Biberich. Here we take the train, and before dark we are at Frankfort-on-the-Main.

IV.

Middle Rhine Continued. Frankfort on the Maine—Heidelberg—Baden-Baden—Strasburg.

IN Frankfort, in the ancient part of the town, is an old but respectable-looking house. Over the door is a coat-of-arms bearing the device of *three lyres;* and underneath the arms is an inscription, "This is the house in which Göthe was born." The arms of the father seem like a prophecy of the genius of the son. Here the childhood and youth of Göthe were spent. Here his early studies were carried on. Here he dreamed his early dreams of life. Here were laid many of those scenes which his autobiography describes. That autobiography was among the books of my boyish reading; and it made Frankfort, and the home of Göthe a sort of dreamland to my boyish fancy. In visiting Frankfort Göthe was more in my mind than any thing else.

The house in which the Rothschild family were born is here too, in the Jews' street, narrow and dark, and crowded with old dwellings, shut in by a gate, formerly, which was closed at an early hour every evening, until the cannon of Marshal Jourdan knocked it down, never to be replaced. And this family have country-seats near the town, and the mother has a splendid mansion outside of the gardens. I chanced to see the Rothschild house at the same time that I went to see the home of Göthe; and thus was I led to compare the Banker and the man of Genius, the wealth of money and the wealth of mind. Both had won success. There was the Prince of Bankers, and there the Prince of Literary men, both from the same town. A noble bronze statue of Göthe is erected in an open space opposite the Theatre. How majestic that figure, how expressive that countenance! And then around the pedestal are bas-reliefs which represent the creations of his genius. The citizens of Frankfort have erected this statue. Will they erect one to the Banker? If it stood there, how would the rotund figure, the absorbed calculating countenance, contrast with the grace and fire of the poet! What bas-reliefs would surround the pedestal?

There is a fine gallery of paintings in Frankfort, established by the munificence of an individual, who bequeathed his collection of paintings and drawings, together with four hundred thousand dollars to his native city. Besides the erection of a suitable building, this fund yields four thousand dollars annually for the increase of the gallery. Thus has he entailed his estate.

In the Kaiser Saal of the Town-house, where the election

of the emperors was celebrated, their portraits are arranged upon the walls from Conrad I. to Francis II. They were painted by Lessing and other eminent artists, and have taken the place of the old and miserably executed paintings. It is an interesting collection, whether viewed as works of art, or as historical memorials.

A short and pleasant drive brings you to the cemetery. The dead-house is well worth examining. Before interment the body is placed in a room, and is so connected with little bells, that the least motion would give notice to the attendant in an adjoining room. The design is to prevent premature interment. Every arrangement is made for promoting resuscitation when any signs of life are given. This is a merciful precaution, if it were only to relieve some minds peculiarly sensitive on this point, from the apprehension of being buried alive. Besides, the instances are not a few where sensation has returned after apparent death. The cemetery itself is neat, but contains nothing very remarkable except some exquisite bas-reliefs by Thorwaldsen, which every one, of course, will take pains to see.

The most beautiful work of art in Frankfort is Dannecker's statue of Ariadne. Ariadne, the daughter of Minos, King of Crete, falls in love with Theseus, one of the seven youths destined as an offering to the Minotaur. She provides him with the clue of thread which, fastened at the entrance of the labyrinth, enables him to find his way out again after he had slain the monster. They fly to the isle of Naxos. Here, while she lies asleep, Theseus forsakes her. She awakes to see his ship fading in the horizon. In despair she roams along the shore. There the beautiful god Bacchus by chance meets her, and enamored with her beauty comforts her, weds her, and bestows upon her immortality. The crown upon her head the god hurls into the skies, where it becomes a constellation.

> "Ariadne! grief and care are dying,
> Thou, my queen! shalt never, never die!
> By yon sun, in morning splendor lying,
> Thou, like him, shalt dazzling reign on high."

Dannecker's work represents Ariadne reclining with easy grace upon the back of the Bacchic panther. She is already immortal, and has the air and look of a goddess. The form and attitude are admirable. Every part is finished with the nicest art, and the marble is forgotten in the life which invigorates the whole. The expression of the face is serious and thoughtful. We may fancy that she is absorbed by the mystery of her new condition. There is perfect content, but perfect delight is delayed by wondering thought.

Every one who visits Frankfort will be delighted with the elegance and cleanliness of the town, and the beautiful suburbs, where the old ramparts have been turned into shady walks, and gardens. In these gardens a fine military band performs in the afternoon. The musicians are arranged in orchestra style, and play from the notes, under the direction of a leader. The music in the open air is charming. The people are walking or standing around, and groups of children twirl around in the waltz or polka, as if by a sort of spontaneity. Soldiers, too, off duty, are leisurely perambulating. To add to the motley appearance, what should I see but a very black, jaunty-looking negro, in uniform, with his military cap placed *à la mode* upon his sooty curls, walking about at his ease like a man among his equals. Where he dropt from I know not, but here he was a German soldier.

At Frankfort we took the train for Heidelberg. We passed Darmstadt, a pleasant city with wide streets and numerous squares, a part of it appearing like a collection of country-seats rather than a compact town. In this respect it answers to my beau-ideal of a town. The road to Heidelberg runs through the *Odenwald* at the foot of that chain of vineclad and wooded hills, which still bear the name of Odin. These hills are sprinkled with ruined castles and towers. They form the eastern boundary of the valley of the Rhine, which stretches away some fifty or sixty miles, where it meets the opposite boundary of the Vosges mountains in France. The route is extremely pleasing from the picturesque hills on the one hand, and the vast plain on the other, studded with towns and villages, and exhibiting the highest cultivation. The Odenwald is a favorite district for pedestrian tourists. It is a region of legend and romance; and the ascent of the hills with their old ruins offer many interesting excursions.

We arrived at Heidelberg about noon. One is at once impressed with the beauty of its situation. The Neckar flows out of the mountain gorges, and just at the point where it enters the valley of the Rhine, there is a narrow ledge at the base of the mountain, on which the town is built.

Several hundred feet above the town, on another ledge, stand the magnificent ruins of the castle and fortress of the Old Electors Palatine. The drive up the valley of the Neckar, and returning by the way of the castle, is one of the most beautiful that can be imagined. On going up the valley you have the mountains before you, and the Neckar winding out of them. On the return you ascend to the second ledge, and before you is the Neckar, flowing through the valley beneath, from which arise the wooded heights; the town is at your feet; the valley of the Rhine stretches out into a broad plain; the two silver rivers run together; still above you are hills crowned with forests; and as you approach the castle you enter enchanting groves, in the midst of which rise up the massive broken walls, and one huge tower lies toppled over in the fosse, of masonry so solid that it seems like a rock split from the side of a mountain. The dimensions of the castle are vast. Some rooms are still inhabited, but the mastery of ruin is plainly enough indicated. The terrace in front is quite perfect, and affords a magnificent promenade, commanding a wide view of the town, and of the valley of the Rhine. Here princes and royal dames once trod. Here were grandeur and pomp. And the town beneath was a splendid capital. But sad associations prevail over all others. The town has been five times bombarded, twice burnt to the ground, thrice taken by assault and pillaged. The castle, ten times surrounded by war, has been three times burnt, the last time by lightning.

The town now contains about fourteen thousand inhabitants, and has no remains of its ancient splendor but one lone building, whose dilapidated front still shows how rich were its original architectural decorations. Heidelberg, however, has a famous university, with professors of great distinction. The little Duchy of Baden—to which Heidelberg now belongs—one hundred and fifty miles long, and its greatest breadth one hundred miles, has two universities.

The beauty of the scenery, the cheapness of living, and the presence of the university, make Heidelberg a very desirable residence for a scholar. For two thousand dollars a family may live here not only comfortably, but elegantly, and keep a carriage and horses.

Our next route was to Baden-Baden. The romantic situation of this town in the valley of the Oos, and just on the borders of the Black Forest, has often been described. All are familiar with it, too, as, perhaps, the most celebrated watering-place in Germany. However high one's expectations may have been raised, they will not be disappointed.

Valleys amid picturesque hills, beautiful groves and forests, cultivated fields, charming drives, paths leading to the most secluded and quiet spots, streams of water, fresh verdure, and every thing showing the hand of taste as well as the lavish bounty of nature, conspire to make this a region of enchantment.

My daughter and myself one morning ascended to the ruins of the old castle, planted on the summit of a high hill above the town, in the midst of a dense forest—a walk of two and a half miles. It was the residence of the ancestors of the Duke of Baden during the middle ages. The ruins are very curious. Solid masonry is joined to the still more solid rocks, so that the walls are in part built by nature herself. Terrace rises above terrace, until, by stone steps, you at length reach the loftiest battlements. Here a magnificent landscape is spread out before you. The valley of Baden-Baden stretches out to the left. The town lies at your feet. The plain of the Rhine, with the majestic river winding through it, is at the right. The delighted eye wanders over hills and valleys, forests and open fields, towns and scattered dwellings—every thing that is beautiful to look upon. As we stood gazing upon the scene, the band of music in front of the *Trinkhalle*, far below, began to play. How soft and sweet were those strains wafted up through the pure air of the morning! It was like music heard in dreams.

Far below the ancient castle, and immediately above the town, is the new castle, one of the residences of the duke. It was built in the fifteenth century. Underneath are curious dungeons. A winding stair conducted us below. Passing through an ancient Roman bath we entered the vaults. Here were the place of imprisonment, the hall of judgment, the room of torture, and the awful pit into which criminals were precipitated. Over the pit was once a trap-door, and in a niche in the wall, an image of the Virgin. The wretched criminal was required to kiss the image, and in the act of doing so, was precipitated beneath, and torn to pieces by knives and lancets arranged for the purpose. The doors are blocks of stone which move easily upon pivots. It makes one shudder to walk through these dungeons, and imagine the scenes which have been here enacted.

The *Trinkhalle*, or pump room, is a splendid building.

Here every one goes and helps himself to the scalding draught. The taste is very much like weak chicken broth. Adjacent to this is the *Conversations Haus.* This building, also, is large and handsome. The grounds around are tastefully laid out. In this building are the celebrated *rouge et noir* and *roulette* tables. Elegantly dressed men and women are walking up and down the large saloon; others are seated in groups within or without. A fine band of music is constantly playing in the afternoon and evening. Some are dancing in an adjoining room. Every thing is calculated to intoxicate the senses. The two gaming tables, which are quite long, are arranged at one end of the saloon, separated from each other by a considerable space. At the centre of each table are seated four persons, two on each side, who conduct the game. At the sides and ends seated or standing are those who engage in play. Two of the conductors manage the roulette or the cards, and two handle the money. Nothing can exceed the calm cold gravity of these men. They pay out the losses with indifference, they rake in the gains without pity. Constantly the wheel is turning, constantly the cards are shuffled, constantly the gold is staked, constantly these men, with features immovable as those of Druid priests presiding over a sacrifice, pay out and rake in. In a few moments thousands are lost or won. There is no talking or whispering, no smiles, no pleasantries of manner. All is profound silence, but the low sound of the wheel and the fall of the ball, the shuffle of the cards, and the monotonous cold voice proclaiming the result, and the chink of the money. And these sounds seem like the voice of fate. While the wheel is yet turning, a man puts down a handful of gold, the ball drops, the gold is lost, and the man with the rake coolly draws it to his pile. Another handful is put down, and with the turn of the wheel, away it goes. Thus thousands are lost in a few minutes. Sometimes fate decides the other way, and the bank loses large sums. It even happens that for the evening the bank is broken. A short time before I arrived at Baden-Baden, a Russian had won twenty thousand dollars, and much to the disappointment of the bank, quitted play and went off to Paris. A year or two ago, a Russian won fifty thousand dollars, but intoxicated with his good fortune, kept on playing until the tide turned. He lost not only all he had won, but exhausted his letter of credit, so that he was compelled to beg a loan of the bank to return home. A suicide now and then occurs in consequence of bad luck. The bank is pleased at losing occasionally considerable sums. It acts as a lure; and as those who win generally go on tempting fortune, the bank is sure to get the better in the end, the aggregate of chances being in its favor. He who gambles for the first time, is ruined if he wins. Bad luck is the best luck to him who has not yet formed the habit.

It is a curious study to a bystander. There I saw a man hoary with age intensely engaged. He could not have been more earnest in the necessary and more appropriate work of preparing to die. People of all ages and of both sexes were there silent and absorbed.

I noticed a young man of dark hair and keen black eyes, and a pale countenance. He put down gold one or two hundred francs at a time. It was swept away. He repeated it again and again; all went against him; he lost thousands. Then he tried silver, with no better success. His brow grew wrinkled, his agony was intense; he looked at a companion and tried to smile, but his smile was ghastly and despairing. He was at the *roulette table.* At length he went away and tried the *rouge et noir.* Here he had moderate luck, and his features somewhat relaxed; but when I left, he had by no means made up his losses.

The countenance of a professed gambler has a remarkable and decided expression—pale, anxious, dreamy, and stern. He is a man always treading on the brink of fate. The very agony of hazard becomes his life. His enjoyment does not consist in possession, but in tempting ruin. His passion is all-absorbing. All his thoughts are melted into one monstrous idea. He almost ceases to be man, and changes into a woful spectre.

I felt most strangely while gazing upon these silent and rapt beings. They had to me an unearthly aspect. It seemed to me as if demons were hovering around and whispering temptations. I had a sense of horror, and yet experienced a wild fascination. It was like standing on the brink of a whirlpool where mermaids were singing. I turned away and walked out into the open air, and looked up to the stars in heaven.

These establishments at the German watering-places are licensed by the governments. The one at Baden-Baden pays about fifteen thousand dollars annually for its license, besides a hundred thousand dollars more to be expended on the grounds and buildings. This will afford some idea of the extent to which gambling is carried on, and of the profits which accrue to the proprietor. It is to be hoped that the disgrace and crime of granting these licenses may be done away.

We left Baden-Baden early in the morning for Kehl, opposite Strasburg. Our luggage we sent on directly to Basil, in charge of an acquaintance. At Kehl we took an omnibus for Strasburg, and crossed the Rhine on the bridge of boats. After a drive of three or four miles, we began to wind our way through the fortifications. Immense labor and skill have made these works apparently impregnable. On entering the town, our passports for the first time were demanded. Every thing has the appearance of a garrison. On the confines of Germany, Strasburg is a very important post. The town itself is not very attractive: but our eyes had been almost constantly directed towards the heavens pierced by that wonderful spire of the cathedral. The cathedral is the only striking object, but this is sufficient to draw a traveller aside. It was already past eleven o'clock when we got into the town, and so we drove off immediately to the cathedral, as its marvellous clock performs all its wonders precisely at noon. We found many persons already assembled, waiting for the hour. This clock has been perfectly restored by a living mechanician of Strasburg. The front in magnitude and appearance resembles that of a richly-decorated chapel. The clock is both a timekeeper and an almanac. But what chiefly attracts attention, is the procession and motions of the various figures connected with it. At the striking of each quarter, a figure passes over the face of the clock: at the first quarter, a little child, at the second, a youth, and last of all, an old man. Two cherubs are seated in front, at about one third of the elevation of the clock; one holding an hour-glass, the other a ball and hammer. Higher up is a figure of Death holding a hammer ready to strike a bell. Just in front of the dial-plate, stands a figure of Christ. On one side, perched aloft, is a cock with burnished wings. Just before the hour of twelve, one of the cherubs reverses the hour-glass, the other strikes the ball, and the cock flaps his wings and crows. In the course of the movements the cock crows three times, and with quite a natural intonation. At the hour of twelve, Death strikes the hour—twelve solemn strokes. At the same instant, the twelve apostles move in procession in front of Christ; each one as he passes turns and makes an inclination of the head, and the benignant image of the Saviour extends its hand to bless them. When Judas passes by, the hand makes the sign of the cross. When all have passed by, the hand is extended again, as if to bless all the beholders. The whole representation is beautiful and affecting. The machinery certainly must be very curious and complicated by which all these effects are daily brought about.

Having seen all the wonders of the clock, we had leisure to walk about the cathedral. The interior is by no means so impressive as the exterior. Many parts of the architecture are indeed grand, but there is not a harmony preserved throughout the whole. There is an elegantly and richly carved stone pulpit, well worth examining.

In one of the chapels some women were engaged in attiring a miserable-looking image of the *Vierge doloreuse*, with a dead Christ in her lap. The attire was chiefly white muslin.

On the head was placed a gilt tinsel crown. At vespers, I found a crowd of women kneeling before the image, gazing at it with strained eyes of adoration.

The exterior of the cathedral produces on one the effect of a beautiful poem. The figures of angels and saints beside and over the doors, are each a study. The whole of the exterior is covered with exquisite carving. It realized fully my idea of Gothic architecture, as a delicate veil thrown over naturally rugged features, and softening every thing into grace and beauty.

The spire, which rises four hundred and seventy-four feet above the pavement, is the highest spire in the world. To the eye it appears to be constructed of iron bars, so hard and so finely wrought are the stones of which it is built. More than four centuries have passed over it, and there it pierces the heavens still, with no sign of weakness or decay. During the day I spent in Strasburg I visited the cathedral again and again; I walked around it more than once, pausing at every point to gaze and admire, and when at length I was compelled to bid it good-by, I felt sad and reluctant. Some weeks afterwards, when descending the Rhine, I caught again a view of the spire, and felt a thrill of pleasure. I had a strong desire to turn aside and take another look at the cathedral. From the time the nave was begun to the completion of the spire, was four hundred years. The other spire will never be built. Mankind will build no more such cathedrals. Monuments of grandeur and beauty; hoary remains of ages never to be revived, let them stand. Our modern attempts at Gothic architecture are like imitations of the Iliad.

Strasburg is half German and half French. The common language is a strange *patois.* There is nothing here to interest one much besides the cathedral, unless it be this curious mixture of habits and language, and the fortifications.

There is but one fine hotel in the place, and that is the *Ville de Paris*, so that travellers need not be perplexed in making a choice.

From Strasburg we took the train for Basle, on the French side of the Rhine. The road here is better than on the other side, and the travelling more rapid. The route lies in a level country bounded by the Vosges mountains. I observed that the land was cultivated in narrow strips, with different grains and vegetables. Upon inquiry I found that this was owing to its being divided among small proprietors, each of whom, in growing a necessary variety, was compelled to make those minute subdivisions of his portion. The cultivation was very nice, and the land made to produce to its utmost capacity. But how different from the ample and substantial farms of our country, each with its house and barn, and belonging to the absolute lord of the soil! We have, comparatively, a careless husbandry, but we have independence and plenty. I was pained to see the strips of potatoes very generally suffering from the *rot.* A failure of this kind must prove a real calamity, where every product of labor is so greatly needed.

We reached Basle about noon, and put up at the Three Kings, the best hotel in the town, and beautifully situated immediately on the bank of the Rhine. The Three Kings, as large as life, are perched aloft in front, and are undoubtedly as genuine as the three skulls we saw at Cologne, and devoted to a much better purpose, for here they promise a regal entertainment.

VII.

Basle or Basil.

THE Three Kings exhibited a very lively scene. Post coaches and other carriages were drawn up on one side· Travellers of various nations were standing on the broad steps and platform of the entrance. Couriers were bustling about, and servants of different descriptions running to and fro. Until night had set in there were constant arrivals of travellers going to or returning from the Alps. Basil is the grand confluence of travellers. Here properly the toon of Switzerland begins. From here you may proceed in various directions—to Schaffhausen, to Zurich, to Lucerne, to Berne, to Neuchatel and Lausanne, and thence to Geneva. We took the latter route.

I had intended, like most travellers, to make no stop at Basil, and to push immediately for the Alps. Mr. Burchard, our consul, persuaded me to remain from Friday, when I arrived, until Monday. This gentleman, a true American at heart, indefatigable, earnest and faithful in all that he undertakes, of a most genial and obliging disposition, intelligent, and well versed in the languages of the country, is singularly qualified for the post he holds. It is to be hoped that no change of our administration will be a sufficient reason for supplanting him.

Should a chargé d'affaires be appointed for the Swiss Cantons, how much better to give the post to a man who is qualified alike by education, experience and residence, than to send some new man into the field who has every thing to learn.

The indiscriminate removal from office upon every change in our administration is an evil attending our free institutions, which we can submit to with a very good grace at home. Some changes are for the better, and many are not for the worse. Individuals suffer, rather than the country at large. But since every man takes office at home under the expectation of giving place to somebody else, sooner or later, the individual has no injustice to complain of. The case is entirely different with respect to our consuls and diplomatic corps. When we have placed the proper man in a post abroad, and he has gained experience and tact, the nation suffers far more than the individual by his removal. It is required of our foreign ministers that they should be men of education, well acquainted with the language of the court at which they reside, and with the French as the common diplomatic language. Profound historical and political knowledge they, of course, should have. When in addition to this they have by long residence become perfectly familiar with their duties, what can be more absurd, as well as more suicidal of our foreign interests, than to displace them merely because we have elected a new President at home? What have our party politics to do with our foreign relations? The frequency of these changes is a matter of surprise and even of ridicule in foreign countries.

One among many evils to be deprecated in sending abroad men who are not acquainted with the language of the country in which they reside, is that they come into contact only with the court and its parasites. Hence, they cannot know the true condition of the country, and the mind of the people, nor possess themselves of the facts which are essential in enabling them to form a correct judgment of political questions and the state of political parties.

The late Mr. Gallatin informed me that when he first took up his residence at the court of Russia as our minister, he set himself at work to acquire the Russian language, and that in three months he was able to read the newspapers printed in that language. He indeed had an extraordinary facility in the acquisition of languages; but, it was characteristic of this truly great man that he would not accept the French—the court language—as his only medium of gaining information respecting Russian affairs.

The modern canton of Basle-town separated from the old canton of Basle, comprises the city, and a territory of only four miles in extent on the right bank of the river. Here the Middle Rhine begins. This too is the head of navigation. The Upper Rhine, with its tributaries, pours down from the glaciers and lakes of Switzerland. The country around Basil is highly picturesque, and cultivated like a garden. The Rhine rushes through the town broad and rapid, and of a beautiful green color. The Black Forest lifts its hills on one side, and the Jura range rises on the other. The town is walled, well built, and has the appearance of considerable trade and wealth. It contains only twenty-five thousand inhabitants, and yet it has a university, with twenty professors. Euler and Bernouilli were once professors here. The present professor of chemistry is the inventor of *gun-cotton*. The public library contains fifty thousand volumes. The Reading-room is finely situated near the Terrace. This is planted with trees and commands a wide view over the Rhine, the town, and the country beyond. In the Reading-room I found newspapers from every part of Europe, and the leading papers of America. Nearly a hundred papers and magazines are taken.

In front of the Terrace stands the Minster, more than eight hundred years old. It is a very curious and interesting building. Here are the tombs of Erasmus, and of the Reformers Œcolampadius, Grynæus, and Meyer. The portal of St. Gallus is adorned with statues of Christ, St. Peter, and the wise and foolish virgins. The equestrian statue of St. George and the Dragon, on the west front, is striking, but somewhat grotesque. Here also is St. Martin and the Beggar.

The gallery of paintings and drawings contains many interesting pieces of Holbein, who was a native of Augsburg, but took up his residence here until he went to England. Among these pieces are admirable portraits of

Erasmus, and of the artist himself. The portraits of his wife and two children, in one piece, is pronounced by artists the finest painting of all. They are represented in a state of want and misery which was real, for the artist suffered much from poverty before his removal to England. In gazing at the group the illusion becomes perfect, and your sympathies are strongly moved. Lifelike reality is the distinguishing characteristic of Holbein. This appears again in his painting of the Passion of our Saviour. It is painted on panels, and comprises eight compartments, representing the scenes of the passion from the arrest to the entombment. The first and the last are the best. The dead body is so real, and the marks of violence on the feet and hands, and the agonized expression of the countenance are so truthful, that one shudders to look at it. This painting was carried away during some convulsion of the state, and repurchased for thirty-six thousand florins.

In this gallery are six frescoes of the original Dance of Death, which once belonged to the walls of the Dominican Church of Basil. There is also a series of colored drawings, which represent all the figures. These frescoes were in being before the birth of Holbein, so that he cannot be the author of them.

On Saturday we drove into the country, accompanied by Mr. Burchard, who kindly took upon himself the office of cicerone. We first drove to the battle-field of St. Jacob, a short distance from the gates. It borders upon the Birs, at an angle made by two roads. Sixteen hundred Swiss forded the stream and attacked sixteen thousand French, commanded by the Dauphin, afterwards Louis XI. The battle lasted ten hours. Only ten of the Swiss survived and fled. They were held in disgrace by their countrymen. Nearly one-third of the French were slain. The politic Louis made peace at once with a people of such determined bravery, and entered into a perpetual league with them. He enrolled a body-guard from among them, a practice continued afterwards by the French monarchs. Vines now cluster around the scene of strife, and the red wine which they produce bears the name of Schweitzer Blut. At a little inn near the bridge, and separated from St. Jacob only by the road, we called for a bottle, and drank the Swiss blood to the memory of the brave. The wine is light and of a pleasant flavor. Suspended to the beams of the inn was a rusty sword, which had been turned up on the battle-field. The Swiss call St. Jacob their Thermopylæ. It filled Europe with the fame of their arms.

We next proceeded to Arlsheim, some six miles distant, by a pleasant road along the stream, with the Jura on our left. On our way we passed the picturesque ruins of Wartsburgh and Reichstein. At Arlsheim we left our carriage at the village inn, ordered dinner, and in the mean time ascended to the deserted convent and hermitage. The hermitage is about half way up the ascent. In it are preserved the bed of rushes and the few articles of furniture which belonged to the devout man. A figure of the hermit dressed in his garments is seated by the table, with a missal open before it, and has quite a natural appearance. The hill, which is a spur of the Jura, has many natural grottoes, which the industry of this man through many years of solitary labor improved and fashioned into beautiful retreats—a fit haunt for poets as well as religious men.

> Intus aquæ dulces, vivoque sedilia saxo;
> Nympharum domus.

The face of the hill is thickly enbowered with trees; paths wind about in every direction; rural seats are placed at intervals; at sudden turns of the path the grottoes are presented; openings among the trees give enchanting views of the valley beneath; the music of brooks and waterfalls catch the ear; and the happy birds fill the trees, and build their nests, and sing their songs undisturbed. It is a place to meditate in, to dream dreams, to drink in all the beauty and quietude of nature.

On a rock is the following inscription: "*Hospes! debes has delicias naturæ, industriæ,*" &c. The name of the hermit follows, which I have forgotten.

One of the grottoes deeper than the rest contains the tomb of the hermit. This was suddenly illuminated by our attendant with lights kept ready for the purpose, and the tomb, with the figure of an angel, and a transparency beyond representing a heavenly radiance, rose out of the darkness. It was evidently a shrine where the villagers resorted to say their prayers.

On the summit of the hill stands the convent, empty and falling into ruins. The little garden is still cultivated by some one, and a small vineyard outside of the wall lies basking in the sun. The view from the convent commands one of the most lovely and quiet scenes in the world. At the left, the valley of the Birs seems shut in by the Jura mountains which wind around westward; at the right, you look down the valley of the Birs toward Basle; in front, lie beautifully cultivated fields, the river flowing through them; Arlsheim and Dornach are at your feet; you look along the sides of the Jura, where several ruins peer out; you turn and look in the rear of the convent, and a valley, hemmed in by the steep sides of the mountain, with a brook gurgling through it, seems to invite you with an air of mystery to explore strange places of beauty, and you feel a longing to know what can be found there, far among mountain fastnesses.

When we descended to the inn, we found a table very neatly spread, and sat down to a dinner prepared after the German fashion, consisting of many courses, excellent in quality, and well cooked. We were surprised to get one of the best dinners, we had met with on the continent, in this plain country inn. We were furnished with a white wine the produce of the fields around, marked *Arlsheimer*, 1825. It was unquestionably the pure juice of the grape, mild and agreeable. The daughter of the host waited at table, a plain, cleanly, and honest-looking young woman, apparently about as old as the wine. We were charged two francs and a half each for the dinner, and one franc a bottle for the wine.

On our return, we passed by *Dornach*, where the Swiss gained a memorable victory over an Austrian army, larger than that of the Dauphin, in 1499, during the Suabian war. Near the Capuchin Convent is a house in which the skulls gathered from the field of battle are still preserved—a strange, ghastly, but not inappropriate monument of the event.

The battles of St. Jacob's and Dornach were alike decisive of Swiss valor and Swiss liberty.

We diverged from the main road at Dornach to reach the Church of St. Margaret. The church is an ancient building. The house of the pastor is attached to it. The whole had an air of comfort as well as sacredness. Our object in visiting it was to enjoy the noble prospect which it commands. The valley of the Birs was again presented us, the Black Forest, and the Jura; but in addition to this the city of Basle lay under our eye, and the landscape was complete. It was now near the setting of the sun, and a day of rare enjoyment was finished by contemplating a scene which combined more beautiful and striking points, very clearly defined, than any I had yet met with. And even now, after I have seen much grander prospects, my mind returns to the view from St. Margaret's Church with a sense of delight which proves to me that I received no ordinary impressions.

Basle is a town strict in religious observances. The gates are closed on the Sabbath, and the inhabitants are assembled in the churches at an early hour. We attended the church of the Huguenots, where the service is still performed in the French language. The building is several centuries old, and considerably dilapidated. The congregation is small, and is composed chiefly of the descendants of the Huguenots who first established the church. The preacher delivered his discourse without notes, and gave us a good gospel sermon. His enunciation was easy, fervent, and impressive. The associations of the place were hallowed, and I felt that I was sitting among Christian brethren.

VIII.

The Val Moutiers—Bienne—Neuchâtel—Lausanne.

LET us recall the general features of Switzerland now that we are about entering it. From east to west it extends two hundred miles from the Tyrol to France, and from north to south one hundred and fifty miles from Baden to Lombardy. Two ranges of mountains traverse this country, and run nearly parallel to each other from the southwest to the northeast,—the Jura and the Alps. The Jura range is about two hundred and fifty miles in length, and forty in breadth, and bold and precipitous on the side which faces the Alps. The Alps longer, broader, loftier, branching out in all directions, and with Mont Blanc as king of the mountains, fill the land. Mountains of snow and ice, seas of ice, glaciers or torrents of ice pouring down into green valleys, valleys beautiful as fairyland, perpendicular precipices of black rock rising thousands of feet; torrents, cascades, waterfalls, brooks, rivers, and lakes, gloomy forests, fields of beautiful cultivation—every wild, grand, and lovely form of nature, is presented in Switzerland. Where in the wide world can another region be found like it?

Our route from Basil lay in the Jura range, along the Birs which has its source in this range above Tavannes. It is really the valley of the Birs, for nature seems to have rent the rocks to open a course for the river. It is called the Val Moutiers, after the village which lies at the head of the principal gorge.

The road which winds through this valley is firm and smooth. It runs along the foot of precipices, close to the edge of the river, and frequently crosses from one bank to the other on stone bridges, to find a level space. Sometimes it is cut along the side of the precipice, where a slope affords a convenient passage.

The Jura, by its spurs and sinuosities, makes a succession of valleys or basins, above which rise the rocky sides and fir-clad peaks. The freshness of the verdure which clothes these valleys is enchanting. The grass and the foliage feed upon the purest mountain streams, and the brightest sunshine. The hamlets and villages which lie scattered about, look as if they had retired from a noisy and impure world and sought here an everlasting repose, and an exemption from the vices and miseries which beset the rest of mankind. It makes one sad to be forced to the conviction that the common human nature dwells here.

The rocks which once separated this succession of valleys

from each other have been cleft asunder, forming narrow gorges where the mighty precipices rise above you like a wall. The road is thus between two huge walls. The whole space between is often occupied by the stream and the road. Some of the rocks are strangely scooped out into grottoes and caverns; some are piled up in a smooth wall; some are jagged and afford a precarious footing for trees and shrubs; while dark forests overhang the brow of the precipice.

The wildest and most wonderful of these gorges is the one which lays open the basin in which the village of Moutiers is situated. The Jura here is cleft to its very foundations, and the strata of limestone are like immense slabs set up on their edges.

It is this alternation of wild gorges and lonely valleys which makes up the enchantment of the Val Moutiers. It is indeed the alternation of the sublime and the beautiful. You forget carriage and horses and all the common contrivances which are bearing you along, and you become sensible only of the succession of grand and beautiful objects and the succession of emotions within you. Nature seems to be a written music blending the wildest and sweetest strains; your outward motion is a motion along the lines of the music, while your heart is all the while joyfully singing the tune. On ascending a steep and long acclivity, by a turn of the road and through a vista of rocks and trees, I got a view of a valley we had just left behind. The softest meadows lay far beneath smiling under a magical sunlight, and swept away under the shadow of bordering woods. Here and there a cottage appeared, and then a clump of trees. I felt as if I had got for a moment a peep into some hallowed spot—some little paradise. I recollect when a boy away in the woods, or angling in mountain streams through the summer days, having fallen upon spots so beautiful that they appeared to me as not of this world, and they awakened in me strange fancies which connected heaven with earth. While looking into this valley, these memories of my boyhood came floating through my mind, so that tears filled my eyes. Then I realized how the effect of the beautiful present to us is heightened by an association with other scenes. These impressions are imperishable. They wake up a strain of melody which is continually lengthening, and every new experience is rendered more exquisite by becoming a part of that which already exists.

After passing Tavannes, and leaving the source of the Birs behind, the road quits the valley, and winds up a steep ascent. Midway, it passes underneath an arch of rocks bearing a defaced Roman inscription. The arch may have been enlarged by art, but it evidently is mainly the work of nature. It is a strange work—a door through the mountain.

At length we reached the last slope of the Jura. How magnificent and thrilling the view which now at once broke upon us from the brow of the hill! The town and lake of Bienne lay beneath us. In the lake reposed the isle of St. Pierre, the dreamland of Rousseau. Far and wide stretched the region watered by the Aar, the Emme, and the Zihl. Behind the whole, rose the glorious Alps. Only the black, gigantic masses were visible; the snow-mountains were hidden in clouds. But there were the Alps! I repeated to myself, There are the Alps—the Alps! How wild were my emotions! I felt ready to leap from the vehicle, to clap my hands, and shout aloud, The Alps—the Alps! I realized that I was in Switzerland; and, oh! how I longed to have those clouds lifted, that I might see the vision which they concealed! The expectations of years were now to be realized. Behind that mass of clouds lay those wonders of creation. As we descended the long hill, my eye passed rapidly over the intervening objects, beautiful as they were, and toiled to penetrate the mystery of the clouds. Those black mountains appeared immense, and yet they did not reach the region of ice and snow. The ice-peaks were in the clouds of heaven.

We gained the bottom of the descent, we wound along through vineyards, and entered Bienne. Here we paused only to change horses and vehicles. We had occupied the coupé of the diligence, which just accommodated our party of three. It was of ample dimensions, and, glazed on the sides and front, gave us a perfect view. We had taken the coupé, two days before, for Neuchâtel. But we had not been informed that this pleasant vehicle proceeded on our route no further than Bienne, and that we were there to be transferred to an inferior carriage. We still occupied what was dignified with the name coupé, but it was narrow, uncomfortable, and open to the weather. The beauty of the drive, however, compensated for every thing. The road followed the shore of the lake. Vineyards covered the slopes of the hills on our right. On our left was the lake, and beyond, the range of the Alps. Our coachman carried a huge whip, with which he constantly amused himself, making strange and rapid evolutions, and giving cracks that the distant Alps might have re-echoed. Whenever we entered a village, his importance and energy increased. The whip made fearful circles around his head, the houses appeared to shake with the concussion, the children ran into the streets, the dogs barked, the whole populace were thrown into a state of agitation. The horses, for whose benefit the great whip might be imagined to be especially designed, took it all very quietly, and seemed quite used to the freaks of their master. The sun had set ere we arrived at Neuchâtel. We put up at the Hotel des Alpes, pleasantly situated near the lake. We had dined by the way at a good village inn. At another inn a pretty Swiss maiden had supplied us with pears and apricots, and a bottle of wine. A cup of black tea, bread and butter, and a comb of the transparent honey in which Switzerland abounds, formed a simple but sufficient supper. Weariness and pleasant thoughts invited a profound and refreshing sleep.

The next morning we took a view of Neuchâtel. The town lies partly against the steep slope of the Jura, and partly upon a level space on the border of the lake. It looks out upon the lake, and the Alps are ever in sight except when veiled in clouds. None but the black masses were yet visible. Neuchâtel, although possessing none of that boldness and grandeur of scenery which distinguish other towns in Switzerland, has a quiet and picturesque effect which renders it very agreeable.

Professor Agassiz, the distinguished naturalist, and who is now a professor in one of our own colleges, was born here.

The Museum of Natural History in his native town is indebted to him for many valuable collections.

Some time during the last century a poor boy named David Pury, without friends or resources of any kind, wandered away from Neuchâtel to seek his subsistence somewhere in the wide world. By industry and frugality he gradually accumulated property, became in time a jeweller and banker in Lisbon, and grew into a large fortune. The boy who had known nothing in Neuchâtel but the home of poverty, when he died became its benefactor, bestowing upon it his whole fortune, amounting to nearly a million of dollars. A hospital and poor-house, and many other public benefits, are the fruits of his charity. Neuchâtel will for ever be his monument, and his memory will live in the hearts of its citizens.

At Neuchâtel we procured a very commodious and easy carriage, with good horses, and a civil and obliging coachman. We had another day of pure enjoyment. Our route was along the northwest shore of the lake until we reached Yverdun at its lower extremity, where we diverged to the south and crossed the high ridge which separates the lakes of Neuchâtel and Geneva.

On the one hand we had the Jura, on the other the lake, and beyond the lake, the Alps, the ice-peaks still in the clouds. The vineyards covered the hills. The whole country was beautiful. The eye was constantly entertained. The temperature was delightful. We enjoyed a holiday, and a holiday seemed to be spread over creation.

Near the outlet of the lake is situated the small town of

Granson. Here is the old castle in which Charles of Burgundy besieged a Swiss garrison, whom, upon surrender, he hung on the trees or drowned in the lake. And not far from Granson we rode over the celebrated battle-field, still marked by three granite obelisks, where the Swiss took their revenge. It is a narrow strip of land on the border of the lake, at the foot of the mountain. On this strip of land Charles led his gay and gallant horsemen. His infantry was planted against the side of the mountain. It was a glorious array of sixty thousand men—the most splendid and well appointed army in Europe. More than a hundred pieces of cannon were drawn up in front.

The army of the Swiss did not number more than a third of the Burgundians; but they were fired with a spirit which nothing could resist—the bodies of their countrymen were still hanging upon the trees.

I asked our coachman if he knew any thing about the battle. He immediately told the story in his rude patois. All the Swiss are familiar with it. Scott, in his Anne of Geierstein, has put the story in the mouth of the rough and clownish Sigismund Biederman. His language, perhaps, was similar to that of the coachman. I will make an extract, therefore, as the best translation I can give:—

"Then there was a huge cloud of dust approaching us, and we began to see that we must do or die, for this was Charles and his whole army come to support his vanguard. A blast from the mountain dispersed the dust, for they had halted to prepare for battle. Oh, good Arthur! you would have given ten years of life but to have seen the sight. There were thousands of horse, all in complete array, glancing against the sun, and hundreds of knights with crowns of gold and silver on their helmets, and thick masses of spears on foot, and cannon, as they call them. I did not know what things they were which they drew on heavily with bullocks and placed before their army, but I knew more of them before the morning was over. Well, we were ordered to draw up in a hollow square, as we are taught at exercise, and before we pushed forwards, we were commanded, as is the godly rule and guise of our warfare, to kneel down and pray to God, Our Lady, and the blessed saints. Charles, supposing we asked grace, was determined to show us that we had asked it at a graceless face, for he cried: 'Fire my cannon on the coward slaves; it is all the mercy they have to expect from me!' Bang—bang—bang—off went the things I told you of, like thunder and lightning, and some mischief they did, but the less that we were kneeling; and the saints doubtless gave the huge balls a hoist over the heads of those who were asking grace from them, but from no mortal creatures. So we had the signal to rise and rush on, and I promise you there were no sluggards. Every man felt ten men's strength. My halberd is no child's toy, and yet it trembled in my grasp as if it had been a willow wand to drive cows with. On we went, when suddenly the cannon were silent, and the earth shook with another and continued growl and battering, like thunder under ground. It was the men-at-arms rushing to charge us. But our leaders knew their trade, and had seen such a sight before. It was: 'Halt, halt—kneel down in the front—stoop in the second rank—close shoulder to shoulder like brethren—lean all spears forward, and receive them like an iron wall!' On they rushed, and there was a rending of lances that would have served the Unterwalden old women with splinters of firewood for a twelvemonth. Down went armed horse—down went accoutred knight—down went banner and bannerman—down went peaked boot and crowned helmet; and of those who fell, not a man escaped with life. So they drew off in confusion, and were getting in order to charge again, when the noble Duke Ferrand and his horsemen dashed at them in their own way, and we moved onward to support him. Thus on we pressed, and the foot hardly waited for us, seeing their cavalry so handled. Then if you had seen the dust and heard the blows! The noise of a hundred thousand thrashers, the flight of the chaff which they drive about, would be but a type of it. On my word, I almost thought it shame to dash about my halberd, the rout was so helplessly piteous. Hundreds were slain unresisting, and the whole army was in complete flight."

A little beyond Granson is Yverdun, where we stopped for dinner. The drive from here to Lausanne affords many fine prospects, and has an agreeable variety of up-hill and down-hill. Villages are scattered all along the way. The Swiss build their houses and barns under the same roof. Hay and grain are often stored away over their sleeping apartments. Sometimes these apartments are over the stables. The villages too are rendered foul and unsightly by stacks of manure reeking in front of the dwellings. The Swiss chalets and villages are beautiful objects in the landscape, but are not very inviting on a close inspection.

At one of these villages, I noticed for the first time our coachman feeding his horses with good rye bread. This I found to be a general custom. An excellent lunch this for horses, and one that occupies but little time.

As the evening approached, the air on these hills became quite cold, so that we were fain to put on our overcoats. Men and women who had been working in the meadows were wending slowly homeward with scythes and rakes; and wains heavily laden were creaking under their burdens. The glorious setting sun tipped the hills with gold, while the valleys lay in shadow. The peaks of the Alps caught the last rays.

The Swiss women have stout persons, and large arms and hands. They go bareheaded, and do all kinds of work in the fields. I frequently saw them swinging the scythe. The young women, with full bronzed cheeks, bright eyes, and long hair, have a good deal of rustic beauty. The old women have leathery complexions, and a haggard, care-worn look. Borrowe remarks of the Gipsies in Spain, that the young women are very beautiful, while the old women are perfect hags. In rustic and rude modes of life, youth has a peculiar freshness and energy. The beauty is the mere beauty of youth. When this fades there is no beauty of expression to supply the loss. The highest beauty of the human face is that of expression: but this depends upon the cultivation and the graces of the soul. The old age which follows a life of thought, of virtuous affections, and of active benevolence, exhibits the human face in its noblest and most impressive beauty. The frail blossoms have fallen to the ground, but the golden fruit now hangs upon the boughs. The sensual loveliness has given place to the pure dignity of intellect, and the benignity of goodness. Indeed, old age will bring out into bare expression the passions, whether good or bad, which have governed the life. All human beings, therefore, will grow beautiful, or ugly, as they grow wise and good, or the opposite. The poor Swiss maidens, and the peasant women of Europe generally, have little control over their destiny. But ye who have life at your command, and would be beautiful and attractive, learn the only true way!

Women work in the fields, but, not only this, cows drag the plough. So it is with the feminine gender of both man and brute. I pitied the poor motherly cow. I contrasted her condition with that of the cows of England and America, roving in fat pastures, and when weary with cropping the grass, lying down under the shade of tress to chew the cud, and then in the evening quietly walking to the farmyard to give cheerfully the treasures of her udder to the milkmaid's pail. And the cow in Switzerland has an ox-like appearance, just as the women are masculine. I asked the coachman, "Why do you work your cows?" "Oh!" said he, "oxen give no milk; they are good for nothing but to work." "But," replied I, "your cows do not give as much milk, nor as good." "Yes, but it is more profitable to work cows, for they give us some milk!"

The peasantry in Europe do not indulge much in the luxury of butter. The Swiss get milk enough to eat with their bread, and with that they are content. In the higher Alpine regions, where the land is devoted to pasturage, the cows lead their natural life, and quantities of butter and cheese are made.

The night had set in when we reached Lausanne. We drove to the Hotel Gibbon. The house was nearly filled with guests, so that we had to mount up several stories to find our apartments.

One of our apartments overlooked the lake. The following morning was clear and bright. I arose and went to the window, and threw open the shutter. What a scene burst upon my eye! Was it enchantment, or was it reality! Was it earth or heaven! I can never forget that moment; neither can I describe my feelings. The beautiful lake lay beneath me. Directly opposite, on the further shore, arose, as from the water's edge, a wall of mountains; and mountain rose behind mountain, and over the whole was the delicate haze of the morning like a transparent veil. I looked down the lake towards Chamouni, and in the distance there was nothing but clouds. I turned towards the head of the lake, and the ice mountains of Savoy were glittering beneath the morning sun. So clear was the atmosphere, and so huge the masses, that they appeared just at hand. The ice mountains! Now I saw them for the first time. The ice mountains piled up, far above all earthly things, in the clear heavens! I gazed in silence. Then I turned away and walked about the room instinctively, to collect my thoughts, and arouse myself from the stupefaction of wonder. I went back to the window—there they were still. How glorious! how beautiful! how pure!—there was no stain upon them. How deep the consciousness that I possessed a soul, and thought, and feeling! I seemed to spread myself over them—to embrace them—to become one with them. God is great: the soul of man is great. O

Almighty Spirit! we are thy work, made after thine image; and here without are thy stupendous works; the heavens are thine—thou hast garnished them; the earth is thine; these everlasting mountains are thine: we see thee in thy works—we feel the glory of thy presence.

Our first excursion was the ascent of the heights above the town. We rode up in a carriage by a steep road. From the platform called the *Signal*, that view is gained which all travellers have celebrated. I scarcely know how to speak of it. There are scenes which can be embellished by description. There are scenes which appear more beautiful in a painting than in Nature. But this is not one of them. The effect upon my mind was similar to what I experienced in looking out of the lofty window of the hotel, but more intense and bewildering, as it was far more extensive and magnificent. There was the same visionary splendor which had struck me at first, especially in the direction of the ice mountains. There is nothing in the world besides like these mountains. No one can adequately conceive of them without seeing them. Here they appeared so near and so distinct, that I felt their presence; not their coldness, for that did not enter into my thought, but their vastness, their mightiness, their purity. They were not of the earth, earthly; they were above the earth; man had not dwelt upon them; they were removed from the region of littleness, of vain ambition, and polluting passion. They were nearest to the skies; the morning sun first touched them with his light, the evening sun left his last splendor upon them. They sometimes hid themselves in the clouds, as if to hold solitary communion with heaven; and when they looked out from the clouds, it was with a countenance of light, majesty, and purity. Sublime and beautiful! Yes, sublime and beautiful! Two ideas, two emotions perfectly united. The more sublime, because at the same time beautiful; the more beautiful, because at the same time sublime. The ideas of incomprehensible vastness and power, joined with the ideas of harmony, purity, and grace. The majesty of God walking in brightness; the power of God building a throne of solid light from earth to heaven. I felt reverence and awe, but I felt love also. At one moment my thought said, How great is God! at the next moment my thought said, How beautiful is God! I experienced an inexpressible delight. I said to myself, How happy I am, that I am! I rejoice in life! I live, I think, I feel! My soul embraces this beautiful world!

I looked down upon the picturesque town—a fine point in the landscape—and yet I cared not to dwell upon it. Why should I gaze at piles of stone and brick, at spires, at paved streets? I looked to the right; there was a green and richly cultivated undulating country; and behind lay the Jura. I looked down the blue lake until its curvature hid it from my eye. Beyond the lake, mountain rose upon mountain, until the clouds shut in the prospect. I looked towards the head of the lake, and there was that region of splendor I have spoken of. There the swift Rhone pours into the lake, the same Rhone which rushes from it at the lower end. The river comes from the bosom of the mountains. The lake lies at the foot of the mountains. The variety of objects, each striking in itself, in this landscape, is wonderful. The variety of hues, too, which adorn it, adds to the magical effect, perhaps constitutes that dreaminess which hangs over it. The splendor of the ice mountains contrasts with the dark precipices of the lower regions—like mighty diamonds set upon a dark ground. The blue lake contrasts with both, and appears like quiet beauty sleeping at the feet of awful majesty. The cultivated and picturesque country, on the Jura side of the lake, contrasts with the wildness and grandeur of the Alpine domains on the opposite side. The Jura range contrasts with the Alpine: the first is of a piece with what Nature does in other lands; the second shows the triumph of her power and majesty here

The town lies upon little hills and in ravines. Here man has erected his dwellings, and piled up and adorned one of his beautiful cathedrals. It is a charming spot, when one thinks of a home—that town of Lausanne. I thought I would like to have a house there, like Gibbon, and pursue my own quiet thoughts and studies. Then when tired of indoor work, I would look out of my windows, walk in my garden, and sometimes ascend these heights to take a wider view of the lake and the mountains. But the town so attractive as a home, what a little thing it appears amid these scenes. How man's feebleness contrasts with the strength that threw up these mountains into the face of heaven! The Cathedral of Cologne, the spire of Strasburg, what toys they would be before these black precipices and these pinnacles of ice! Let not man build cathedrals or towers, or obelisks or pyramids here; this is no place for his works.

Nature has forestalled him. If he build he will, indeed, add to the variety of the landscape; but let him do his best, and he will only serve the humble office of increasing the effect of the might of Nature, by bringing it into contrast with his own weakness. Build cathedrals or palaces here! When the avalanches fall, the mountain echoes will laugh you to scorn. No, no; build here commodious and tasteful dwellings, if you please, but let them be unpretending. Do not try to show your might and your pride; here the might and majesty of the Almighty are too palpably seen. And if you want a temple to worship in, go to the roof of your house, or into a closet with a window open toward the mountains; or, better still, go into some solitary place, where the trees shut you in from human view; but where through vistas you can see all without. And was there ever a grander temple built than this? Jura on one side, the Alps on the other, green slopes of meadows and vineyards, and the blue lake between, and the serene heavens overhead! Here kneel down and pray, or muse in speechless devotion. What mean those who talk to us about consecrated places? This glorious world, has not God made this himself, and consecrated it himself?

It is a human contrivance to take the beautiful world for base uses—for mere agriculture, commerce, and ambition and violence; and then to inclose some little spot between four walls and call that a place of worship. Men endeavored to shut out God from his earth and heavens, and to imprison him in a temple where they might visit him as they pleased. When God condescended to human weakness and permitted a temple to be built upon Sion, it was announced that it could not contain him. When the Son of God was upon earth he went out into the mountains to pray.

Now that I have spoken of the Alps and all this glorious scenery around, I feel inclined to speak of nothing else in or about Lausanne. Just at this point, it has occurred to me to look at the third canto of Childe Harold, and I am almost startled as I recognize there my own thoughts and feelings. What I have written above came from my own soul, and I have within me the evidence that the poet uttered true words about man and nature.

> "I live not in myself, but I become
> Portion of that around me; and to me
> High mountains are a feeling ——"

> "Are not the mountains, waves, and skies, a part
> Of me and of my soul, as I of them?
> Is not the love of these deep in my heart
> With a pure passion?"

It is this melting of the soul into the grand and beautiful of nature, or this reception of the grand and beautiful into the soul itself, by which we seem to become one with that without us, so that "High mountains are a feeling," that contains the mystery and yet the explanation of all that ecstatic delight which we experience amid such scenery. The ideas of the infinite and the beautiful within us now find their embodiment. Coleridge has expressed the same truth in his Hymn in the Vale of Chamouni:

"O dread and silent mount! I gazed upon thee,
Till thou, still present to the bodily sense,
Didst vanish from my thought: entranced in prayer
I worshipped the Invisible alone.
Yet like some sweet beguiling melody,
So sweet, we know not we are listening to it,
Thou, the meanwhile, wast blending with my thought,
Yea, with my Life and Life's own secret joy;
Till the dilating Soul, enrapt, transfused,
Into the mighty Vision passing—there
As in her natural form, swelled vast to Heaven!"

From the material form which in its indefinite vastness becomes to us an expression of the infinite, the soul ascends to the infinite itself. In the greatness of its idea it becomes conscious of its own greatness, and seems to clothe itself with those majestic forms in which its idea is reflected.

IX.

Lake Leman—Geneva.

FROM the *Signal*, the view of the head of the lake is perfect. This is the grandest part of it. Is this the scene of the thunder-storm which Byron describes? I have thought so, since he mentions Clarens immediately after. The rent in the mountains, where the "swift Rhone cleaves his way," appears, however, to refer more naturally to the wild gorge near Collouges. It is probable that he intends to grasp the whole lake and its sublime scenery in his description. But while standing on these heights above Lausanne, although the heavens were clear and the sun shining in his strength, the idea of a storm among these mountains rushed into my mind, and I repeated to myself the wonderful lines:

"Far along,
From peak to peak, the rattling crags among,

> Leaps the live thunder! Not from one lone cloud,
> But every mountain now hath found a tongue,
> And Jura answers, through her misty shroud,
> Back to the joyous Alps who call to her aloud!"

The conception is very grand, and unsurpassed, if equalled, by any similar description in human language. The storms enthrone themselves, each on his mountain, and as if in wild sport, "fling their thunderbolts from hand to hand:" the mountains roar and give out their echoes as if rejoicing o'er the birth of an earthquake: the big rain dances to the earth: the lightning gleams like phosphorescence over the surface of the lake: and the Jura and the Alps from all their peaks shout to each other. All is life: the agencies of nature become mighty spirits; and darkness, and lightning, and thunder, and tempest—all that is terrifying to man, is but the stir and glee of their sport among the hills. To witness such a storm amid such scenes were worth more than years of ordinary dull life.

To the admirers of Rousseau this is a classic region. Byron was one of them. His admiration of Rousseau led him to write verses which throw a more genuine charm over Lake Leman and its shores than any thing which Rousseau has written. Byron's poetry is noble. What charm is to be found in the sentimental Sensualist, to a man of thought and true taste, I never yet could comprehend.

The names of Rousseau, Voltaire, Gibbon, Madame de Stäel, and Byron, are all associated with the picturesque shores of this lake. But of all these, Byron, by his Prisoner of Chillon, and his third canto of Childe Harold, is the only one who has really given a lofty, tender, and classic interest to these scenes. Together with an inimitable power of description, there is a depth and almost sacredness of sentiment which show the better elements of his nature, and place him very far above Jean Jacques.

The following stanzas breathe the very spirit of these scenes. I have in my mind now a sense of the beauty which dwells there—a beauty whose power I felt at Lausanne and Geneva, by day and by night, and while sailing down the lake and back again. These express it all:

"Clear placid Leman! thy contrasted lake,
With the wild world I dwell in, is a thing
Which warns me, with its stillness, to forsake
Earth's troubled waters for a purer spring.
This quiet sail is as a noiseless wing
To waft me from distraction; once I loved
Torn ocean's roar, but thy soft murmuring
Sounds sweet as if a Sister's voice reproved,
That I with stern delights should e'er have been so moved.

"It is the hush of night, and all between
Thy margin and the mountains, dusk, yet clear,
Mellowed and mingling, yet distinctly seen,
Save darkened Jura, whose capt heights appear
Precipitously steep; and drawing near,
There breathes a living fragrance from the shore,
Of flowers yet fresh with childhood; on the ear
Drops the light drip of the suspended oar,
Or chirps the grasshopper one good-night carol more;

"He is an evening reveller, who makes
His life an infancy, and sings his fill;
At intervals, some bird from out the brakes
Starts into voice a moment, then is still.
There seems a floating whisper on the hill,
But that is fancy, for the starlight dews
All silently their tears of love instill,
Weeping themselves away, till they infuse
Deep into Nature's breast the spirit of her hues.

"Ye stars! which are the poetry of heaven!
If in your bright leaves we would read the fate
Of men and empires,—'tis to be forgiven,
That in our aspirations to be great,
Our destinies o'erleap their mortal state,
And claim a kindred with you; for ye are
A beauty and a mystery, and create
In us such love and reverence from afar,
That fortune, fame, power, life, have named themselves a star.

"All heaven and earth are still—though not in sleep,
But breathless as we grow when feeling most;
And silent, as we stand in thoughts too deep:—
All heaven and earth are still: From the high host
Of stars, to the lull'd lake and mountain coast,
All is concenter'd in a life intense,
Where not a beam, nor air, nor leaf is lost,
But hath a part of being, and a sense
Of that which is of all Creator and defence.

"Then stirs the feeling infinite, so felt
In solitude, where we are *least* alone;
A truth, which through our being then doth melt
And purifies from self: it is a tone,
The soul and source of music, which makes known

> Eternal harmony, and sheds a charm,
> Like to the fabled Cytherea's tone,
> Binding all things with beauty:—'twould disarm
> The spectre Death, had he substantial power to harm.
>
> "Not vainly did the early Persian make
> His altar the high places and the peak
> Of earth-o'ergazing mountains, and thus take
> A fit and unwall'd temple, there to seek
> The spirit in whose honor shrines are weak,
> Uprear'd of human hands. Come, and compare
> Columns and idol-dwellings, Goth or Greek,
> With Nature's realms of worship, earth and air,
> Nor fix on fond abodes to circumscribe thy prayer!"

The stir of the feeling infinite, mingled with the feeling of the beautiful, fed by every object which here meets the sense, whether of earth or sky—where earth and sky are so in harmony as to appear, indeed, parts of the same world—and these lifting up the soul to Him who is of all Creator and defence,—this expresses the emotions of every one whose mind grows into unison with Lake Leman and the scenery in which it lies embosomed.

In sailing down to Geneva the contrast between the northern and southern shore struck me as the source of the peculiar charm which belongs to this lake beyond all others. The first presents beautiful slopes mantled with vines, broad meadows, fields of corn, smiling villages and enchanting country-seats; the other is a scene of mountains rising above mountains, in some places starting from the water's edge, in others leaving a narrow margin with fields and villages, until you approach

Geneva, where the hills settle away as if to reveal the full glories of Mont Blanc.

The day we sailed down the lake, Mont Blanc and the other ice peaks were lost in the clouds, except at one point where, through a gorge of the adjacent hills, we caught a view for a few minutes, of the snowy crown of the king of mountains. At first I was not certain whether it was the loftiest mass of clouds or the mountain itself, and I turned to a gentleman and asked, "Is that Mont Blanc?" "Yes," said he, "that is Mont Blanc." And then I noticed that it glittered in the sunbeams as clouds never glitter. There it was above the clouds of heaven—nothing of it visible but that one shining peak above the hills and mountains, above the highest clouds, piercing the azure arch of the sky, looking down upon all earthly things, and seeming to thrust itself into the very path of the sun.

The country near Geneva is one succession of villas beautifully situated, embowered in trees, and all looking out upon Mont Blanc. The appearance of the town itself, upon approaching it from the lake, is quite imposing. One portion of it called the upper town, and where are generally to be found the residences of the aristocracy, is situated upon eminences of a considerable elevation, and shows proudly in the distance. The lower town is composed of narrow streets, with lofty houses, and is the seat of trade. The hotels, stores, and dwellings on the Quai, and particularly in the *Quartier des Bergues*, are new and elegant. The town lies on the two banks of the Rhone, which are connected by bridges; and just where the river shoots out of the lake is a long bridge spanning the lower point of the lake, and resting midway upon a little island. The approach to Geneva, and the entrance from the western side, give the most pleasing impressions. These are not diminished upon a further acquaintance with it, although it contains no peculiar objects of interest. It is, in itself, a pretty town, and the situation and the environs are so beautiful, and the whole region of the lake so magnificent, that Geneva can never want attractions.

Geneva is a small state: but although it fills only a little place on the map of Europe, it fills a large place in the history of civilization and religion. The whole canton, in its greatest length, is less than twenty miles, and contains some sixty thousand inhabitants, of which the city contains about the half.

The republic of Geneva had its origin in the municipal government of the city. A prince bishop, as a feudatory of the empire, was the chief magistrate until the Reformation drove him away. The House of Savoy also claimed supreme authority, as derived from the counts of Genevois, a line which became extinct in the fourteenth century. It was in defending the rights of Geneva against the Duke of Savoy, that the patriot Bonnivard became a prisoner in Chillon for six years, from 1530 to 1536.

The Genevese finally triumphed, and the man who had been chained to a pillar in the dungeon for so many years, and whose solitary tread had worn a path in the pavement, was released with acclamations. He came forth to see Geneva free and reformed. At his death he gave his library to the Republic, and made it the heir of all his goods on condition of founding therewith a college after a plan which he himself had projected. His library, which contained many rare editions of the classics, became the foundation of the public library which now contains forty or fifty thousand volumes. Bonnivard did not suggest to Byron the theme of his poem. He remarks in a preface, "When this poem was composed, I was not sufficiently aware of the history of Bonnivard, or I should have endeavored to dignify the subject by an attempt to celebrate his courage and his virtues." With respect to a poem so perfect and so beautiful, it is difficult to regret any thing; but, if any thing is to be regretted, it surely is that Byron was not acquainted with the history of Bonnivard when he wrote the Prisoner of Chillon. He could not have made a more affecting picture of suffering, but he might have infused an element of historic heroism, and celebrated in his immortal verse a man who deserved so much of his country and of mankind.

Geneva has produced a host of distinguished men in theology, science, and letters, whose names are familiar to the world. It is remarkable how pre-eminent the name of Calvin stands among them all. Whatever amount of severe criticism may be passed upon him, there is the fact, that this man—a poor man, who lived poor and died poor, and with no other source of authority than what was found in his writings, his preaching, and his conversation—simply the authority of mind, did virtually govern Geneva both civilly and ecclesiastically; was a terror to the Roman Catholic church, and a tower of strength to the Reformers; was honored as a great authority in theology by the most eminent men of his own day, and has been honored as such by multitudes in every subsequent age; and is at this day a great and venerable name in the most free and enlightened nations of the world. No one can doubt his intellect and scholarship, no aspersion can be thrown upon the purity of his life. When his enemies speak against him, they assail his doctrines; but these are to be refuted by argument and not by personal abuse. Or, they ridicule his sumptuary laws, and inveigh against the tyranny of his laws for the regulation of public morals. This is the man, say they, who limited ten persons to five dishes, interdicted plush breeches, rebuked from the pulpit those who violated the Sabbath, punished adultery with death, and exposed the gamester in a pillory with a pack of cards tied around his neck! But, this is a question of legislation which must be judged of relatively to the times and occasions; and, was the state strengthened or weakened, at a time when it could afford to lose no strength, by laws which enforced frugality and morality? Did any good citizen feel the pressure of these laws? When every thing else would fail, the case of Servetus is adduced. Now, God forbid that any one should ever justify the burning of Servetus: but do not insist that Calvin, to be a good man at all, must be in all things beyond the age in which he lived. Remember, that neither in his own age, nor in the subsequent age, did his worst enemies lay this to his charge; that Servetus had already been condemned by a Roman Catholic government under a similar accusation, and would have met the same death had he not fled; and that his condemnation at Geneva was under an existing law of the state. The principle of religious toleration, and of the separation of the church and the state, had to be vindicated afterwards. The sun of a glorious day had arisen, but it was still shorn of its beams by the mists of the morning. And it is just in this way that I would judge of Calvin and all the Reformers: compare them with the men of their own age, and they are immeasurably ahead of them in light and freedom; but the very fact that they were at the beginning of a great movement, that they were at the point where mankind were just emerging from the darkness of ages, is a reason why they should not be an absolute authority to us. Calvin, could he reappear, would not be the same man in our day that he was in his own. How stolid are we, if with centuries of experience, and with new light, we make no advances upon them! Those are not the true followers of the Reformers who shut up the free thoughts of their own minds, and have only wit enough to repeat verbatim the words which were spoken centuries ago; those, rather, are their true followers, who imbibe their fearless spirit of inquiry, and who dare to differ from them, for sufficient reasons, as *they* dared to differ from the learned and mighty hierarchs around them, and from all the tomed fathers, if need be.

Calvin gave out a certain theology according to his philosophy and criticism. Why should not a thinker now, as well as in past times, frame a theology, by a philosophy and criticism, perhaps, more fully developed and perfected?

There is one fact worthy of notice in the history of Calvinism;—it has been the creed of the heroes and martyrs of freedom. This is to be explained by a cardinal element of this creed—the absolute sovereignty of God, resulting from the doctrine of absolute divine decrees.

This doctrine, as expounded by Calvin, appears to us, when carried out to its logical consequences, to annihilate the human will, and to introduce a system of pantheism. But the Calvinists have, by no means, carried it out to its logical consequences; but they have employed it in a practical way to set forth the sovereignty of God—a doctrine, unquestionably, fundamental to all true religion. Thus divine sovereignty became with them an all pervading idea—it pervaded their preaching, their hymns and their prayers, and was framed into a test of their religious experience. But the men who bowed to an authority so holy and august, who were penetrated by the sentiment that God governs all things in heaven and earth, and that it is the first duty of the human being to merge his own will into the Divine will—these were not the men tamely to submit to any human priest or despot. The very passivity with which they yielded to a Divine authority, became a most energetic activity against the pretensions of any other authority. The government of God over them was the government of the Infinite—and of truth, justice and love, as attributes of the Infinite—the Lord God was lord of their conscience; how contemptible must the authority of popes and kings have appeared to them when attempted to be exercised over the conscience!

The doctrine of Divine sovereignty is not indeed exclusively appropriated by Calvin's view of the Divine decrees: that sovereignty really appears more exalted when exercised over beings of perfect freedom of will. But the extreme doctrine of the great Reformer was calculated to fix the mind upon it with great intensity, and to signalize it as the distinctive feature of his creed.

Our estimate of Calvin, therefore, would lead us to give him a very exalted place among the great and good men who have devoted themselves to the propagation of truth and righteousness, while claiming for ourselves that same freedom of opinion for which they were ready to suffer and to die.

The hotel des Bergues is a very large building, occupying a fine and commanding site. It has the reputation of being the best hotel in Geneva. I am inclined to think it is reposing somewhat upon its reputation. I have no doubt there are other hotels as good, if not preferable. Here we found a party of friends from Savannah, Georgia, who had sailed a fortnight before us. We had been on their track for some days, and we were most happy to come up with them at last.

They had been detained by the sickness of a colored man-servant. Instances of cruelty to slaves are very apt to be recorded. But are we equally forward to record instances of kindness? Here was one worthy to be noticed. This man had been sick with a southern fever before he left home, and was in a very delicate state of health in consequence of it. His owner took him abroad purely on account of his health. His services were not needed, and he was not in a condition to render any important services. At Lausanne he had been attacked again with fever. He appeared to be convalescing, and they removed to Geneva. Here he experienced a relapse and became very ill. The best physician was called in, and a nurse provided. The qualities of the nurse were not satisfactory; and the two ladies of the party, who were strictly southern ladies of refined breeding and habits, devoted themselves to their sick servant, day and night, and performed for him all the tender offices which sisters could perform for a brother. His disease was subdued, and when we arrived, he was just beginning again to move about. We travelled together in Switzerland for a month, and during this time I observed this colored servant treated with all the kindness and consideration that could be bestowed upon any human being.

We found our friends making preparations to start for Chamouni the next morning. We accordingly engaged a carriage to accompany them. The excursion cannot be made in less than three days, two of which are occupied in going and returning. Early in the morning our friends set off; but two of our party being decidedly on the sick list, we were compelled to remain behind. In the end, we regretted this less as we had glorious views of Mont Blanc from Geneva—more glorious, it is said, than can be gained at the foot of the mountain itself, where the proximity prevents the eye from taking in the whole outline. The valley of the Grindelwald, too, which I shall notice hereafter, compensated us for the loss of Chamouni. By many the former is preferred to the latter. I find Lord Byron among this number. In one of his letters he writes:—"We have been to the Grindelwald and the Jungfrau, and stood on the summit of the Wengen Alp; and seen torrents 900 feet in fall, and glaciers of all dimensions; we have heard shepherds' pipes and avalanches, and looked on the clouds foaming up from the valleys below us like the spray of the ocean of hell. Chamouni, and that which it inherits, we saw a month ago; but, though Mont Blanc is higher, it is not equal in wildness to the Jungfrau, the Eighers, the Shreckhorn, and the Rose Glaciers. Besides this, I have been all over the Bernese Alps and their lakes, and think many of the scenes—some of which were not those usually visited by the English—finer than Chamouni."

We left the hotel, and procured lodgings about a mile from the town, in a most delightful and quiet spot. The building is surrounded with fine grounds and trees, and was once a chateau. It is kept by a Mr. Argand, whose wife is an English woman, and one of the neatest and kindest beings in the world. It is much resorted to by the English. The situation commands a view of the town, the lake, the country beyond, and the Alps. Our window opened towards the Alps. Here we remained five or six days, driving out, walking, or lounging under the trees enjoying the *dolce far niente.*

The weather was clear, the air soft and temperate, and heaven and earth full of cheerfulness. Every night the sun cast his last rays upon the ice mountains in full view: and when he went down, they pierced the heavens—as Coleridge hath it—like a wedge, an ebon mass, the kingly Mont Blanc, towering above them all. In the morning there were clouds about them, and they were indistinct, until the sun got up into the heavens, and then through the bright day they were pure silvery masses. But when the sun got low in the western horizon, they would take those pink and roseate hues which made them appear of such marvellous beauty, that one might have fancied them the stately gates of heaven, before which the angels were singing evening hymns.

But there was one evening of all others, which I can never forget, when Mont Blanc came into view with a distinctness, magnitude, majesty and beauty, which even by the inhabitants was regarded as a rare vision. The atmosphere, I suppose, must have been remarkably free from humidity, and exceedingly transparent. Mont Blanc seemed to lie just behind the hill beyond the lake, so near, that one ignorant of the real distance might have imagined that a short ride would bring him to the foot of it. The whole mass of the mountain appeared to rest against the face of heaven, as if it were some great barrier placed there before an opening. Or, it appeared like some vast substance just floated out of the skies, and resting upon the earth while its top was yet in the azure arch. It was a thing more of heaven than earth. It was too glorious and beautiful to belong to earth. There was nothing earthly about it. The hues changed as the sun descended lower and lower, but a most delicate rose-tint predominated. At least, this hue is more distinctly in my imagination than any other, and therefore it must have lasted longer. On the side of the mountain there was a deep bosom like a sloping plain, on which it would have appeared natural if myriads of happy beings in shining garments had been trooping up and down. And from this plain the high peak of the mountain shot up as if forming a connection between earth and heaven. It did not appear to me a thing of ice and snow; it had a warm, sunny look. It was as grateful to the eye as the soft golden clouds which lie on the western horizon at the close of a summer day. It was something one could never tire of gazing at: it fed the eye with harmonies of colors. The only fear was that night would come too soon and throw her dark veil over it. It was worth the whole journey to Switzerland to see. Now that I have seen it, I have in my mind an image of sublimity, glory, and beauty which was never there before, and which I could have got in no other land. How rich I am in this possession! But how is the conception to be conveyed to him who has not seen it? No painter can paint it, because he cannot convey the magnitude by any witchery of his art; no poet can sing it, for how can he put the colors of heaven into his verse? What image my words may call up in the mind of another I cannot tell. The best effect will be if I shall induce him to go and see for himself.

It is a pleasant walk from Aux Charmilles, the name of our chateau, to Chatellaine, on the right bank of the Rhone. The bank here is very high and steep; and from a little platform, with a railing about it, you look down upon the junction of the Arve with the Rhone. The Rhone empties into the upper end of the lake a muddy stream; it shoots out of the lower end purified, and blue as indigo. The Arve, turbulent and furious, comes rushing down from Chamouni as muddy as the upper Rhone. When it joins the blue Rhone, the two rivers, for a considerable distance, flow side by side—the muddy Arve along one bank, the blue Rhone along the other, until at length they are commingled, and the Rhone flows on a turbid stream to the sea.

There was a captain of the British navy lodging with his family at the same house with us, very intelligent and very social. He had been knocking about the ocean for many years at the equator and the poles, and had seen abundance of icebergs in his day. He never went to Chamouni, nor to the Grindelwald. He said he had had his fill of adventures and grand sights, and enjoyed now his quiet anchorage more than any thing else. It was natural for him to feel as he did. He was right in his way. But to him whose life has been too much of an anchorage, motion is delight. An anchorage at Geneva, however, could not be regarded as an ordinary affair. One cannot help seeing grand sights there. Much was yet to be seen; but we all felt no little regret in leaving the old chateau and its kind entertainment, the environs of Geneva, the placid lake, and the sunlit face of the mountain king.

X.

Morat.—Aventicum.—Swiss Confederation.

FROM Geneva we returned to Lausanne by the steamer. From Lausanne we went to Berne. Our party now consisted of six persons besides George, the colored man. We stopped for the night at Payerne, and the next morning proceeded to Berne.

Our route from Neuchâtel to Lausanne lay on the Jura side of the lake of Neuchâtel. Our route from Lausanne to Berne lay on the Alpine side of the same lake, close by the small lake of Morat, which is separated from the former lake by a narrow strip of land. Berne is thus east of Neuchâtel, and nearly on a line with it.

At Morat the battle-field is indicated by a granite obelisk, bearing an inscription and the date, 1822. It is erected on the very spot where the ossuary stood in which, for three hundred years, the bones of the slain had been preserved as a monument, in like manner with Dornach. The Burgundians had, for ages, been accustomed, when passing this way, to carry off some of the bones to their own country; and postilions had purloined them for knife handles. In 1798, the Burgundian legion in the French army destroyed the ossuary to efface the memory of the defeat of their forefathers. The bones which remained were, in 1822, buried under the obelisk.

At Morat the defeat of Granson was repeated, only it was more dreadful and fatal. When the Duke of Burgundy heard of the approach of the Swiss, he left his entrenchments and marched out upon the narrow level on the borders of the lake, prompted by that wild and gallant spirit which characterized him. The Swiss covered the heights above. The men of Uri and Unterwalden sounded their horns, and the whole mass came down upon the Burgundians like an avalanche. They overran the cannon, and leaped upon mailed knights and men-at-arms. The Burgundians, crowded together in the narrow pass, were crushed like insects, or driven into the lake. Fifteen thousand were left dead upon the field; thousands perished in the lake; a few succeeded in swimming the lake and escaped by Neuchâtel. The bold Charles never recovered from the effects of this defeat. The battle of Nancy next followed, in which he lost his life.

"While Waterloo with Cannæ's carnage vies,
Morat and Marathon twin names shall stand;
They were true glory's stainless victories,
Won by the unambitious heart and hand
Of a proud, brotherly, and civic band."

Morat lies near the upper end of the lake. Avenches, the Roman *Aventicum*, is situated near the lower end. The ancient walls can yet be traced for four miles, which extended to a circumference of six miles when the city under the Roman rule was the capital of Helvetia.

When the legions of Germany, A. D. 69, proclaimed Vitellius, the Helvetians, not yet acquainted with the murder of Galba, stood forth in his defence. Cæcina, the legate, routed their forces with prodigious slaughter. Aventicum offered to surrender, and sued for mercy. Cæcina gave sentence of death against the principal inhabitants. Among the rest was one Julius Alpinus, who had a daughter named after himself Julia Alpinula, a priestess of the goddess Aventia, the tutelary divinity of the city. She interceded for her father. Cæcina would not relent, and the father was executed. The daughter died soon after of a broken heart;

"And then—oh! sweet and sacred be the name—
Julia—the daughter, the devoted—gave
Her youth to Heaven; her heart, beneath a claim
Nearest to Heaven's, broke o'er a father's grave."

The story is gathered from the following sepulchral inscription, found many centuries after among the ruins of Aventicum:

Julia Apinula: Hic Jaceo. Infelicis patris infelix proles. Deæ Aventiæ Sacerdos. Exorare patris necem non potui: Male mori in fatis illi erat. Vixi annos XXIII.

Morat and Aventicum are two great historical monuments. The modern history and the ancient stand here side by side.

Until the fifth century the Roman power prevailed, with the exception of the central valleys, where a rude independence was maintained. At the breaking up of the Roman Empire, Helvetia was divided between the Burgundians, who came from the shores of the Baltic, and the Alemanni who had planted themselves on the banks of the Rhine. Then Clovis the king of the Franks conquered the Alemanni, and gained possession of the greater part of Helvetia. New races thus rooted out or mingled with the natives and destroyed the Roman civilization. Under the successors of Charlemagne, the feudal system was established in Helvetia.

In the eleventh century, the whole country was annexed to the German Empire. The Suabian house of Zähringen now governed Helvetia as a feudatory of the Empire. This continued until the line became extinct in the thirteenth century. Next, the country was governed by various counts, of whom the principal were the Counts of Savoy, Neuchâtel and Toggenburg.

In 1264, Rudolf of Habsburg became the most powerful noble in Helvetia, and nine years afterwards was elected emperor. Here begins the house of Habsburg. We passed the ruins of the ancient castle of this House on the route between Basle and Zurich.

After the death of Rudolf, his son Albert attempted to annex the free towns and states of Helvetia to the patrimonial domains of Habsburg. Now commenced the great struggle for Swiss freedom.

In the vicinity of the lake of Lucerne is a wild and mountainous region, divided into the three cantons of Uri, Unterwalden, and Schwyz, called, collectively, the Waldstätter or Forest Cantons. These cantons had been free from time immemorial. It is probable the Romans never subdued them. They were now under the protection of the German Empire. They therefore acknowledged the Emperor, but they refused to acknowledge Albert as patrimonial Duke; and demanded the imperial, and not ducal judges, to be sent to administer justice. Albert sent them as imperial judges two noblemen, creatures of his own—Gessler and Beringur. Ministers of justice by name, these men were guilty of the grossest acts of injustice and oppression.

Then Werner Stauffacher of Schwyz, Arnold Von Melchthal in Unterwalden, and Walter Furst of Uri, conspired for the deliverance of their country. In a small green meadow on a ledge at the foot of a precipice, the spot called the Grütli is still pointed out, where the three confederates took their solemn oath. The story of Tell, who slew Gessler, is told at every fireside. Soon the whole Waldstätter was in a state of insurrection. The officers of Albert were driven out, and their houses razed to the ground; but by a noble and humane forbearance, they were expelled without personal injury. It was an insurrection without bloodshed. Albert, while on the point of marching in person to avenge himself on the Waldstätter, was assassinated by his nephew.

Seven years after this, his son Leopold was defeated at the battle of Morgarten, by the people of the Waldstätter. The three Forest Cantons now formed a federal union, and the inhabitants henceforth go under the name of Schwyzers. Hence are derived the names Swiss and Switzerland, which are now applied to the people and country at large. These Cantons constituted the grand centre of the Swiss confederation.

In 1332, Lucerne withdrew from the House of Habsburg, and joined the confederation.

The feudal nobles after this entered into a league against Berne. The Bernese led on by Rudolf Von Erlach gained a decisive victory at Laupen. A bronze statue of the hero with a suitable inscription adorns the open space in front of the cathedral. The duke of Austria was again defeated by the inhabitants of Zurich. Successively, Zurich, Glarus, Zug and Berne joined the confederation. There were now eight independent cantons, and a federal Diet or Congress was appointed in 1352. In 1375, the Bernese defeated the army of the French adventurer, De Coucy, at Frauenbrunnen. In 1386, the men of Lucerne gained the victory of Sempach over the Austrians, where Leopold II. was slain. Two years afterwards the Austrians were again defeated at Näfels. This was followed by a truce of twenty years with the Swiss. The Swiss extended their possessions by purchase and conquest. The Canton of Appenzell next revolted against the Abbot of St. Gall. During the fifteenth century, the Valais revolt and join the confederation; the people of Rhætia revolt against their feudal lords, and form the league called the *Graubund*; the battle of St. Jacob is fought with the Dauphin of France; Austria, in another war, loses all her possessions except the town of Winterthur, which she mortgages to Zurich; the victories of Granson and Morat are won over Charles the Bold; the Swiss defeat the Milanese at Giornico; and the Emperor Maximilian is finally defeated in the Tyrol and at Dornach. This ends the wars of the Swiss for their independence. In the mean time several other cantons join the confederation.

It is a remarkable history. These men fighting for liberty were uniformly victorious, and that, too, over the most splendid armies of Europe. While the rest of Europe was subjugated, they threw off feudalism and monarchy, and vindicated the capacity of the people for self-government.

They are a hardy and warlike race by nature; and the face of their country—its mountains, lakes, and rocky passes—gave them great advantages over invaders: but they, probably, are not superior to other nations of Europe in native intelligence and social and moral capabilities. Their love of liberty grew by conflict, and their national dignity and self-respect by victory and success. And this formed their superiority. The misfortune of the people of Europe in general is, that they cannot win for themselves the opportunity of making that experiment of free institutions which the Swiss won under the peculiar circumstances which favored their struggle. And when an occasional outbreak takes place, or a revolution is attempted, and the people are defeated by organized force and diplomacy, the cry is the people are not yet prepared for free institutions. But when will they be prepared? and by what discipline is this preparation to be made?

The Swiss were prepared five hundred years ago. The Swiss have been a free people for five hundred years.

The introduction of the Reformation into Switzerland led to civil commotions. The Roman Catholic and Reformed cantons made war upon each other. From 1531 to 1712 there were three religious wars. It was a struggle for freedom of conscience. In the end the great cause was won. Religious toleration was added to civil liberty.

There are now twenty-three cantons in the Swiss confederation. Of these seven are Roman Catholic, namely, Lucerne, Uri, Schweitz, Unterwalden, Zug, Tesino, and Valais. In the remaining sixteen the Protestants are greatly in the majority. Of the entire population the Protestants constitute about two-thirds. Nearly two-thirds of the population also speak the German language.

Under the French Republic, Switzerland was overrun by the French. Bonaparte, by his act of mediation, constituted the Swiss confederation of nineteen cantons under the protection of France, and annexed Geneva, Neuchâtel, and Valais to France. The allied powers at the Congress of Vienna, restored Switzerland to its ancient limits.

In the Waldstätter the purest democracy has always prevailed. Here the entire male population constitutes the popular assembly. In most of the larger cantons representation had been based upon property. Twenty years ago universal suffrage was introduced. The city of Basil made a strong opposition, and finally separated from the country district and became a distinct canton.

The confederation, as it now exists, assembles a Diet at least once a year, by turns, in Berne, Lucerne, and Zurich. The Diet has power to declare war, to make peace, to enter into alliances with foreign powers, and to appoint foreign ministers and consuls. All difficulties between the particular cantons are settled by the Diet. Each canton casts a single vote. A simple majority decides all questions except those of war, and peace, and foreign alliances, when three-fourths is required. The deputies cast their votes according to the instructions of their constituents. A council, together with a chancellor and secretary, is appointed by the Diet, from the canton in which it meets for the year, to carry out its resolutions. This council is called the *Vorort.* On the demand of five cantons the Vorort has power to convene an extraordinary Diet.

This is the general constitution of Switzerland. It will be seen that it is highly democratic. The Almighty, who has reared its enormous mountains, has made them the fastnesses of civil and religious freedom in the midst of surrounding despotisms.

God and nature have secured it against foreign intervention beyond all other European countries. Switzerland is a standing proof of what the people can do for themselves when let alone by priests and despots.

And Switzerland is in every respect a prosperous country. Its husbandry resembles that of England. Every spot capable of cultivation is made productive: and where the plough and the sickle cannot reach, the green pastures sustain innumerable flocks and herds. It is filled with fine towns, villages, and country habitations. No country has better roads. It has also arts, manufactures, and commerce. And, finally, it is distinguished for its literary institutions and for men of learning.

The remark is frequently made that the Swiss have degenerated from their ancient virtue, under the influence of French manners, and the cupidity awakened and fostered by the influx of travellers. The remark is just, to a certain extent. But it must be recollected that travellers fall in with the worst specimens of Swiss character. Hotel-keepers and all their dependents, persons who keep carriages and horses for hire, watchmakers and jewellers, and the whole tribe of small traders, are the individuals with whom travellers are continually brought into contact. It is not strange that those who make it a business to impose upon travellers as far as possible, if taken as representatives of Swiss character, should lead to very unfavorable conclusions. But it is to be hoped that Switzerland, as well as other countries, would present very different forms of character in those classes which the ordinary traveller never meets with. The extraordinary scenery of Switzerland attracts to it more visitors than any other country in the world, who spread themselves through every part of it. It is natural, therefore, that many persons should everywhere be on the lookout to earn money by their services. Travellers are themselves very much to blame for the lying and cheating of which they complain. The wish to appear rich is a pernicious vanity, and reckless expenditure encourages extortion. I soon found it necessary to examine the hotel bills carefully, and frequently detected errors made to my own disadvantage; but I never had any difficulty in getting them corrected by calmly pointing them out.

The practice of begging is obviously owing to injudicious giving. Well-clad children rush out of comfortable chalèts, and hold out their hands for alms. They are by no means objects of charity, but they must be successful in their applications on some occasions, or they would not continue them. If travellers will give where they ought not, merely to show their indifference of their pence, decent children will be degraded to beggars.

Guides, postillions, and persons of like character, whom I had occasion to employ, were always civil, obliging, and faithful. Except where there were fixed rates, they always had an asking and a taking price: but this is human nature every where.

My conclusion, therefore, is, that the cupidity, lying, and cheating of the Swiss are only what might be expected under the circumstances; and that travellers have it very much in their own power to restrain and correct them in these vices.

I do not believe their national character is lost. They have still a hardy and brave peasantry, who, when the occasion comes, will show the ancient virtue of Granson, Morat, and Dornach. That they have, too, cultivated classes, and not a few distinguished and good men, is unquestionable.

The history of Switzerland, no less than its scenery, is Alpine. Such a history is a constant inspiration to a people.

"The high, the mountain-majesty of worth
Should be, and shall, survivor of its woe,
And from its immortality look forth
In the sun's face, like yonder Alpine snow,
Imperishably pure beyond all things below."

XI.

The Oberland.

ON approaching Berne, we gained our first view of the OBERLAND—*highlands*—or Bernese Alps. The road passes over a considerable elevation. The day being unclouded, with a transparent atmosphere, we saw the whole range with perfect distinctness. There were no intervening objects to interrupt the view: all the peaks rose up against the sky in dazzling whiteness.

At Chamouni, the ice-peak is called *Aiguille—needle* :—In the Oberland, it takes the German name of *Horn*, which is the same with our English word *horn*, but is applied by the Germans to mountain-peaks also.

The *Wetterhorn*—the peak of tempests, the *Schreckhorn*—the peak of terror, the *Finster Aarhorn*—the gloomy peak of birds of prey, the Eigher, the Mönch, the Jungfrau, and the Blumlis Alp, all lay before us. It was a more perfect and extensive view of the ice-peaks than we had had at Geneva. No single mountain in this range equals Mont Blanc, but there is no part of Alpine scenery which, taken together, produces such a magnificent impression. This is owing to the fanciful forms of the peaks, their brilliancy, and to the fact that, from several points of view, one can take in the whole range at once.

When Berchtold, the founder of Berne—so goes the tradition—laid the foundations of the city, he slew a huge bear upon the site. Hence it was called Berne, or the Bear. The bear is the armorial bearing of the canton, is the effigy upon its coins, and forms the embellishment of signs, fountains, and public buildings. The principal fountain in the city is surmounted by the figure of a bear in complete armor, with a sword by his side and a banner in his paw.

In one of the ancient watchtowers there is a clock which reminds one of the clock at Strasburg: a wooden cock claps his wings and crows, and a procession appears in front of the dial-plate; but it is a procession of bears. There are two live bears, also, kept at the public expense in a very pleasant place prepared for them. Here they sit erect, good-naturedly show their teeth with a sort of effort to laugh, and gratefully receive gifts of cakes and apples.

Berne, besides being one of the cities in which the Swiss Diet holds its sessions, is also the residence of the foreign ministers. The city is built upon a promontory seventeen hundred feet above the level of the sea. The sides are very steep, but covered with a green sward. The houses are substantially built of stone, and rest upon arcades which form covered walks in front of the shops. There is here a Gothic cathedral of great beauty. The principal entrance is ornamented with reliefs of the Last Judgment and of the Wise and Foolish Virgins. Among the representations on the windows there is one which excites a smile as a poignant witticism. The Pope is grinding the four Evangelists in a mill, whence they issue in the shape of wafers which a bishop collects in a chalice.

The Aar nearly surrounds the town. There is a noble bridge of granite thrown over the river and the gully through which it flows, nine hundred feet in length; the central arch is one hundred and fifty feet wide, and ninety-three feet high. Near the cathedral is a terrace built of solid masonry, one hundred and eight feet high. It is a charming promenade, particularly at sunset, when the Alps in full view are tinged with those magical roseate hues of which I have already spoken. All the ramparts are now converted into agreeable walks. The most beautiful walk is the *Enghe*, outside the Aarberg gate. It is an elevated terrace and looks out upon the town and country around, with the Alps in the background.

The streets of Berne are well paved and cleanly. Rills of water flow through many of them. There are also numerous fountains, some with quaint ornaments. One of these, the Ogres fountain, has the figure of a giant devouring a child, while his pockets and girdle are stuck full of children, whose countenances and struggles make a most grotesque expression of terror.

Berne has also a University and a Museum, and a Public Library containing 40,000 volumes.

Altogether it is one of the most picturesque and interesting towns in Switzerland, and must form a very agreeable residence.

Thun is some sixteen miles distant from Berne. At Berne we engaged two carriages. When the carriages drove up one of them had but one horse. Some difficulty had occurred. Without waiting for the explanation, as we had only a short stage to make, I jumped into the one-horse carriage. The horse was a small, black, sluggish-looking animal, and the driver a stocky, queer little fellow. When we started, the long and slow paces of the horse augured very unfavorably for speed, and by the time we had reached the granite bridge with a hill on the opposite side to ascend, I begun to insist upon going back to get another horse. The little coachman was very good-natured, and begged me to have patience, assuring me that the horse would go better as he grew warm and got his joints loosened, and that he would beat the two-horse carriage. So, I yielded, and walked up the hill to relieve the poor animal. When I got in again at the top of the hill, the slouching animal began to show his mettle, and, sure enough, we left the other carriage behind, and reached Thun a very considerable distance ahead. This was another illustration of the saying, not to trust to first appearances. The little coachman, too, was a treasure in his way, full of good humor and very talkative.

The road from Berne to Thun leads through the valley of the Aar, and is a delightful drive. The valley presents the freshest meadows and pastures, and is filled with villages, and picturesque Swiss dwellings, with their broad overhanging roofs. Each story has a piazza sheltered by the projection of the roof, and the stairs are on the outside from one piazza to another.

Beyond the valley the snowy Alps were constantly in view, with the dark limestone mountains—the Stockhorn and the Niesen in the foreground.

The Hotel de Bellevue, with two or three dependencies, all beautifully situated, and surrounded by extensive walks and gardens, and commanding a fine view of the Aar and its valley, is the great establishment at Thun. The proprietor has erected a neat Episcopal Chapel on the grounds for the accommodation of the English who resort here, where service is performed every Sabbath during the summer.

Besides this hotel there is the Pension Baumgarten, kept by a son of the proprietor of the Hotel de Bergues, in Geneva. The situation of the Baumgarten is equally pleasant, not far from the Bellevue, and surrounded in like manner with gardens and walks. These hotels are outside of the town. We selected the Baumgarten as the more quiet of the two. It is well kept, and a favorite retreat of English families. With two or three exceptions, besides ourselves, there were none but English here. Among them was a clergyman and his daughters; Colonel R——, a retired Irish officer on half pay, with his English wife, both full of good humor and pleasantry; Sir Claude W——, of the East India Service, also retired, with a young and beautiful wife; and others of respectability and agreeable manners. All were social, and our time within doors passed cheerfully. I say *within doors*, for here we were shut up for several days by a storm of rain and sleet, which began the very night of the day we arrived. The day had been the warmest I had experienced in Switzerland, when suddenly the wind rose and brought the storm. The next morning the ice mountains were hidden in the clouds, and the limestone mountains were covered with a deep snow to a considerable distance below their summits.

We heard much of this storm afterwards. Several parties of English ladies and gentlemen were caught by it on the Grimsel and other passes. The roads were blocked up with snow; some struggled on waist-deep; but most were obliged to seek the nearest refuge, until the roads were cleared by the shovel, or trodden down by the mules.

We met some of these adventurers at Interlachen. They appeared much elated with the dangers they had passed through, now that they were safely housed, particularly the ladies. To be caught in a snow-storm on the Grimsel, or on the Great Scheideck, was something worth remembering—something worth relating in after years. A day in the passes under a bright sunshine was mere romance: in a snow-storm it became heroism.

To many Englishwomen of strong frames and robust health, crossing the passes appears to be the great charm of visiting Switzerland. From the conversations I overheard in the saloon of the hotel, I was led to suspect they were more penetrated by the love of adventure than by the love of the sublime and beautiful. Still I could not help admiring the vigor and spirit which carried them through all difficulties.

Colonel R—— and his agreeable English wife, had been over all the passes of the Oberland. They talked of it as a frolic, but they were not insensible to the grandeur of the scenery.

By and by the snow began to disappear on the lower ledges of the Stockhorn and the Nieser, the air grew milder, and the sun began to show himself again. We took the steamer for Interlachen, and sailed up the enchanting lake of Thun. But before we had proceeded half way, the rain poured down again, and we reached the Hotel des Alpes only to be immured for the rest of the day. This hotel is situated directly opposite the Valley of the Lütschine, and commands a view of the Jungfrau. In the evening the valley was filled with mist which rolled up to the top of the mountains. Early the next morning the top of the Jungfrau peered through the clouds with the sun shining upon it. We immediately ordered carriages for Lauterbrunnen.

The Lütschine, swollen by the rains, rushed along wildly and furiously. Two or three miles up the valley is the junction of the Black Lütschine from the Valley of Grindelwald with the White Lütschine from the Valley of Lauterbrunnen. The clouds collected thick again, with occasional showers. The appearance of the valley was grand and wild beyond description. Our road lay on the bank of the Lütschine, at the foot of tremendous precipices rising into the clouds and mist. At every turn of the road, we saw torrents, in some places pouring down steep slopes; in others, hanging like a strip of foam against the perpendicular rock; and again, in others, rushing down gullies, hiding themselves for a moment beneath rocks and foliage, and then bursting out to the light as if emerging from the bosom of the earth. On the other side of the river, the mountains recede a little, and precipices of rocks alternate with wooded slopes. Up these slopes the mists rolled like billows dashing upon the shore. The amazing walls of rock, beside which the proudest cathedral would be but a child's toyhouse, the huge rocks scattered about, which had toppled from the precipices—each an old minster in itself, the torrents and cascades, the overhanging clouds resting upon the edges of the precipices, the boiling mist, the river raving through the valley, the gloom that seemed to fill the air—all gave an impression of power, majesty, and awfulness which was like the presence of the Supernatural. These were indeed the forms of nature, but it required no great stretch of the imagination to believe that mighty spirits were playing with the elements.

At length we reached the entrance of Lauterbrunnen. Here the road runs between two walls of perpendicular rock, from which the streams are every where dangling in white foam, forming a beautiful contrast with the dark face of the rock. These are smaller specimens of the Staubbach. Making our way up this narrow deep and dark valley where the sun is not seen until several hours after he has risen, we catch, at length, a view of the Staubbach—the *dust stream;* we reach the hotel. I jump out of the carriage, and between a run and a walk, hasten to the foot of the fall. By the way are several little shops where Swiss toys are sold, every one of which addressed me and offered their articles for sale; then beggars waylaid me; and last of all, a boy with a horn began to blow for my edification. Good heavens! exclaimed I, do these people think I came here to buy toys, to listen to beggars, and to be entertained with horns! And so I did like Bunyan's Pilgrim, who put his fingers in his ears and ran through the teasing crowd calling out Eternal life! Eternal life! I fixed my eyes steadfastly upon the Staubbach, and looked above the petty annoyances.

The torrent was unusually full, and falling sheer from the precipice nine hundred feet, came down in fine spray scattered over a wide circumference. In my eagerness to get as near it as possible, that I might bring it between myself and the sky, I found myself suddenly enveloped in a mist-like shower, which soaked me thoroughly.

On the brow of the rock, dense clouds were hanging, so that it seemed as if the fountains of heaven were opened. It is of wonderful beauty:—a fit place for the beautiful Witch of the Alps to be evoked.

Looking into the valley of Lauterbrunnen higher up, the appearance was that of a tumultuous ocean of mist and spray. The Jungfrau was hidden; but, ever and anon, the mist and spray gave way, and then appeared the dim outlines of mountains, and between them dark depths. It was like catching glimpses of a sublime and mysterious immensity.

There is a wide difference between the Staubbach and Niagara. The one, a brook falling nine hundred feet, is a thing of beauty rather than grandeur; the other, a wide, deep and mighty river, falling one hundred and fifty feet, is a thing of power and sublimity as well as beauty.

The Englishman Tupper—the author of Proverbial Philosophy and some other pieces, has pronounced Niagara properly an object of beauty, and seems to doubt the applicability of the epithet sublime. He does not in this remark reach the true element of the sublime, which is the idea of the Infinite.

Indefinite space and magnitude, or the exhibition of an indefinite strength and force, whether of mind or nature, by the very fact of surpassing our ordinary standards of measure, call up this idea with its corresponding emotion. It is an error into which some fall, to imagine that the sublime must always collect around it images of wildness, terror, and destruction. These images, as representing indefinite power and force, are connected with the sublime, but not because they belong to wildness, terror, and destruction. Where order, harmony, and beauty are connected with indefinite power and force, the idea of the infinite is no less prone to be awakened; and the emotion of the sublime is enkindled with an undisturbed fulness. Terror, when excessive, often subdues the sublime emotion, but beauty and order always harmonize with it, and serve to enhance it. Infinite space, infinite duration, and infinite intelligence and power displayed in the starry heavens, are sublime without terror. And why should not infinite power, producing order and beauty, be sublime as well as when displayed in destruction and terror? Nay, more sublime, since now there is no conflict of emotions. It is the immeasurable power of Niagara, "notching its centuries in th' eternal rocks," that gives it its sublimity. Its spray and rainbows clothe it with beauty, but do not lessen the sense of amazing power. The spray and the rainbows of the Staubbach clothe it with beauty also; but it has not the sublimity of Niagara, because not an object awakening an equal conception of power.

Near the entrance of the valley of the Lütschine, on an eminence overlooking a space of green meadows, are the ruins of the *Castle of Unspunnen.* There is a story current of the last baron of Unspunnen, how that his beautiful daughter and only child Ida went off, clandestinely, with his enemy, the knight Rudolph, of Zähringen, and became his bride. And then long years of bitter and cruel strife followed, until the knight, taking Ida and his infant son, presented himself, unattended and unarmed, at the gates of Unspunnen. The affection of the father was aroused by the sight of his daughter and the infant, and his anger subdued by the confidence which his foe reposed in his generosity. A reconciliation followed, and the son of Rudolph was received as the heir of Unspunnen.

But a still higher interest attaches to these ruins, from the general belief that Byron made the castle the residence of Manfred. It is in the very neighborhood of the Jungfrau, of the Staubbach, and of all that wild and majestic scenery amid which the poem is laid. And it is the only old castle there. Its solitary position, its solemn and melancholy air, might well attract the eye of the poet. And Manfred is the most solitary of beings, and the poem a most solemn and melancholy poem. Filled with grandeur and beauty, and a wonderful work of art, I, nevertheless, never read it without feeling completely wretched. And it seems to me to be wrung from the poet's own heart, as if every line had cost him a pang.

It was a strange passion of Byron to exaggerate his own faults and to misrepresent his better qualities. He seems to have been possessed with the belief that the world was bent on abusing him, and in a sort of madness he helped on the abuse. And this he did not merely by a reckless life, braving public opinion, but by painting characters in which his own identity was sure to be recognized, and yet distorted and enlarged so as to make a hero of crime or of wretchedness, or of both united.

In Manfred, this character painting upon himself attains its highest and grandest development:—Manfred the solitary, despising yet pitying mankind, with an intense love of the beautiful, and that love uniting him to one being in guilt and sadness, and ending in some mysterious crime, and a misery like the misery of the damned; Manfred attaining to high mysterious and unlawful knowledge and power, calling upon the fierce spirits of the elements, walking among the dizzy cliffs of the Jungfrau, gazing at the Staubbach upon the mild beauty of the Witch of the Alps, and then on the very summit of the Jungfrau mingling with the Destinies, Nemesis and Arimanes, and all in pursuit of forgetfulness and annihilation; and failing in these, calling up the dead to ask forgiveness, to inquire after her fate, to know if they are to meet in another state, at least to hear once more her voice; and then at last dying himself, triumphing over the spirits of hell, and departing into the unknown world to be his own torturer, his own hell. It is grand and terrible, second only, perhaps, to Milton's picture of the "Archangel ruined," but more sad and affecting. Manfred is alive to the beauty of nature, has a quick sense of his own sins and wrongs, and condemns himself, in utter despair, under the consciousness of irremediable crime.

He is a lofty nature crushed by the weight of guilt. He suffers extreme agony, but is calm and majestic in suffering. In the language of the good Abbot:

> "This should have been a noble creature: he
> Hath all the energy which should have made
> A goodly frame of glorious elements,
> Had they been wisely mingled; as it is,
> It is an awful chaos—light and darkness—
> And mind and dust—and passions and pure thoughts
> Mix'd and contending without end or order,
> All dormant and destructive."

Was this a picture of Byron himself in his exaggerated imagination of himself? But there is one thing in which there is no exaggeration, and that is the dark skepticism which haunted his soul. In Manfred is the restless spirit of the poet himself—believing in immortality, half believing in retribution, confident of that retribution at least which is self-inflicted—

> "The mind which is immortal makes itself
> Requital for its good or evil thoughts"—

With moral sensibilities for a better creed, and yet held in the torturing grasp of doubt. "At times there is something mournful and depressing in his skepticism; but oftener it is of a high and solemn character, approaching to the very verge of a confiding faith. Whatever the poet may believe, we, his readers, always feel ourselves too much ennobled and elevated, even by his melancholy, not to be confirmed in our own belief by the very doubts so majestically conceived and uttered. His skepticism, if it ever approaches to a creed, carries with it its refutation in its grandeur."*

Wonderful is the power of the poet when even the scenes of the Jungfrau receive a new interest from his words! But the poem grew in his mind in the midst of this scenery. The internal mood found its apt representations in the forms without. The mind, too, has its ice-peaks, its avalanches, and its boiling mist, "like the foam of the ocean of hell."

* Prof. Wilson.

XII.

The Oberland Continued.

THE next morning the mist rolled up the mountains and dissolved in air, the sun shone out bright, and the Alps had that apparent proximity which indicates a clear atmosphere and settled weather.

We accordingly took an early start for the Grindelwald. Unspunnen lay in the shadow of the mountains, silent and melancholy as ever. We entered the valley of the Lütschine. Here the aspect of every thing was changed. The river and the mountain torrents had expended some of their fury. Most of these torrents, where they cross the line of the road are bridged. There was one which the day before we had been compelled to ford with some apparent danger, for the carriage was swept down several feet, and the horses staggered. To-day it was a harmless babbler. The remaining mist curled lightly up the mountain sides, like an offering of incense which the mountains were paying to the serene and smiling heavens. The tops of the precipices were visible, and their dark faces were softened by the cheerful light of the morning. The tufts of foliage were bright and fresh, and glistened with the exhaling rain-drops. The cascades hung against the steep precipices every where like threads of light. The birds were singing out their joy to the returning sunshine. And the majestic Jungfrau in her virgin whiteness rose right before us, rearing her head into the heavens, like innocence conversing with God. Nor only the Jungfrau, but peak after peak burst upon our sight. It was a scene of glory and beauty, such as mine eye had never beheld before. It seemed as if we were entering an enchanted land, or as if the doors of paradise itself were opening to us.

We reached the junction of the Black and White Lütschine, and turning to the left, crossed a stone bridge, and entered the valley of Grindelwald. The Lütschine was at our right, deep in the valley, while the road wound along a ledge of the mountain. The precipices rose on both sides to an amazing height—several thousand feet, from whence the streams were descending in every imaginable form: sometimes rushing through a gully, a roaring torrent; sometimes falling from ledge to ledge a succession of waterfalls; and sometimes falling sheer several hundred feet, and then meeting a slope of the mountain, and curling down its side to the bottom. On our right, above these precipices, peered the snow-peaks, except when we descended too far under the shadow of the mountains. There were meadows below, and pasturages above us scattered over with chalets.

Nature here seems to be dealing in ideal works. Man has his works of utility, and these are chiefly his works. Sometimes he becomes the artist, and aims only at beautiful and sublime expressions. The artists are the few, the useful workers the many. The artists, indeed, are useful workers also, under a lofty and just estimation, for they minister to the most exquisite and rational enjoyments, and to the highest culture and good of human kind; while the mere useful workers aim at the good of man the animal—a creature to be clothed and fed. Nature is bountiful to man the animal, but no less so to man the creature of thought and beautiful tastes.

In ordinary scenes, we are so occupied with the harvest-fields of the plains, the mines, quarries, and timber of the mountains, and the mechanical power of the streams, that we come to look upon nature as only the grand useful worker. But in the valley of Grindelwald, the commonness of nature is gone, and here, at least, she becomes the idealist—the artist.

The road to the Glaciers takes various turns, presenting the different peaks, which appear to be quite near, and you are expecting every moment to come up to the foot of the snow mountains, and you begin to wonder that what appears to be so near should be constantly receding. Then suddenly the road bends to the right, the scene opens, and the Lower Glacier is directly before you—a frozen torrent pressed down into the green meadow—and the mountains of snow stand revealed!

Then the road descends into a hollow, and then ascends

again, and the whole of the Grindelwald is presented—an amphitheatre of Alps! On the south side of the valley rise the three enormous mountains—the Eigher or Giant, the Mettenberg—above which, as from a base, rises the Schreckhorn—and the Wetterhorn. Between these mountains, the two glaciers crowd down their icy masses into the valley. Above the Lower Glacier, a portion of the Mer de Glace is seen, and beyond, the peak of the Finster Aarhorn. On the right, the Jungfrau towers aloft eleven thousand feet above the valley: below her summit are the Silber-hörner—*the silver peaks*, which are called the *breasts* of the Jungfrau. The Silber-hörner glittered in the sunbeams, and appeared like drifts of spotless snow.

It was about the hour of noon, and from the Mettenberg the avalanches were falling—loosening in masses upon the airy heights, and then scattered into snow-dust.

We visited the Lower Glacier, which is four times as large as the Upper. After leaving the green meadow, there is a space covered with rocks and gravel, which have been forced down by the ice; above this is the foot of the glacier—a vast, scragged wall of ice, in which are deep caverns in every grotesque form, with pillars of ice. The water is constantly dripping from the roof and trickling down the sides. It is the melting of the glacier in the crevices which forms these caverns. While the ice is melting at the extremity, the pressure from above still moves down the frozen masses, so that the advance of the glacier keeps up a wall of ice on about the same line from year to year. Near the farther edge of the glacier is an immense arch of ice quite regularly formed, and—if my memory serves me right—seventy feet high, from under which the black Lütschine rushes into the sunshine.

On ordinary mountains, the rains which fall are collected into fountains and lakes, and run off in brooks and rivers. On the Alps, the rains are turned to snow. There are no fountains and lakes, but the whole superincumbent mass, obeying the law of gravity, topples off the steep peaks in avalanches; presses down into the hollows between the mountains, and forms the Mer de Glace—the sea of ice; and the sea of ice receiving constant accumulations and pressure from the heights above, urges down into the valleys and forms the glacier. The snow obeys, in general, the same law which the mountain streams obey. The glaciers are the grand outlets of the mountains of snow. They descend into the temperature which melts them, and their ice-caverns are the fountains of the rivers. The sea of ice and the glacier form one body, the latter being the extension of the former. The surface of the glacier is broken into crevices, and covered with pinnacles of ice, which are caused by the movement of the glacier over an uneven surface, the melting below, and the action of rain and sunshine above. The appearance is grand and terrific. The movement of the glacier ploughs channels in the rocks, and carries along rocks, stones, and gravel. These channels have a peculiar appearance; and being found in localities where glaciers no longer exist, indicate a lower temperature at some former period, when these mighty masses made their way through districts where the fields now produce corn and wine.

The mountains of snow and the fields of ice are fringed with forests of fir. Next to these are green pastures dotted every where with chalets. The verdure has that peculiar hue which belongs to cold mountain regions, soft and moss-like. The contrast between the ice and the green forests and pastures has a magical effect. Often on the summit of a seemingly inaccessible precipice a green spot appears, an oasis amid tremendous rocks; but a chalet, and cows and goats feeding about, show that man has found somewhere a path to reach it, and has made it a home. No green spot is left unappropriated.

The passes are depressions in the mountains over which mule and foot paths, and in some instances carriage roads, as the Simplon, and Splügen, are carried. By ascending these the mountains of snow are more nearly approached, you look upon them midway of their height, you look down upon the seas of ice and the glaciers, and into deep and awful valleys. The summit of the pass of the Wengan Alp is more than six thousand feet above the level of the sea. This pass leads from Grindelwald to Lauterbrunnen. The Faulhorn, situated between Grindelwald and the lake of Brienz, is more than eight thousand feet high. Some of these passes may be made with perfect safety, others are attended with danger. When the atmosphere is clear the views are described as magnificent in the highest degree. When enveloped in mist, or caught in a snow-storm, there is no pleasure but that of toil and adventure, which is probably greater in the retrospect than in the experience. The ladies of our party were not English enough to endure the fatigue, and to meet the hazards; and as Mr. H—— and myself could not well leave them to their fate, while we went scrambling over the mountains, we concluded to defer these adventures to some other occasion.

When I shall have made these passes I will have a story to tell about them. Now I can conceive of nothing more beautiful and majestic than the appearance of the Alps rising from the meadows and forests of Grindelwald—pyramids and obelisks which the hand of the Almighty hath built up. The more you gaze upon them, the more entranced do you become. The eye and the soul dilate with the mighty and glorious vision.

We left Grindelwald with reluctance: but we did not say farewell for ever: we cherish the hope of re-visiting these scenes. In descending the valley, every object was placed in new points of view. In Switzerland there is endless variety, arising from the changing views as well as the changing objects. In winding up and down the valleys, you seem to carry on a mystic dance on all sides of beautiful and grand forms;—the cliffs take every shape, the waterfalls make a fantastic play, and the snowy tops of mountains start into view like apparitions in the clouds to surprise you.

One of these apparitions startled me as we were approaching the lake, on our way back to Thun. I chanced to look towards the Grindelwald, where the mountains had been for an hour or two veiled in clouds, when a shining speck caught my eye, high up in the heavens above the clouds, and as I supposed, at first, above the tops of the Alps. The clouds opened a little more, and I perceived it was a snow-peak. I never before had such an impression of the height of the Alps. Our judgment of height, as well as of magnitude generally, is relative. From childhood nothing has appeared so high to us beneath the heavens as the clouds. From the place where I was, I could not see any of the lower mountains;—I saw only a mass of clouds, and the snow-peak above them. The comparison, therefore, was simply with the clouds themselves. How high did it appear? The height varied with my thought, but sometimes it seemed to occupy the elevation of the sun, for it broke out of the clouds as the sun is often seen to do.

While sailing on the lake down to Thun, as the sun sunk low in the west, the whole range of the Oberland gradually emerged from the clouds. Peak after peak sprung up into the levelled beams of the sun, and the horizon was studded with golden pinnacles which seemed to rise from a sea of clouds. The shores of the lake rejoiced in the same beautiful sunlight; and when we reached the lower end of the lake, the Aar, as it shot from its bosom, appeared like a swift messenger hastening away to far-off lands, to tell them a story of the lake and the mountains.

There is an old castle in Thun—some eight centuries old—standing upon an eminence in the midst of the town—to which you ascend by steps: and near the old tower is an old church, with a terrace on which some yews are planted. This terrace looks out upon the lake and the Alps. I went up there to witness the effect of the setting sun upon the ice-mountains which now lay exposed to view in a clear atmosphere. It is a sight one can never grow tired of. I looked out from between two young yew-trees: the old town lay at my feet; then came the river, emerging from the lake above the town, with wooded banks and beautiful country-seats scattered along; then the lake of Thun, now dark under the shadow of the Niesen; then the farther shore rising into forest slopes, and these again into limestone hills and mountains; then the Alps, with mist at their base above the lower mountains; and last of all, the snowy tops in the heavens, bathed in purple and roseate sunshine.

The Blumlis Alp was nearly opposite, and as clearly defined as possible. It is a curious formation. It had this evening the appearance of a vast fortress with enormous square towers, all hewn out of white marble. I called it the Ehrenbreitstein of the Alps. But what is Ehrenbreitstein, compared with this! I looked right into the bosom of this Alpine fortress. The towers cast their shadows sharply into the immense court beneath. The roseate hues of the parts exposed to the sun, contrasted beautifully with those shadows.

When the sun had set on all other objects, his rays still lingered on these lofty towers in rose and purple. Gradually these delicate hues crept up the sides of the towers, then rested a moment on the top, while all beneath was dark, and then were gone—like the last flash of an angel's wing, disappearing in immensity. Truly, I exclaimed, Switzerland is God's masterpiece!

XIII.

Lucerne.—Zurich.—Basil.

THE beauties of Thun and Interlachen, are celebrated. Of the two I prefer Thun. The valley of the Aar, the exceedingly variegated and beautiful country around, the perfect view of the Oberland which it affords, form a combination of objects unsurpassed by any scenery in Switzerland.

Interlachen—*between the lakes*—is also between the mountains, a charming, secluded spot. It would be a perfect retirement from the world, if the world did not here rush in upon you. During the summer, its numerous hotels and *pensions* are crowded with persons on their way to the Alps or returning from excursions. While we were there the mountains were so covered with mists, and we were so deluged with rain, that I am aware I cannot do justice to it. The morning we went to Grindelwald, however, revealed it,

It is a perfect gem in its way, but it has not the variety of Thun. It is hemmed in by the mountains, and lies under their shadow ; while Thun, as from an eyrie, looks out upon them.

At length we took our departure from the Oberland. Our route lay towards Lucerne. The queer little fellow who drove the little black horse from Berne to Thun, was one of our coachmen. He had the black horse again, but matched with another which he deemed of similar extraordinary qualities.

Our first stage was to Lagnau, twenty miles from Thun, where we passed the night. After tea, we were about retiring, when a loud concert of voices singing Swiss songs came up from the public room below. On going down we found a dozen men or more seated at a long table, on which were placed some bottles of common Swiss wine, and who were making merry after the labor of the day. Their drinking appeared moderate, and the wine was more acid than strong. There evidently was no inebriation. At the head of the table was seated the Corypheus, a burly, jolly fellow. Some two or three began the song, the rest joined in the chorus, which was sung in that clear, musical, and ringing falsetto peculiar to the Swiss.

At our request they sang one of the airs of the *Ranz des Vaches.* This name is given to a class of melodies, of which there are many different airs, having their origin in the Alpine valleys. The name signifies *a row of cows*, referring to the order in which the cows march home at the milking time, when the shepherd calls to them through the Alpine horn.

This horn is made of wood five or six feet long, and wound around with bark. In the Valley of the Grindelwald, girls twelve or fifteen years old, with brown faces, bright eyes, and hair streaming in the wind, trotted beside our carriages, singing airs of the *Ranz des Vaches* as long as we kept tossing *batz* to them. The singing of the girls in the open air was wild and sweet. Our company at the inn of Lagnau had more stentorian voices, but they sang well and kept good time. Some of the songs were very pretty. Some were comic. Great good humor prevailed, and they appeared to sing from the love of it. Long after we had retired to bed we heard the merry choruses below.

Indeed, I felt more disposed to listen to the singers than to go to sleep. The beds in Switzerland are a sort of square box, always made for short men, or made on the principle that every one must fold up his legs when he goes to sleep. Now, being somewhat tall, and accustomed to stretch out my legs in bed, which, I believe—the Swiss notwithstanding—is the true principle, I very often found myself, indeed, *in a box.* This night, the box was shorter than ever, and I had no relief but to protrude my feet far, far beyond this *Procrustean* measure. When my feet grew tired of this pendulous condition, I placed myself diagonally; then again I tried the folding up system, and so I spent the night in vain efforts to dispose of my limbs. And all this was carried on, not on a feather bed, but under it, for the Swiss and Germans put the feathers above. The music was my only solace, until a light was struck in the adjoining room, where the ladies engaged in a battle with the fleas. This occupied the remainder of the night, and I forgot my sorrows in listening to the uproar and exclamations of the combatants. I knew the number of the wounded, but the number of the slain has never been reported.

The next day we reached Lucerne before sundown. In driving up to the Hotel de Suisses, our little coachman was intent upon making a display: so he whipped his jaded horses and came dashing up in fine style; but not calculating all the turns he had to make, he came very near running into another coach, which he prevented only by a sudden check. The spirit of his horses was gone, his whip dishonored, and with an odd expression of deep mortification on his face he slouched up to the door.

The Hotel de Suisses—considered one of the best in Switzerland—was thronged with travellers. We had taken the precaution to write to Lucerne a few days before to engage apartments. We accordingly were well accommodated, our apartments being situated to overlook the lake. Mount Pilatus and the Righi were before us. The lake has wonderful wildness. Pilatus and the Righi were usually hidden in the clouds.

We sailed up the lake, one day, to the bay of Uri, and to Altorf. The lake twists about among the mountains. Dark and majestic are these mountains, which shut up in their bosom the waters gathered from the melting glaciers. Imagine the wildest and grandest mountains piled together and covered with firs. Next imagine them to be split irregularly, making a huge fissure; and let all the mountain streams pour into it, and then you have the lake of Lucerne.

In many places, the precipices and mountains rise abruptly from the water: then again there are level spots of meadow at the foot of the mountains, or scattered on their bosom like emerald gems. Often you seem to be sailing right against the mountain side, when suddenly turning a bold point of land, a new scene opens, and other mountains rise aloft.

Schiller's Wilhelm Tell, a noble composition in itself, and embodying a portion of history of which human nature must ever be proud, derives an additional charm from the scenery of this lake. One of the scenes is thus described: "A meadow surrounded by forests and high rocks. On the rocks are paths with rails, also ladders, on which the country people are seen descending. In the background the lake appears, and over it hangs a rainbow of the moon. The prospect is closed by high mountains, behind which still higher rise the mountains of ice. Deep night has settled upon the scene, and only the lake and white glaciers are shining in the moonlight." And this is true to reality.

The lake is properly called the *Vier-Waldstäter-See—the sea of the four Forest Cantons;*—Lucerne, Uri, Unterwalden, and Schwyz, lie about it. Superior to all other lakes in the grandeur and beauty of its scenery, it is consecrated by the associations of freedom, heroism, and virtue.

> "Each cliff and headland, and green promontory,
> Graven with records of the past,
> Excites to hero-worship."

The river Reuss, which issues from the lake, divides Lucerne into two parts. The town commands a prospect of the beautiful lake, of mountains, and the snowy Alps of Schwyz and Engelberg. A summer might be spent here in excursions amid the grandest scenery of nature.

The bridges of Lucerne are numerous, and are singular on account of the pictures which adorn them. These are suspended against the timbers supporting the roof. The Kapell-brücke, near the Hotel de Suisses, contains seventy-seven pictures. In passing from the hotel to the opposite bank you see a series of pictures taken from Swiss history: in returning you see another series representing the acts of St. Leger and St. Maurice, the patron saints of the town.

The church beyond this bridge is surrounded by curious cloisters which contain a number of monumental paintings. One of these struck me as very beautiful. There are two figures, the one a man, the other an angel. The face of the man is youthful, expressing reverence, faith, and goodness: the face of the angel is transcendently lovely, expressing purity, benignity, and sympathy. The human, although pure and beautiful, belongs to a race sinful and sorrowful, and doomed to trial; the angelic tells of a being that had never known personal sorrow and trial, had never sinned, and had nothing to repent of, or regret—a being sympathizing with evils not his own. What an experience that must be which can say, I have never known sin and sorrow—I have wept for others, but never for myself!

The monument erected to the memory of the Swiss Guards who fell in defence of Louis XVI. is worthy of the praise which has been bestowed upon it. It exhibits the masterly conception of Thorwaldsen, and the execution, although by another artist, is not unworthy of the conception. It is cut out of a rock in the side of a hill, and represents a colossal lion, twenty-eight feet long and eighteen high. The noble animal, wounded and dying with a spear sticking in his side, still grasps between his paws a shield bearing the fleur-de-lis. The names of the officers of the Guards are inscribed below. At the foot of the monument a basin is scooped in the earth, which receives the water which trickles from the rocks. The scene is solitary and quiet.

There is an old man dressed in the uniform of the Guards, who attends upon visitors, and claims to be the last survivor of those who escaped the massacre. He speaks French, and, of course, is full of the story. He says he was a drummer in the regiment, and sixteen years old when the catastrophe took place.

Lucerne is a Roman Catholic canton. In the town, out of more than eight thousand inhabitants, there are only some two hundred Protestants. There is a little German Protestant church where the English service is performed at hours when the congregation do not occupy it. We attended this service Sabbath morning. I have remarked the strictness with which the English attend their own little chapels planted at the places of principal resort in Switzerland and other parts of Europe. In a foreign country they do not forget their religious habits nor the church of their fathers. These chapels in Switzerland are open for the English service, only during the travelling season. Young clergymen are generally sent to officiate in them. Besides the stipend, which depends upon the voluntary contributions of the worshippers, they have the advantage of spending a summer in the neighborhood of the Alps.

The preacher in Lucerne was remarkable for his intonation and mannerism—faults which age and experience may moderate, but which are not likely to be cured.

I have been struck by the tones which belong to and distinguish classes of preachers. I have observed a tone peculiar to many of the Dissenters in England, and which is never found among the ministers of the Established Church. The Established Church, again, has its own stereotyped tone. The German Lutheran clergymen have their tone; and the German Catholic priests their sing-song monotony in opposition to it. They are all a departure from nature, and all more or less disagreeable. I believe the effect of preaching is very much destroyed by this. Let a man speak as he feels. Why should he act a part? Nature is full of beautiful variety. We get into this mouthing by overstraining nature: and then growing tired of excess, we take up our repose in monotony.

We had had of late some disagreeable, misty days. But the day on which we started for Zurich was clear and cool. We took the route by the pleasant lake of Zug, and over the *High Albis*.

The drive, of about thirty-three miles, was one of unalloyed pleasure. The road is carried up and down the Albis in zigzags, and is an admirable one. The summit, over which the road passes, is twenty-four hundred feet above the level of the sea, and a thousand feet above the lake of Zurich. From this summit we looked down upon a vast landscape embracing the town and lake of Zurich and the Alps. The view is panoramic, and extends over a large portion of Switzerland.

The lake is twenty-six miles long, and only three broad. Its banks are green slopes, beautifully cultivated; and so numerous are the villages, country-seats, and dwellings of various descriptions scattered along the water and against the slopes, that the whole appeared, from the point at which we stood, like an immense straggling town adorned with vineyards, gardens, and trees.

We got out of our carriages and walked some distance, to enjoy more fully the prospect. And then when we betook ourselves to the carriages, and drove down the Albis by the zigzag road, we were constantly entertained by new views as we changed our direction. We passed the battle-field where Zwingle was killed. Then we got involved among the dwellings and country-seats on the border of the lake: the gardens grew more limited, the houses more clustered, and so, by charming gradations, we found ourselves in the town of Zurich with its fifteen thousand inhabitants.

The Hotel Baur, at which we put up, is large and elegant, and, to our taste, the best hotel we had found in Switzerland. On the roof is a Belvidere, from which you look out upon the town, the lake, and the country. It was here that we enjoyed again those splendid sunsets which I have already described, and saw the Alps once more clothed in those delicate hues which make them an unearthly vision.

The proprietor of the Baur was engaged in completing an additional building of large dimensions on the shore of the lake. The grounds of this establishment extended to the water's edge, and were tastefully laid out in walks, flower-beds, and clumps of shrubbery. I then thought how delightful it would be, some future summer, to cross the Atlantic, ascend the Rhine, make another tour through Switzerland, and repose some weeks by the lake of Zurich. The time and money which are wasted at Saratoga and Newport would be sufficient to accomplish this. How much better, instead of returning to the city satiated and jaded with fashionable dissipation, to return from such a tour with renovated strength, and with an imagination filled with images which can never fade, which invigorate thought, and minister delight whenever we recur to them!

In Switzerland, as in other parts of Europe, you hire rooms at a hotel, and then dispose of your time as you please. You may take your meals at the hotel, or elsewhere, according to your fancy or your convenience. Nothing is compulsory but the hire of your rooms. Here you may live with perfect retirement, freedom, and comfort. There is in Zurich a library of more than forty thousand volumes. The roads are perfect, and the drives in every direction enchanting. Or, if you are fond of sailing and fishing—behold! the beautiful lake is before you. Do you love walking—Zurich is surrounded with charming promenades: or, you may ascend the Albis and walk along its brow as far as you please, growing stronger and stronger at every step, for there is no lassitude in this air. Or, do you wish to make wider and bolder excursions—see! the Alps are there inviting you. Culture, beauty, grandeur, and the sense of health and vigor, all are here. Inspired by these representations, do you say—Come, let us make up a party and away to Zurich? I reply, Come then; I am ready at your call. Why breathe this hot, dusty and polluted air, when God has made such a country as Switzerland to breathe in?

We do not make enough of the world which God has given us. How we waste existence in the endless pursuit of wealth, ambition, and pleasure, imagining enjoyments neither fitted to our nature, nor to the conditions of our being; while we forego the sweet influences of the heavens above us, the beauty of the earth spread around us, motion and breath in the pure air freely given us, the melody of running streams, and the happy thoughts of a mind set free from toil and care. While we are preparing to live and enjoy, life wears out, and a thousand enjoyments slip from us never to be recalled. Duty and enjoyment have a common principle, in that they are not to be waited for in the future, but are to be found under the sunshine of to-day.

How many of the beautiful towns of Switzerland are similarly situated: Geneva, where the Rhine issues from Lake Leman; Thun, where the Aar issues from Lake Thun; Lucerne, where the Reuss issues from the Vier-Waldstätter-See; Constance, where the Rhine issues from the Bodensee; and Zurich, where the Limmat issues from the Lake of Zurich. The Alps, which form the splendor and majesty of Switzerland, are the parents of all its beauty—feeding the lakes and streams, which freshen and adorn the valleys.

Zurich, like the others, is agreeable as a town, and like them, too, derives most of the attractions presented to the eye from the situation. In this land nature has done so much, that even the best works of man are turned into insignificance.

But Zurich has historical associations dear to freedom and religion. The old banner of Zurich was the banner of the Reformation in Switzerland; and here lived Zwingle—the hero of that Reformation—one of the finest and loftiest characters that appears in history. The cathedral in which he preached was to me a place of the deepest interest.

Zwingle was not made by Luther; nor was the Reformation in Switzerland made by the Reformation in Germany. The man and the movement sprang from the soil, and grew in the air of Switzerland. There appears to be a law which governs human thought and events, by which a great conception is born in several minds at once, and men from different quarters rush to the same point of action. Evidently, human thought had been working to a common conclusion, for when the Reformation began, communities and states were electrified by it. Eminent scholars in different parts of Europe were reaching the truth by the study of the Hebrew and Greek Scriptures; and the corruptions of the Church of Rome had become so gross that they began to strike the common sense of the people.

The great and true-hearted Zwingle was born in an Alpine valley, two thousand feet above the lake of Zurich, near the source of the Thur, where his eye from infancy looked upon the savage grandeur of rocks, glaciers, and the mountains of snow. His father was a shepherd of many sons and daughters; a man of uprightness, and a patriarch of the village.

The house in which Zwingle was born is still standing. Like other rude dwellings in these mountain regions, where the winter storms are violent, the roof is covered with large stones to give additional security to the shingles. I did not make a pilgrimage there, but I have seen many such dwellings. In these mountain fastnesses we look for strength of character, as well as strength of limb and nerve.

The boy Ulric gave indications of uncommon intelligence. His father gave him up to the care of the Dean of Wesen, his uncle, to be educated. In due time he was sent to the University of Basil. From thence he went to Vienna, and finally returned to Basil, where he finished his scholastic studies. He became an elegant classical scholar, and well versed in the philosophy and theology of his day.

At twenty-two years of age he was ordained priest and pastor of Glaris, not far from Wildhaus, his native village. Here his talents and schorlarship drew the attention of she Bishop of Sion, and he soon was informed that the Pope had granted him a pension of fifty florins to aid him in his studies. This money, accordingly, was spent in the purchase of classical and theological books. He was now a solitary student of the Alps.

His repose was disturbed by the sounds of warlike preparation; for the Swiss were gathering under the influence of the Bishop of Sion to join the standard of Pope Julius II. on the plains of Italy. Zwingle was zealously opposed to these enlistments in foreign war. His patriotic spirit could not bear to see the flower of the Swiss youth perish in battles in which their country had no interest, and he lamented the dissolute manners which were introduced by those who returned to their native mountains. He had already published a poem and an allegory setting forth these evils. But, as the pastor of Glaris, he was compelled with the Landaman to join the march. Such was the custom.

His visit to Italy revealed to him many abuses. On his return, he devoted himself to the study of the Greek. "I am resolved," so he wrote to one of his friends, "to apply myself so closely to the Greek, that no one but God shall call me off from that study; and this I do, not from a love of fame, but for the sake of divine learning." It was ever afterwards a great principle with Zwingle, that the study of the New Testament in the original was the spring of the Reformation. When charged with being a Lutheran, he replied, "I am no Lutheran, for I understood Greek before I heard the name of Luther." And thus he grew and ripened into a Reformer in the solitary study of the Greek Testament, while a Catholic priest in an Alpine village. This is a great and pregnant fact, both in relation to the man and the cause. The Reformation in Switzerland began in these studies of the priest of Glaris.

In 1515, when thirty-one years of age, he again accompanied the confederate Swiss to Italy. He harangued the soldiers. He preached to them before the battle of Marignan. In this battle, so fatal to his countrymen, he stood by them. He was a soldier and priest at the same time. He disapproved of the war, but his bold spirit would not suffer him to hide himself from the standard of his country.

He returned home filled with indignation at the slaughter

of the Swiss in the ambitious wars of the Pope. The ignorance, licentiousness and pride of the priesthood, were still more apparent to him.

Now he gave himself up to expounding to the people the Gospels and Epistles. Here was the fruit of his studies. He did not directly attack the Church, but he preached the Gospel to the poor.

Between the lakes of Zurich and Wallenstadt is a naked undulating plain, on which stands the Abbey of Einsiedeln. In the ninth century a hermit had built his cell here, where he was murdered by robbers. The cell was afterwards rebuilt by monks of the Order of St. Benedict, and a convent and a church founded in honor of the Virgin.

When the Bishop of Constance and the monks were assembled at prayers, the night before the day appointed for the consecration, they were startled by a heavenly chant performed by invisible beings. The next day when the Bishop began the service of consecration, a voice cried out three times, "Stop! Stop! Christ himself has consecrated it." The music they had heard was the angelic hymn of consecration. A bull of Pope Leo VIII. confirmed the legend and forbade any one to doubt it. In consideration of the miracle, he granted plenary indulgence to all who should repair to the shrine of Our Lady of Einsiedeln. For nine centuries, pilgrims from the surrounding countries have resorted to it. Its wealth consequently became enormous, and its Abbot, usually selected from noble families, was made a prince of the Holy Roman Empire with a seat in the diet.

In the church of this convent, Zwingle, one year after his

last return from Italy, was called to officiate as priest and preacher. Conrad of Reichburg, of ancient and noble descent, was the Abbot. He prided himself upon breeding fine horses, and was given to hunting. He was an honest, independent and hospitable baron, rather than an ascetic priest; and averse alike to the pretensions of Rome and to scholastic discussions. The Baron de Geroldsek, the administrator of the monastery, was pious and fond of learning. His great aim was to convert the convent into a society of learned men. He permitted the nuns of the nunnery of Einsiedeln to read the Bible in the vulgar tongue. He became a convert to the Reformation, and died with Zwingle in the field of Cappel.

Zwingle soon saw all the superstition and folly of these pilgrimages. He derived his income from the contributions of the pilgrims, but he did *not hesitate* between his interest and his duty. Boldly did he preach to the pilgrims upon the inefficacy of all they were doing—their weary journeys, their offerings and prayers to the Virgin, their fasts and penances—"Christ alone saves us," cried he, and "Christ saves every where." The multitudes were astonished. Some shrunk away in pious horror; but greater numbers returned to their homes proclaiming the blessed truth, that "Christ alone saves, and saves every where." The shrine of Our Lady of Einsiedeln was well nigh deserted. Thus did the truth extend more and more, the eloquence of Zwingle was blazed abroad, and the number of his friends increased. It is wonderful how little opposition he, at this time, met with. His course indeed was eminently prudent as well as faithful, for he laid out his strength in expounding the Scriptures, and in pointing out the way of salvation.

From Einsiedeln he was called by the canons of the cathedral of Zurich, to become their preacher. His election had met with opposition on account of his innovating spirit. Nevertheless, he prevailed by a large majority. When he was received by the chapter, his duties were explained to him. These were, to collect the revenues, to exhort the people to pay all tithes and dues, and to increase as much as possible the income arising from visitations to the sick, and from masses for the dead. Without directly replying to this, he declared that his intention was to set before the people the life of Christ, and that for this purpose he would begin by lecturing upon the whole Gospel of Matthew. "It is to the glory of God and of Christ," said he, "and to the salvation of souls, that I desire to consecrate myself."

Here began the great work of Zwingle. Preaching Christ and him crucified, he overcame all opposition. He came to Zurich as a priest of the old religion, and was regularly inducted into the cathedral service. But he preached as the early fathers of the church, and as the apostles preached—he preached only the true Gospel.

What followed was a result to be expected. The people, instructed in the Gospel, became true converts under the Gospel. Both Zwingle and his hearers were carried along by a genial and happy current of light and love, and without violence. Whenever he was opposed, he simply appealed to the word of God, and therefore was always victorious. Zurich became reformed, and the doctrines of the Gospel, from thence as from a centre, spread far and wide. The man who had been the instrument of so great a change could not but have paramount influence. By wisdom, foresight, fearlessness, and decision, united with a clear and powerful eloquence, he was fitted to be a leader of the people. The union of church and state every where existed. In a democratic state like Zurich, how could its most distinguished citizen, while this union existed, keep aloof from state affairs?

But there were many events taking place around him which led him, as it appears to me, unavoidably into those political movements for which he has been blamed even by his admirers. The forest cantons, bigoted in their attachment to Rome, forbade the preaching of the gospel, and in several instances condemned the faithful servants of Christ to be beheaded or to be burnt at the stake. They even went so far as to form an alliance with Austria, their ancient enemy, to put down the reformers in Switzerland. Then Charles V. appeared on the stage, making the most mighty combinations in Europe, to extinguish the Reformation. The Protestant states in Germany, and afterwards the states of Holland, were compelled to unite in defence of the natural rights of opinion and conscience. Was it wrong in Zwingle to aim to bring about a similar union in Switzerland, and even to effect a union of all the Protestant states of Europe? The Catholic states were making war upon the most holy and valuable of all natural rights.

Zwingle and his adherents did not aim to propagate the gospel by the sword. They trusted alone to the free preaching of the gospel. As members of the state, they stood forth only in the defence of natural rights.

The battle of Cappel was a battle for liberty of conscience, against those who had invaded it. Zurich lost the battle and Zwingle was slain, but the cause, in the end, triumphed. He accompanied the troops to battle, in obedience to the custom of his country, as he had before accompanied the troops of Glaris to the fields of Italy. He fell at Cappel, a martyr in a holy cause. The spirit of his enemies was clearly shown in the brutal ferocity which committed his mangled corpse to the flames, and then scattered his ashes to the winds.

Zwingle, from the beginning to the end of his career, was a consistent and heroic advocate and defender of the truth of God, and the rights of man.

From this episode, into which I have naturally been led by the associations of the place, as well as by feelings which I could not well suppress, I return to the journal of a traveller.

From Zurich we went by railroad to Baden. Our friends accompanied us thus far, and then took leave of us. Their route lay in the direction of Constance. After visiting Munich, Dresden, Berlin, and Vienna, they were to spend the winter in Italy. How happy we would have been to have accompanied them. But we were bound for France, and thence home again. Italy is to us still an object of expectation.

The route from Zurich to Basil is one of great natural beauty, and of historical interest. At Baden the Limmat has forced its way through the mountain to join the Rhine. On one side of this gorge stands the ruins of a castle, once the stronghold of the Princes of Austria. The Swiss Baden, like Baden-Baden, and Baden in Austria, is resorted to for its baths.

Next after Baden is the ancient town of Brugg. Below the town, the Limmat, the Reuss, and the Aar form a junction, and then they all flow on as the Aar, and join the Rhine. Where the Reuss unites with the Aar stood the Roman Vidonissa. Near Brugg is the abbey of Köningsfelden, founded in 1310, on the spot where the emperor Albert was assassinated. On the height of Wüpelsberg stand the ruins of the castle of Habsburg, built in the eleventh century by Count Radbod, an ancestor of the family, whence came Rudolph the first emperor of that house. A small estate, had these Counts of Habsburg, who took possession of the throne of Charlemagne.

At the foot of the Wüpelsberg are the baths of Schintznach, the most celebrated of the watering-places in Switzerland. The number of these places in Germany and Switzerland is astonishing. They all have their uses and attractions, and they all are resorted to.

At Brugg we crossed the Aar by a long wooden bridge, and wound our way up the long hill of Bötzberg. It was here that we began to meet crowds of pilgrims, of all ages and of both sexes, on their way to the shrine of our Lady of Einsiedeln. After this we passed them continually. Most of them were from the French side of the Rhine. They carried packs containing provisions and other necessaries. They were all of the lower order. We could hear them at a considerable distance repeating their *Paternosters*, and *Ave Marias.* It was like the hum of bees swarming, and as rapid as the repetition of the alphabet, or multiplication table by children. On they trudged with fixed countenances, apparently weary and heavy laden, some with packs, some with age, and perhaps, too, with a sense of their sins,—on they trudged day after day to the sacred seat of the Holy Mother to find rest unto their souls. O that the voice of a Zwingle could again penetrate them as of yore, "Christ alone saves us, and Christ saves every where." The average number of pilgrims annually at Einsiedeln is 150,000. In 1834, 36,000 resorted there during one fortnight.

From the summit of the Bötzberg we saw for the last time the glorious Alps. During our ascent they had come into view, and for nearly an hour they lay before us. There again were the Eigher, the Mönch, the Wetterhorn, the Schreckhorn, the Jungfrau, the Blümlis Alp. As we descended the other side of the hill, gradually we lost sight of them:—at last only their snowy peaks shot above the brow of the hill; we descend a little lower, they are gone. For some time I felt sad, and I said to myself, When shall I see them again!

We left the Bötzberg; we were again on the banks of the Rhine. The evening drew on. The cornfields, meadows, and vineyards of the canton of Basle were around us; and as the sun went down, we were under the protection of the Three Kings of Cologne, or rather of mine host of the Three Kings in the goodly town of Basle.

XIV.

Country and Home.

THE attachment of the Swiss to their country and homes is well known to all. Every one is familiar with the story, that Swiss soldiers in foreign armies are prone to desert if by chance they hear the airs of the *Ranz des Vaches.* And this Switzerland does look like a country which one would love to call *his* country; and these Swiss towns, and villages, and glorious valleys, have a homelike aspect. Attachment to country and home is a strong and dear feeling of the human heart. Home, indeed, is home every where, for it is made up of the circle of parents and children; and it is possible to remove it from country to country and yet to preserve it. But, nevertheless, the home feeling is strengthened by the attachments of friends and neighbors, and by attachment to the country in which we make our home. It is strengthened also by local associations, and by natural objects of beauty and grandeur. The spot where our fathers have lived before us, the old house in which they were born and in which they died, the lands on which they toiled—these gather a sacredness around them. And when mountain and valley, and lake and river, and mountain-streams, make up a glorious scenery, the imagination and the heart become wedded to the soil by a charm whose power is then only fully realized when the connecting tie is broken. If, in addition to all this, one's country has an old and heroic history, is filled with native literature and native arts, and with the memory of great and good men, is fostered by benignant political institutions, and is under holy religious influences, so that patriotism and piety join hand to hand,—then are the ties of country and home complete.

Such a country and such a home the Swiss have had. And yet, with the other nations of Europe, they are beginning to emigrate to America in large numbers. Even from the Oberland they are flocking to our shores. They seek to escape from an overcrowded population; they desire a more abundant subsistence more easily obtained; they want more space and freedom of action; they distrust their own security amid the vortices of European revolution; they wish to escape from the liabilities to war and invasion, and to sit down undisturbed amid the arts of peace. The time was when their mountain fastnesses were the only home of liberty; but now they are filled with dreams of the glorious West, where liberty is still more secure, and where all that man wants is more abundant; and thus restlessness and hope conspire to lead them away. But I cannot believe they can leave their native valleys without regrets and tears. And yet the human heart is often a rude thing. Man the animal overcomes man the creature of thought and feeling. It is, too, a great thing to have independence and plenty.

I was sitting on the elevated box beside the coachman—according to my practice in Switzerland, in order to enjoy a better view of the country—on our way to Basil, when learning I was from America, he expressed a strong desire to emigrate.

Myself.—Why don't you go, if you wish to?

Coachman.—Ah! if I only had the money.

Myself.—It costs but little. The sailing ships take emigrants very cheap. You can get from here to America for one hundred and fifty francs.

Coachman.—But how shall I get so many francs?

Myself.—You have a family, I suppose.

Coachman.—No, but I can only just live myself on my wages. How much do you pay for yourself and your ladies in the steamship?

Myself.—Twenty-five hundred francs.

Coachman—(*in astonishment*).—Twenty-five hundred francs! Holy Virgin! If I had so much money, I would give up work, and live like a lord.

When I told him how easily a laboring man could earn thirty dollars in our country, and how possible it was for him even to get together five hundred dollars, he listened as if I were telling stories about an El Dorado. This explains the willingness of the Swiss to emigrate. But will they form an attachment to country and home like that which possessed them in their native land? Will they not often long to see the glacier, and the snowy Alps, and the green valleys between the mountains, and to hear the sound of the Alpine horn, the music of waterfalls, and the thunder of the avalanche? Will they not sing the Ranz des Vaches, and long to go home?

The question has often arisen in my mind, Are the tendencies of society in our country calculated to create a strong home feeling, and intense love of country? With my present impressions, I am not prepared to give a favorable answer. I state these impressions that I may do somewhat to correct an evil which I fear really exists among us.

First as to the home feeling. There are not many places in our country which have old associations about them connected with particular families. And where these do exist they are invaded by that spirit of enterprise which carries away the young men to distant cities and new states in the pursuit of wealth and distinction. We are a restless people from the very conditions of our country. We seek for change and dare fortune. We do not seek wealth as a means of creating a home, and finding repose. Business is our occupation, and increase of riches opens but a wider field of activity. We accumulate that we may accumulate more.

We build houses and occupy them with no idea of permanency, but with the idea of some future speculation. The street in which we build may become a great business street; or we may, somehow, have an opportunity of selling again at a profit. We buy an estate in the country; but if possible we will locate it near some railroad, or expected railroad, and hold ourselves ready to turn it into village lots, or divide it in any way, or make any disposition of it which may make increase of value. Windfalls of this nature have been so frequent in our country, that we cannot buy without dreaming of them, nay, we calculate upon them. We are a people who buy and sell, and get gain. Beyond all nations that ever existed, we are a money-making nation. Possibilities with us are endless. Possibilities open to every one. The newsboy may yet be the greatest man upon change; he may be the Mayor of the city; he may be the President of the Union. But the race for money takes precedence of every thing, for here the chances are most numerous. It is more or less with the whole country as it is with California. There are gold mines in which every one may dig, and rich enough to reward the labor of many. Let us dig away then. Who can tell without trying where the largest lumps of gold are to be found?

Now it is plain that in all this we are not founding homes. We are not building houses to grow old over the heads of our descendants; we are not planting trees that their hoary branches may wave around the old homestead from generation to generation. We hardly know where we shall be in a dozen years hence; and Heaven only knows where our children will be. In other countries those changes are extraordinary events, which, with us, are an ordinary experience. Families there may be scattered, here we know they shall be scattered.

As, then, we are not founding homes, how can the home feeling exist among us? Is not this precious element of our being going to decay? Are not even our fireside charities supplanted by the prevailing genius of our country? When Æneas fled from the sack of Troy, there were two treasures he did not forget to carry away with him, his old father Anchises, and the Penates—*the household gods.* He first of all thought of founding a new home.

As to love of country, there are similar indications. We are, indeed, proud of our country, and quite ready to fight for it, if need be. But what does our country contain for us—what is it that we value in our country? Is it dear to us, and are we proud of it on account of its history—those old heroic and virtuous memories; on account of its institutions—its government and laws, its religious freedom, its educational privileges, its arts and literature, its noble public monuments, its development of a higher phase of humanity, its glorious example to the world, its power to work upon the destinies of nations, and its own destiny as the mighty Palestine, where the oracles of truth and liberty are preserved for the universal good? Or, is it dear to us, and are we proud of it as the great mart of trade, and because here are our profitable investments and our sources of revenue?

Our conduct must decide the question. Do the great objects I have mentioned above inspire us? Do we live for the greatness and glory of our country in these points of view? Are we public spirited citizens engaged in the preservation of our old honors, and in promoting all that enlightens, elevates, and adorns a state? Do we enter manfully into political and municipal affairs for the public weal? Are we willing to take upon ourselves great trusts, and to devote ourselves to the good of the state? Do we aim to build up great institutions, both for our own times and for after times? Are we ambitious to set forth our country as a mighty and benignant power in the world to crush oppression and hold up the oppressed?

As it now stands with us, we are letting all the offices of society run into the form of trades and professions. Our merchants, and our men of business of every kind, are just intent upon their business. While this thrives, they are content. Another class of men, often the most worthless and incompetent, take upon themselves to manage the municipal and state affairs. This becomes their trade—their profession—their mode of getting gain. Great abuses may exist, but the man of business is prospering nevertheless. He buys and sells with profit: he lives in his ceiled house secure. What does he care whether this man or that is elected to the State Legislature or to the general Congress? What does he care how the city government is administered? Public peculation, dirty streets, and general neglect of the vital public interests, do not reach him. He can endure it all while trade flourishes, and the stocks stand well. How can the men who are engaged in profitable business of any kind afford to mingle in politics, to hold public offices, or see to the well-being of the city or state? Let the rabble who have nothing better to do, attend to this. And as to the great and noble institutions which give birth to a national character by permeating society with elevated principles and refined tastes, and by quickening the moral, intellectual, and social life—let the poor scholars and artists attend to these as they best can: this is their trade, and they must contrive to live by it. Let the worst come to the worst, the state and the city will last as long as we last; our fortune, at least, is made: let posterity take care of itself.

I will admit, of course, that there are exceptions to this, I will even admit, if you please, that the picture is strongly drawn; but who can deny that a spirit like this is prevalent among us, and that we are feeling the effects of it?

The same intense commercial activity, the same love of gain which destroys the home feeling, destroys the spirit of a manly, high-minded, and devoted citizenship. Our country or our city is a place to stay in for certain purposes, but we do not cause our heart's blood to flow together in one genial tide of ardent and devoted patriotism.

When we visit other countries we are charmed by the institutions of learning, by the glorious works of art which we see every where, and by the elevated tone of society. We return and say, What charming lands we have travelled through, what beautiful things we have seen, how ripened and perfect are all things there. But taught by what we have seen, why do we not set about creating the same things here? And when we come to make a comparison between our country and other countries, we content ourselves with saying, they indeed have better institutions of learning, they have more perfect arts; but we have more freedom, and we have more to eat and drink.

But how is it, that with our greater freedom, our greater abundance, our more ample field of action, our young and mighty energies, we do not strive to rival them in all that goes to elevate, embellish, and perfect society?

London, at an expense of thirty thousand dollars annually,

has clean streets. Is it a part of our freedom in New-York to expend one hundred and eighty thousand dollars annually, for the same purpose, and yet live with streets that might breed a pestilence?

The great cities of Europe have universities, great libraries, and collections of art. Are these symbols of despotism? Is it a part of our freedom to deny our youth the means of a high cultivation, and while we decry the transatlantic aristocracies, do all that we can to foster a vulgar aristocracy of money, and the tyranny of a rabble municipality?

In England, the nobles, the men of learning, the men of wealth, make it their glory to take part in the affairs of the state. Nothing there is so honorable as to serve the country. Is it a part of our freedom to forsake the assemblies of the people, and to resign the public offices to peculators and sciolists? In a country like ours where every individual forms a part of the state, because every individual contains a portion of the universal sovereignty, it ought to be the pride as it is the duty of every one to take part in the concerns of the state, not in the leading strings of a party led on by a self-interested demagogue, but in the spirit of a clear-sighted and magnanimous patriotism. Each man ought to feel that he has a duty to perform, and he ought to perform it fearlessly and with a hearty interest. We ought to feel that we have a country to take care of, and a country worthy of all our devotion. Let us receive a baptism from the spirit which animated our fathers—those men who laid the foundations of our institutions.

If any one asks, What remedy shall be applied to correct

these evils? I reply, that the first thing is to become convinced that the evils exist, and to measure their bearings. After this we may seek for a remedy.

In respect to the home feeling, a difficulty must be acknowledged to exist, necessarily growing out of the conditions of our country. Our rapid growth, our vast improvements, and our wide-spread territory, are at war with permanency, and bring about constant changes.

The absence of the law of entail prevents also the growth of old estates. In our country the love of home must grow up with the love of country. It may have a more particular determination in the interest we take in the city, or the particular locality in which we reside. Let us take, for example, the city of New-York. Here are great capabilities and opportunities. This city, in point of commercial activity and population, is fast advancing upon the greatest cities of the world. Let us not look upon it as a mere mart of trade. Let us consider how it may be adorned by public buildings and works of art. Let us make it the seat of great institutions of learning and the arts. Let us aim to diffuse the spirit of a higher cultivation. Let us make it an intellectual as well as a commercial metropolis. Let it become as remarkable for its beauty and magnificence, for its taste and order, for a graceful and enlightened society, as it now is for active trade and growing wealth; and let the beautiful shores of its waters become the seats of men of cultivation as well as men of wealth. When this is accomplished, then we have thrown about it charms and attractions which strike the imagination, and enkindle enthusiasm; and which make it a region that we feel we can call our home. The city of Athens—the city itself was the home of every Athenian. The city was his pride and glory. And why was it? Because, there was the Acropolis with its temples, and the whole city was adorned by the hands of its artists. There was the grove of Academus. There was its theatre—not like our theatres, places for the exhibition of buffooneries and farces, but a vast space, open to the heavens, where the whole population assembled to hear the compositions of Æschylus, Euripides and Sophocles. There was the Areopagus. There were the assemblies of the people where Æschines and Demosthenes reasoned and thundered—in no barbaric vulgar style—but in pure classic Greek, with cultivated oratory, before a people who were competent judges of eloquence and grace. Athens had commerce and arms, merchants and heroes; but it was philosophy, poetry, eloquence and art which so polished and enriched it, and invested it with such splendid attractions and dear associations, that it was the only home in the wide world that an Athenian could find.

The unfortunate sons of Israel, in past centuries, had no resource but in prosecuting traffic and gain. They went wherever traffic and gain attracted them. They were without a country and a home, and their pursuits harmonized with their fate. We have a country and a home; but the concentration of all our passions and energies in the mere love of gain will make us, like them, ready to wander up and down the face of the earth; the ties of kindred and country will be easily broken; and all things under heaven will be measured and valued by a commercial standard. We shall even build churches and schools of learning to improve property rather than to cultivate human souls. Our very charities will become a speculation. The true remedy is, to begin at once to act upon higher principles. The love of home and the love of country will be revived and confirmed when we engage earnestly in those great and beneficent works, which will make our country a grand and sacred thing, and fill it with those fresh, beautiful, and holy places, where we shall be drawn to build our habitations, for thought and for usefulness, and where our ashes at last may be gathered to an honorable repose.

XV.

Down the Rhine.—Belgium.

WHEN I turned my back upon Switzerland, I felt like one leaving home. I had now been several weeks among those stupendous mountains, and wandering through those green sequestered valleys. It was to me a new experience. Such scenery I had never seen before. Indeed, such scenery is nowhere else to be found. In respect to its natural features, it seemed more like home to me than all other lands, because, more grand and beautiful than all others. Where we find most to love, there we find most of home. The soul is most at home amid the grand and beautiful, because it finds itself there reflected. It sees itself, and it sees God, the Infinite Soul. It flows out into the objects around, and becomes one with them. It is conscious of its own greatness and beauty. The Alps are its fellows, the avalanches its playthings, the green valleys its sense of beauty, the sound of streams and waterfalls its own music, in which it is perpetually expressing joy and adoration.

Does not the soul always feel sad when it leaves the beautiful behind—whether it be the beauty of Nature, or the beauty of Art, or the beauty of "the human face divine"—the index of the loving heart?

We had one month before entered Basle from the French side of the Rhine: we now descended on the German side, and passing through Freiburg, before nightfall were again at Baden-Baden. The throng of visitors had passed away, but a very considerable number yet remained. The region had lost none of its beauty. I took some charming walks, the early part of the next day.

In the *Conversations Haus*, I found the *rouge et noir* and *roulette* tables still surrounded by absorbed and eager gamesters. There was the same awful stillness, the same joyless faces. Chink, chink, the money was still changing hands. They appeared like men offering sacrifices to the Destinies.

Speaking with a gentleman about these gambling establishments, he related to me a story which illustrates the infatuation of play. A porter in Paris who earned about twenty-five francs a week, went, at the end of a certain week, with what he had accumulated, into a large gambling-house to try his luck. The play all went in his favor, and he came out with forty-five thousand francs in his pocket. He immediately deposited the money with a banker whom he happened to know. After a few days, he called upon the banker and asked for ten thousand francs, that he might go and try his luck once more. The banker strongly dissuaded him, but all in vain. He gave him the ten thousand francs, telling him at the same time that he would not let him have any more of his money for that purpose. The man lost his francs, and came back to the banker for more. The banker refused, told him he would not suffer him to ruin himself, and urged him to invest the remainder in some kind of business. The man insisted upon having his money, and at length told the banker he wished to rob him of his own. The banker grew angry, returned him all his money, and bade him begone. He lost the whole, and the next day he was at his old employment again.

At Baden-Baden we took the train for Manheim, passing through Carlsruhe. The station-houses were decorated with wreaths and garlands, in preparation for the Duke, who was expected that way. We saw the carriages designed for himself and suite. The one he was to occupy was decorated with the ducal arms. In Europe the carriages on the railroad are taking the place of all other vehicles. Kings and princes travel now in this way as well as other people.

I noticed in the Duchy that the fields were mostly worked by women. The men are called off for garrison-duty. Emigration to America is going on very actively from the Duchy. I was informed that whole villages were nearly deserted. In Mayence is an office for emigrants where they take passage for America. In many places I observed placards were posted designed to dissuade the people from emigrating. They contained accounts of the manner in which emigrants are cheated at New-York by agents, and of the unhealthiness of the climate in our Western states and territories. At one of the stations I noticed a laborer on the road eating his dinner. It consisted of a chunk of black bread and some hard pears. He was nevertheless a hearty-looking young fellow, and ate with a good appetite.

We reached Manheim in the afternoon. It is a dull-looking place, situated on very low ground at the junction of the Neckar with the Rhine. It was once a strongly fortified position, and the capital of the Palatinate. Its fate, like that of Heidelberg, has been a sad one, having been several times bombarded, and twice burned to the ground in two centuries. How this rich and beautiful country has been desolated by war, truly called the pastime of princes! The people—the poor people, have had to endure the suffering and bear the burdens.

At Manheim we took the steamer. Night had set in when we reached Mainz. It being Saturday night, we remained here during the Sabbath. We took apartments at the Europäischer Hof—a fine hotel, and which boasts of the distinction of having entertained Queen Victoria.

Travellers on the Rhine are very apt not to stop at Mainz at all, but to land at Biberich, as we did when ascending the river, and to proceed on immediately to Frankfort. Indeed, there is not much to detain one here. The cathedral, built of red sandstone, has many interesting monuments. Those of the Archbishop Electors are particularly so, both from their historical associations and from the effigies of the archbishops represented in full costume. The cathedral itself is admired by architects as a fine specimen of ecclesiastical architecture. There is also a fine bronze statue of Gutemberg, the reputed inventor of movable types. It is cast after a design by Thorwaldsen.

The public gardens around the city are very agreeable. The town is very compactly built, and the streets are narrow and crooked. It drew my attention particularly as a garrison town. The fortifications are very strong. It is connected by a bridge with the opposite shore, where there is a fortification commanding the bridge. It is, I believe, the most important fortress on the Rhine after Ehrenbreitstein. It has been a place of consequence in military operations from the days of the Romans. It now belongs to Hesse Darmstadt, but is garrisoned by the German confederation. The troops, eight thousand in number, are partly Austrian and partly Prussian.

Sabbath morning we went to the cathedral for a short time, where many of the Austrian troops were assembled. There is but one Protestant church in the place besides the garrison church of the Prussians. We attended divine service at the latter.

The orchestra was composed of the military band. The music was admirable. There were but few instruments besides the organ. The church was filled by the soldiers. They all had prayer and hymn books, and, according to the German custom, they all united in the singing. Their conduct was perfectly orderly, and they appeared attentive and devout. They were young men of fine robust forms. At their homes they had been trained to religious duties, and their early habits had not forsaken them here. The preacher delivered an appropriate sermon with much earnestness, and his prayers were devout.

It was an affecting sight to me. I could not help thinking what a terrible scourge these military establishments are. These strong young men are taken from their homes, while their mothers and sisters are left to work the fields. How many tens of thousands of just such young men have been slaughtered in the wars which have swept over this country from age to age! And here on garrison duty, not only is their labor lost to the country, but their support is a drain upon the produce of the fields, to which they contribute nothing.

These would be happy regions if nations could live without being embroiled in war. War, war, this is the great curse of Europe. Could we calculate all the cost of war in the loss of labor, in the destruction of the lives of the laborers, in the expense of maintaining armies, and in the destruction of property by battles and sieges, and the march of troops,—what an enormous sum it would be! And then imagine all this to have been appropriated to the arts of peace—to human improvement, and how different the condition of nations would have been! We live in the bosom of a rich and bountiful Nature who has enough for all; but in making war upon each other, we make war upon her: we desolate the kind mother who would nourish us all as her happy children.

The first archbishop of Mainz, St. Boniface, was a missionary. The Pope made him primate of Germany. His successors became earthly princes, and ruled over a territory containing four hundred thousand souls. Their revenues were immense. They maintained a powerful body-guard, and surrounded themselves with the trappings of royalty, and still they were priests. In the Diets these archbishops presided. They were at the head of the princes of the German empire. Did the true church exist when its kingdom became a kingdom of this world?

At the table d'hôte of the Europäischer Hof were several military officers. Mine host, according to the German custom, dined with us. After dinner they lighted their cigars, and commenced a game of cards together—that is, the officers and mine host.

We landed Saturday evening within a few yards of the hotel. Our luggage was carried up by the public porters. I was surprised at the unusual charge. I found that according to the police regulation the same charge is made for porterage to every part of the town: one yard or one mile, it is all the same. The tariff, however, is based upon the presumption of the greater distance.

Monday morning we were again upon the Rhine. We were now transferred to another line of steamers below the bridge. The descent of the Rhine was rapid. We now had the advantage of the swift current which in the ascent we had to stem. The scenery still struck me as beautiful. I was still interested in the old ruins upon the hills. The foliage was not so bright: the first touch of the declining season was apparent. I found that the promise of the vineyards was poor, owing to the rains, and the coolness of the season.

There was one thing which I could not avoid remarking—that the scenery of the Rhine, although equally picturesque, did not appear as bold as before. My impressions of Switzerland made every thing appear diminutive.

We reached Cologne in the afternoon. We paid another visit to the cathedral, and were more than ever struck with its beauty. Then we took the train for Aix-la-Chapelle, where we arrived some time after dark, and put up at Nuellin's hotel, opposite the fountain.

Next morning we were awakened by a band of music. I got up and went to the window, when I saw persons walking up and down a colonnade, while every instant, some were disappearing, and others starting up, through what had to me, where I stood, the appearance of a trap-door. I dressed myself, and crossed over to the colonnade. There were spacious apartments at either end of it open to the visitors. Within a railing was collected the band of musicians. What had appeared like a trap-door turned out to be an abrupt descent, by stairs, to the steaming fountain. I looked down below, where I saw people receiving one after another tumblers of the scalding fluid, which they cooled and drank like people taking any other hot draught. It is right to get all the good we can wherever we go; and so, if an additional portion of health were to be had at Aix, by simply drinking a tumbler of hot water, why should I not take it? I therefore suddenly disappeared like the rest, and received a tumbler which I could hardly hold in my hands—it was so hot. I tasted it—then drew back in dismay: the water at Baden-Baden was weak, insipid chicken broth; this was chicken broth fiery hot, and spiced with sulphuretted hydrogen. But all around me were drinking it down very composedly, one tumbler after another. I observed, too, that as soon as they had completed their potations, they went aloft and walked about where the delicious music was floating through the air. Then I concluded that the band played while the people were drinking, to allay nervous irritability, and to take them "with ravishment," like Milton's fallen angels, and suspend the torment. So, I opened my ears wide to the music, and bravely swallowed down a tumbler full of stuff that might well serve in purgatory to punish drunkards. If I had need of the music before I drank, I had much more afterwards. The music, indeed, did some good, but the best remedy was a substantial breakfast at Nuellin's. The potation, however, wrought in me the whole day, at least so thought my companions, for to them I appeared unusually irritable and fiery towards porters, coachmen, and all that tribe who generally try the good-nature of travellers.

The waters of these hot springs, after furnishing the baths and supplying the drinkers, escape in sufficient quantities to accommodate the washerwomen. The water, containing an alkaline salt, as well as being very hot, saves them both soap and fuel. The odor of the linen thus washed, to be sure, is not pleasant to strangers, but the inhabitants of Aix, accustomed as they are to drink sulphur and inhale sulphur, can have very little objection to wearing sulphur likewise.

The name of this old city—which the Germans change into *Aachen*—is compounded of the Celtic word *Ac*,—the same with the Latin *aqua*,—and *la chapelle*, the chapel, referring to the cathedral founded by Charlemagne, in the latter part of the eighth century. The Roman name is said to be Aquisgranum, after Granius, who, under Hadrian, in the second century, is supposed to have founded the town. So the waters of Granius have become the waters of the Chapel.

Aix in France, and Aix in Savoy, both have medicinal springs: hence the name given to them.

Aix-la-Chapelle, the place where Charlemagne was born, where he died, and where his tomb was erected, has associations which are familiar to all readers of history. It is now included in the dominions of the king of Prussia.

The tomb of Charlemagne was opened by the emperor Frederic Barbarossa, in 1165. The skeleton of Charlemagne was found seated on his throne, clothed in the imperial robes, the royal sceptre still grasped in the fleshless hand, the crown upon the skull, the sword still belted on, and the pilgrim's pouch still fastened to the girdle. What a spectacle of the vanity of human greatness and power! The throne—an armed chair—is still preserved in the cathedral; the other regalia are deposited at Vienna.

The bones of Charlemagne, together with other relics, namely, a locket of the Virgin's hair, a piece of the true cross, the girdle of Christ, the rod which smote him, and the sponge dipped in vinegar, and several more, are preserved in the treasury of the sacristy. On these relics the emperors of Germany took the coronation oath.

The *grand reliques* are another collection, comprising those which were presented to Charlemagne by the Patriarch of Jerusalem and Haroun, the king of Persia.

These are shown once in seven years, from the 15th to the 27th of July. At the last exhibition 180,000 pilgrims were present. The next exhibition takes place in 1853.

Travellers can make their calculations accordingly, if they feel curious about these matters.

The cathedral did not interest me much, except on account of its antiquity. The pillars of porphyry, collected by Charlemagne from the east, and from the Exarch's palace at Ravenna, are very beautiful.

Aix, for the most part, is a sombre looking town. A traveller, on entering it, however, receives a different impression, on account of a new street which leads from the railway to the theatre and to the principal hotels. This is wide and very elegantly built.

On our way to Antwerp, we passed by Liege, and Mechlin or Malines. We had a very good view of Liege. Situated at the junction of the Ourthe with the Meuse, in a very fertile valley, it has always been a place of consequence, and celebrated for its manufactures. Here reigned the bishops, raised by the emperors of Germany to the rank of sovereign princes.

Their dynasty continued down to the time the French took possession of the country, at the close of the last century. The reign of the bishops was by no means peaceful, for the brave and enterprising citizens were ever striving for their freedom. It is one of those conflicts which Scott introduces into his Quentin Durward. The bishop, at this time, was a Bourbon supported by Charles the Bold. Charles marched against Liege to quell the insurrection of the people, and to avenge the death of the bishop.

Brave and stern was the defence of the men of Liege, but the Burgundians and French succeeded in storming the city, slaughtered the inhabitants, and burnt it to the ground, with the exception of the churches and convents. Liege then contained 120,000 inhabitants. The present number is between seventy and eighty thousand. Louis XI. fomented the very insurrection which he aided in putting down. Such was the game of princes, and such the fate of the people. Sir Walter Scott, in this novel as well as in others, does not give sufficient prominence to the cause of the people. It is painful to find fault with the amiable and gifted novelist, but it must be confessed that his sympathies were with knightly deeds rather than with the struggles of liberty.

In passing Malines we caught a glimpse of the cathedral with its unfinished tower. It is three hundred and forty feet high. It was designed to be six hundred and forty feet; but there it stands, and will stand like the tower of Babel, until time shall crumble it to the ground. The cathedral was built by the sale of indulgences. The completed works of Gothic architecture are vast and astonishing; they were the labor of centuries; and yet the designs outran even the zeal of superstition.

The appearance of the open country of Belgium is very pleasing, and reminds one of England, by its high cultivation, order and neatness. The peasantry under a limited monarchy, and with a good king, are in a happy condition, and experience few of those evils which afflict other parts of Europe. The position of Belgium, however, exposes her to invasion from the neighboring mighty powers, or makes her a convenient battle field in any rupture which may take place between them. To France, Belgium seems to have a sort of natural affinity, and France seems ever ready to swallow her up when any plausible pretext shall arise. Her security, therefore, depends more upon the balance of European powers than upon her own independent strength.

On entering Antwerp, one is struck with the great strength of the fortifications. In this respect, it is similar to Strasburg. But these fortifications in time of peace, with their green embankments and slopes planted with trees, and a sort of labyrinthine effect of the many angles, constitute an embellishment of the town, and afford many a pleasant promenade. The principal streets have a very striking air of elegance and magnificence. The houses are tasteful, and built in a substantial manner of a light-colored sandstone called *Kareelsteen*, which is obtained at Boom, only a few miles from Antwerp. The town is in good repair, and has a considerable amount of manufactures and trade, and yet one experiences an instinctive feeling that some great change has come over it. There is not that activity and bustle which would be expected in a city of such magnitude, and such displays of art and wealth in its buildings, both public and private. In driving from the railway station to the Hotel du Parc, near the cathedral, we passed through the heart of the city, and it appeared to me then that there was a Sabbath-like stillness pervading it. It is a city whose life does not fill out the measure of its capacity. It is, I suppose, something like Venice, although by no means in such a state of decay. The same impression is felt, still more deeply, upon visiting the *Quays* upon the Schelde, and the basins and careening docks constructed by Napoleon. Here are preparations for a commerce which no longer exists.

In the eleventh century, Antwerp was a small republic. In the fifteenth and sixteenth centuries, she was the unrivalled seat of commerce. Then she had 200,000 inhabitants, her merchants were princes. Two thousand vessels annually entered her port; the money put in circulation annually was more than five hundred millions of guilders; and five thousand merchants assembled every day on the Exchange.

The Duke of Alva gave the first blow to the prosperity of Antwerp. In 1576, it was given up to three days' pillage by the Spanish soldiers. "Antwerp, at the time of this catastrophe, was in the most flourishing condition. Companies of merchants from almost every commercial nation resided in it, possessing storehouses and factories filled with the most precious commodities. Great numbers of the citizens, too, were the wealthiest in Europe. Their magnificent houses were adorned with the most costly furniture; and their shops and warehouses stored with gold and silver stuffs, and all other kinds of valuable effects, collected from every corner of the globe. Upon these the Spaniards seized without any discrimination of the owners, and without considering whether the persons whom they pillaged were friends or enemies. The plunder that lay open and unconcealed was immense; but it was far from being sufficient to satiate the avarice of the Spaniards. They exercised the most unrelenting cruelty upon all whom they suspected to have concealed their treasures; and nothing was to be heard in the city, but either shrieks and groans of the sufferers, or the lamentations of those whom they compelled to behold the torments of their husbands, wives or children. Contemporary historians have described some of the several species of torture which they inflicted; but the reader's modesty would be offended, and his humanity shocked by the recital. In this manner were these men, for three days and nights, employed in plundering and butchering by turns, a people who were subjects of the same prince as themselves, and from whom—whatever ground of complaint they might pretend against the council of state—they had never received the smallest injury or provocation. Nor does it appear that their officers interposed to moderate their excesses, till the soldiers exhausted with fatigue, were about to give over of themselves. The money in specie which was extorted, amounted at least to eight hundred millions of guilders, besides an immense quantity of gold and silver, in plate, stuffs and furniture, which the owners were not able to redeem.

The loss which the people of Antwerp sustained by the burning of so many buildings, was not less than what they suffered by the rapacity of the soldiers. The most beautiful part of the city was burnt to the ground; and great numbers of shops and warehouses containing the richest goods, were consumed to ashes."*

The imagination dares not dwell on the horrors of this savage brutality. But the calamities of Antwerp did not end here. In 1585 it capitulated to the Prince of Parma after a siege of fourteen months. The Protestants were compelled to leave the city, and carried their wealth and enterprise with them into Holland. In 1648 the final blow was

* Watson.

struck at its prosperity, when, by the terms of the peace of Westphalia, the navigation of the Schelde was closed, and Amsterdam absorbed its commerce. The French, indeed, re-opened the navigation of the river in 1792, and Antwerp was recovering a part of its original prosperity, when the revolution which separated Belgium from Holland again concentrated in the Dutch towns the commerce which before Antwerp had shared with them. At present Antwerp contains less than eighty thousand inhabitants. The number of ships which entered its port in 1829, before the revolution, was about one thousand. In 1831 this number was reduced to less than four hundred.

But, although its commerce has decayed, there stands yet its glorious cathedral, and it has yet the fame and paintings of Rubens.

From the windows of my apartments in the Hotel du Parc, I saw that beautiful spire, four hundred feet high, every hour of the day, whose delicate carving Napoleon is said to have compared to Mechlin lace. Day and night I heard the musical chimes of its ninety-nine bells. Pauses indeed there were—short pauses, and then they would strike a new variation. In the intervals of slumber, in the night, I would hear them; they even mingled with my dreams. Sweet and clear, they seemed to come from the upper regions of the air, and produced a constant ravishment of the sense.

The appearance of the spire is eminently beautiful at night, when the sky is clear, and bright with stars. Then it lies against the heavens, and all the interstices are specks of light. I think it must have been this view of it which led Napoleon to make his comparison.

The interior of the cathedral, five hundred feet in length, and two hundred and fifty in breadth, with its lofty choir and nave, produces a sublime effect.

Over the high altar hangs one of Rubens' famous pictures, *The Assumption of the Virgin.* This picture he is said to have finished in sixteen days. The deification of the Virgin in this and other pictures, I confess, is so painful to me as to distract my mind from the splendors of art.

But in another part of the cathedral there are pictures where an art almost divine has wedded itself to a divine subject. I mean the two great pictures of Rubens, *The Elevation of the Cross*, and *The Descent from the Cross.*

The Elevation of the Cross is in three compartments—the central one being the cross. On the left are the two thieves represented in the background. One is partly nailed to the wood, and struggling with the executioners. The other, ghastly pale and horror-stricken, is about to be thrown down. On the right, Mary and John stand together; the first pale, and in silent, unutterable despair; the second excited, astonished, and dismayed—beholding, and yet scarcely believing, the awful reality before him. Here, too, are the Marys and the aged Salome. Mary Magdalene bows her head as if incapable of beholding the sight. Mary, the wife of Cleopas, has an infant at the breast. She is aghast with horror; and even the infant is overcome by an inexplicable distress. Salome exhibits intense sympathy, touched with the calmness of age.

Christ is nailed to the cross, which is partially elevated. The large, sorrowful eyes are raised to heaven. The contrast between the horror and struggles of the thieves, and the sublime submission of the august sufferer is strongly expressed. The nails have just been driven through the living flesh; he is suspended by them, while the soldiers in every variety of muscular action, are straining to erect the cross. With him there is no appearance of resistance: he is as a lamb led to the slaughter.

Rubens is remarkable for his coloring, and the reality which he gives to his paintings. Yes, reality, that is the word which expresses all. I stood and gazed in silence. I forgot the artist and his canvas. I had no thought of playing the critic. I too was standing by the cross. I was looking on the face of Christ. I shuddered and was awestruck before the sublimest and most momentous event that ever transpired. There he was, wounded for my transgression, suffering for my guilty soul. Now mine eye saw, what before I had only heard of by the hearing of the ear.

The Descent from the Cross is considered by artists the greatest work of Rubens. He has here achieved a wonderful triumph of art in wrapping the body in white linen without hurting the coloring of the flesh. "I consider," says Sir Joshua Reynolds, "Rubens' Christ as one of the finest figures that ever was invented: it is most correctly drawn, and, I apprehend, in an attitude of the utmost difficulty to execute. The hanging of the head on the shoulder, and the falling of the body on one side, gives it such an appearance of the heaviness of death, that nothing can exceed it."

But here, as in the other picture, I was impressed by the reality of the scene. In reflecting upon these pictures and the effect they produced upon me at the time, I perceive that I then for the first time understood the qualities of a great artist, and the power of his works. We may read books on art, we may comprehend æsthetical principles in general, we may form an acquaintance with many very good pictures, but never can we be truly said to know what art is, until we see with our own eyes what art has done by the hand of the great and unquestionable masters—those who have re-created nature, or made her more perfect on her own principles.

Antwerp contains many beautiful churches. Among these *St. Jaques* is the most remarkable. The interior is very splendid, and adorned with marble columns of exquisite workmanship, and delicate and curious carvings in wood. These churches are filled with paintings by Rubens, Vandyke, and other artists.

The Academy of Painting is a large edifice, formerly a convent, and contains a very large collection. The works of Rubens and Vandyke here are numerous.

There are four great paintings of Rubens in Antwerp which form a series, and to which in my own mind I gave the name of *The Epic of Redemption.* The first is in the church of St. Jaques, and represents the scene of the scourging. It is too painful to look at. The blood trickles under the lash, and the blue marks of the bruised flesh not yet bleeding are reality itself. The patient and illustrious sufferer is meekly bent to receive the scourge. What a sight! I could not endure it—I turned away.

The second is the elevation of the cross already described. The third is the crucifixion of Christ between the thieves.

This is in the Academy. A soldier is just piercing the side of Christ. Another is breaking the legs of one of the thieves, who in his mortal agony has torn one of his feet from the nail which fastened it to the tree. This figure is horrible. The other thief is quiet and turns his dying eyes to Christ. The head of Christ is bowed in death, and the whole frame relaxed. Mary Magdalene is at the feet of Christ and convulsively stretches out her hand as if to prevent the spear from entering his side. The figures of the mother of Christ, St. John, Mary the wife of Cleopas, and of the centurion, make up the principal group. This Sir Joshua Reynolds pronounces "one of the first pictures in the world, for composition, coloring, and what was to be expected from Rubens' correctness of drawing."

The fourth of this series is the Descent from the Cross. The mysterious and sublime facts of Christianity inspired the genius of Rubens. He is the Milton of painters.

The series of historical paintings in the Louvre have merits indeed as works of art; but the subjects could not call out the great powers of Rubens. The flattery in them is so extravagant and fulsome, that to me they were positively disagreeable. I can admire the painter's art when employed on common or indifferent subjects; but I am not enough of a connoisseur so to lose myself in the display of art, as to rise above an offensive subject. And this I deem the natural and highest effect of a painting, when it causes the observer to forget art itself, and brings his mind into direct union with the subject.

Antwerp is one of the places in Europe for the study of

paintings. I think, too, it would be agreeable as a residence.

Could Napoleon have carried out his stupendous design, Antwerp would have recovered its ancient glories. It would have become the commercial metropolis of his empire, and his naval arsenal and depôt. Now it seems destined to a quiet existence, unlesss war should arise, when it would be important as a fortress.

Brussels is a fair city on the little river Senne, with steep streets leading from the lower to the upper and more elegant portion, where the noble, wealthy, and fashionable reside, and where the hotels are situated. All say it has the air of Paris; but as it has only one hundred and forty-five thousand inhabitants, including the suburbs, it is only Paris in miniature. And yet, in the heart of the town, where you are affected only by the objects immediately around you, and can form no judgment of the entire circumference, it may be called Paris to all intents and purposes, presenting as it does a similar style of building, a similar display of elegant shops, and pouring upon your ear the rapid and easy inflections of the same language. Flemish is indeed spoken by the mass of the population, but not in those places where a stranger is apt to resort. There is a difference, however, as far as language is concerned, which will very soon begin to appear:—in Paris you will hear but little English, in Brussels a great deal. The English love to make this a residence; and, since the battle of Waterloo, they must of necessity come here, while making their annual, or rather their perennial pilgrimage.

Brussels has fine churches, magnificent palaces, and other

public buildings of note. It has a pleasant park and boulevards. The Royal Library contains two hundred thousand volumes. In the Burgundian Library, which is now united to the Royal, are eighteen thousand manuscripts, of great value. They are richly bound, and many of them embellished with exquisite miniature paintings. I found nothing in Brussels of equal interest with these manuscripts. They are named after the Dukes of Burgundy who began the collection at an early period.

At the time we visited Brussels there was a grand exhibition of paintings and statuary, to which all the artists of Europe had been invited to contribute. It was a competition for public attention with the grand exhibition in London. The collection was immense, particularly of paintings. There, of course, was a great variety of merit. Among them were paintings of a high order. I noticed many from the Dusseldorf artists. But, I had just come from viewing the great works of Rubens; and, I believe I was not in the mood to do justice to any modern paintings. They all appeared to me too fresh and too fine. They appeared too much like paintings. They did not affect me with the sense of reality like the works of Rubens. But even a great painting gains more of this effect from age, when the glare of the paint is gone, and only the lines and coloring remain.

I suppose many feel disposed to ask me the question, did you visit Waterloo? No, I did not. I had read many descriptions of the battle; I thought I understood the battle as a battle sufficiently well for all the interest I had in it. The marks of the battle are mostly obliterated. Little additional knowledge can be gained by visiting the field. But then—it may be asked—did you not feel a curiosity to stand on the spot where this glorious battle was fought—did you not desire to feel the inspiration of the associations? I can only tell the truth about my feelings. The field of Waterloo has for me no glorious and inspiring associations. I admire the Duke of Wellington, the immovable bravery of the English, the gallantry of the Prussians. But I never could see what great triumph Europe gained there. I believe a great many who were filled with enthusiasm at the time, have since doubted the results. I am not prepared to say that I wish Napoleon had gained the day. This is not what I mean. But I would that Wellington and Napoleon, that England and France had never been brought to such an issue. I cannot discuss the subject here; I can only express an opinion which I think is capable of being sustained, that England at an early period might have consolidated a peace with France that would have been immeasurably better for herself, and for the liberties of Europe, than the terrible wars which resulted in the prostration of Napoleon, and nothing more. Napoleon was the choice of France; he was hailed as a deliverer by Italy and Poland; he shattered the old tyrannies of the continent; and he propagated throughout Europe more liberal ideas than had before existed. He brought out ripened results from the French revolution. His excessive ambition, his tremendous struggles for domination were stimulated by the dogged determination of England to overthrow him. Now, when a usurper of the same name holds France, and that, too, not with the genial grasp of the first Napoleon, why does not England stand forth again the defender of legitimacy? Is not the cause the same? Has she learned wisdom by her past experience?

At the Congress of Vienna, England was associated with Rome and the despots of Europe. There was no power that represented the liberties of Europe. And what followed this congress of the nations? The Bourbons returned to France, to re-enact a tyranny which soon led again to their expulsion. The Czar returned to his undisturbed autocracy. Austria resumed her leaden sceptre. The princes of Germany forfeited their pledges made to the people, who had sustained them. Spain and Portugal lay down again the corpses of nations. The Pope regained a power under which England herself is now writhing. And England was covered with glory, and loaded with a debt which has ever since caused her gigantic strength to tremble.

Europe, at this moment, is more unsettled than ever, and is only waiting for the man and the opportunity.

So we left Brussels behind, without seeing Waterloo. In one day we went from Brussels to Paris. This is an admirable railroad, and the speed is great. We passed many important places, and skimmed over the surface of a wide stretch of country. The appearance of the country is not very interesting. It has no striking features. It is a dull level, under fair cultivation, indeed, but it wants the freshness and beauty of England.

By-and-by, late in the afternoon, we become aware that we are approaching the great city. There is not that smoky, dingy atmosphere lying before us, which indicated our approach to London, but we catch glimpses of domes and spires. On we rush—domes and spires thicken upon the view: at length an immense mass of buildings lies spread out before us, and we seem to be dashing right into them. Suddenly our speed slackens—we are under the shadow of the city, and in another moment we are under the roof of the vast station-house—the train stops—the carriage-doors are unlocked, and we step out into Paris.

XVI.

Paris.

We step into Paris;—but the first step is not made into any inviting place:—it is a large room under the same roof with the station-house, where all the trunks and parcels are deposited to undergo the inspection of the custom-house officers. Ladies who enter Brussels seldom leave it without Brussels lace. And, then, in entering France, there is apt to be a little trepidation respecting the above-named inspection. The lively Flemish woman of whom the lace was purchased, had assured us that there would be no difficulty, since we had not purchased as traders, but, as would appear at once to the officers, only for private use. Passengers stopping short of Paris had to undergo an inspection upon entering France. How they fared I know not. But at Paris, when my trunks and parcels were all collected, I handed over a box of cologne as unquestionably subject to duty, and opened one of my trunks, adding, at the same time, that I was an American travelling for my pleasure. The officer immediately conducted me to the bureau, where I paid a small duty on the cologne, and received a permission to pass all my baggage.

And now we are in a carriage, driving through what appears to us, wearied as we are, an interminable range of streets, in the direction of the Tuilleries. We seek for lodgings in two or three hotels without success: Paris, like London, is thronged with visitors—several thousand Americans, it is said—how many English, I know not. At length we get rooms at the *Hotel de Lille et d'Albion*, in the Rue St. Honoré. They are the only rooms unoccupied in the house—so said the little woman with sharp black eyes, who kept the hotel. They are very elegant—a large parlor, and two large bed-rooms, *en suite.* They must all be taken together, and the price is exorbitant. We took them for one day.

The next day, through the intervention of a friend, we succeeded in hiring furnished apartments—just vacated—in the Rue St. Honoré, near the Tuilleries. We, of course, had the entire floor, which comprised a parlor, a dining-room, four bed-rooms, a kitchen, three rooms for servants, and an ante-room. We had more room than we needed, but the entire suite had to be hired. The same friend procured us a man-servant, who was a man of all sorts of work, and a good cook in the bargain. The same night we were settled as pleasantly as if we had been in our own home. The rooms were amply and tastefully furnished. We had every convenience. After the French fashion, every mantelpiece had an elegant clock, besides various ornaments, so that we had no less than four clocks ticking at the same time.

Our breakfast and tea we always took at home. We dined at a restaurant whenever we pleased. More frequently, however, we dined at home, when our servant prepared for us some substantial dish of meat, with vegetables, while soup, entrées, and dessert were procured at a restaurant. We had infinitely more comfort than we could have had at any hotel, and at a cheaper rate.

We remained in Paris a month, and we succeeded in hiring our apartments for just that time.

The convenience of living in Paris is admirable. The French, beyond all other people, understand the economy of life. In London we hired apartments also, but the arrangements were not so complete nor so convenient. In Paris, you are as much isolated, as much at housekeeping, as really at home, as if you lived in a separate house. This is owing, in the first place, to the style of building. The ground floor is appropriated to shops or offices. The form of the buildings is quadrangular. The entrance is by an arched way in the middle into an inner court shut in from the street by massive double doors, and is wide enough to admit carriages. From this court winding stairs ascends to the top of the house, with platforms connecting with the ante-rooms of the different stories. This stairs answers the purpose of a private street, with which each story is connected as a separate dwelling. The different stories are as completely shut out from each other as different houses, standing side by side in the same street, are with us. The accommodations in each story are complete for all the purposes of a private family. The houses differ in size, so that more ample or limited apartments may be obtained according to the number of the family. That I hired more ample accommodations than I required was owing to the fact of my being obliged to make my arrangements without delay, and for a particular time, so that it was prudent to embrace what so fortunately was offered to me at once. Those who contemplate a longer residence, and who take time to look about, can make very exact and economical arrangements.

Sometimes apartments are hired unfurnished, or furnished only in part; but there is no difficulty in hiring furniture or any articles necessary to housekeeping. There are persons who make it their business to hire out every thing of the kind. The rates are all fixed. An inventory is taken of all the articles when you take possession of your apartments, and again when you leave them, a copy of which is furnished you. You, of course, are responsible for all loss, and for damage beyond necessary *wear and tear*. To provide against all imposition, you can examine the articles for yourself when the inventory is taken.

Persons may live in a very elegant and expensive style in this way, or they may live economically and yet neatly, tastefully and comfortably. All humors and tastes may be suited. Small families and of moderate means, can, in this way, go to housekeeping without the trouble of buying, owning or arranging any thing, and for a longer or shorter time, as suits their convenience. In fine, it is a state of things which answers exactly to the wants and conditions of a great city.

It is to be hoped that in our city of New-York, apartments may, ere long, be arranged and let out in the same way. Could it become as general as it is in Paris, it might be done with an approach to the same economy.

It did not appear to me that articles of food were generally cheaper in Paris than in New-York. Many articles are much dearer. Tea costs four times, coffee three times, and sugar twice as much. Some things are cheaper, but I think the average is nearly the same. House rent and servants' wages are much cheaper. But there is a very exact calculation as to quantity, so that there is no waste. And herein consists the great difference. In Paris you will have enough, without superabundance, and every thing is appropriated and turned to account.

On the ground floor at the foot of the stairs is a room occupied by the *concierge*, or porter, who has charge of the outer gate, and an oversight of the whole building, and who is always on duty.

We were no sooner established than we felt at home and at our ease, and with an entire command of our time. Located near the Tuileries, a few steps brought us at any hour of the day within its beautiful promenades. The Louvre was just at hand, where I could devote any spare hour:—a most extensive and magnificent gallery of art thrown open and free of expense, and as accessible as if I myself had been the owner of it. When I felt inclined I could stroll into the Bibliothéque Nationale, seat myself at a table, call for a book, and amuse myself as long as I pleased, and nothing to pay. I was in the centre of Paris with every thing at my command.

When we wished to drive out, in a few moments a neat carriage was at the door, for which the hire was two francs and a half per hour. And so driving and walking were intermingled as we saw fit.

Paris is the world where you can see every thing, and get every thing, where all the conveniences of life, and all the means of culture are provided. It is a place too where those who seek for pleasure can readily find it under every form. The amount of dissipation in such a city must be enormous, and yet it is so regulated and veiled as not to obtrude itself grossly upon the public eye. The French in their pleasures are finished epicures, who know how to prolong enjoyment and to nourish the capacity for enjoyment to the last pulsation of existence.

Paris wears an air of refinement and cultivation which meets you every where. The long, elegantly built, well paved, and cleanly streets, and particularly the wide and airy boulevards which occupy the ground of the ancient ramparts demolished in the reign of Louis XIV., and which were once planted with double rows of magnificent trees on either side; the splendor of the public buildings, and particularly the palaces with their extensive gardens adorned with statues; the triumphal arches and monumental columns; the quays on the Seine giving the appearance of a river flowing between massive and smoothly-built walls, with frequent wide stone stairs leading down to it; the bridges which connect the banks, and the view presented from them, up and down the river, where, in one direction, are palaces and gardens, and, in another, tall dwellings of various descriptions;

the magnificence of the shops, the very manners of the shopkeepers—the mantuamaker and milliner—the tailor—the bootmaker—the servant who waits on you—the concierge—the poor fellow who lounges about public places, and opens the door of your carriage in expectation of a sous—the manners of every body, from high to low—a sort of polish, ease and readiness—a speech abounding in courteous expressions, and graceful compliments; in fine, every thing, and every person show the marks of the metropolitan city—the imperial city—the city of fashion, art and grace.

The *imperial* city—who can believe it is republican? On the public buildings, on the churches, are the words *Liberté*, *Egalité*, *Fraternité*, but the buildings and churches notwithstanding are imperial, and the words appear out of place. It makes one smile to read them. Stand in the grand entrance of the Tuileries, and look up through the wide avenue of the gardens to the Place de la Concorde, where stands the obelisk of Luxor, and beyond the avenue of the Champs Elysée to the grand Arc de l'Etoile—a view of two miles—and what do you see but imperial grandeur? On every side are soldiers. The vast pile stretches right and left—a façade of three hundred and thirty-six yards. Pass through the main entrance to the court of the Tuileries on the east side, and here you see the long and gorgeous wings of the palace stretching out to meet the Louvre, forming an immense square where an army can be reviewed, and where Napoleon was wont to review his troops. Here, too, is the Place du Carrousel, where stands the Arc de Triomphe, supported by eight splendid Corinthian columns, with bases and capitals of bronze. It is surmounted by a triumphal car, and four bronze horses, modelled after the famous horses of the Piazza of St. Mark at Venice, which once stood here. The arch is covered with representations of Napoleon's victories. Next, walk from the Tuileries to the Arc de l'Etoile, and mark the splendid statuary as you pass through the gardens. When you have ascended to the Place de la Concorde look to the left, and you see beyond the Seine the Chamber of Deputies, on the right the Madeleine—beautiful specimens of Grecian architecture. In the Place are two magnificent bronze fountains, where dolphins, and tritons, and nereids are grouped around. Between the fountains stands the obelisk. Here again are statues. And now you ascend the broad avenue of the Champs Elysée to the Arc de l'Etoile—the proudest monument erected by Napoleon;—its height, one hundred and fifty-two feet; its breadth, one hundred and thirty-seven feet; its depth, sixty-eight feet. Behold it ornamented with groups of figures wrought on the surface. There is the Genius of War summoning the nations to battle: and there they are arming and rushing together. There is victory crowning Napoleon: Fame and History are recording his deeds, while conquered cities lie at his feet. The battles of Napoleon, the forms of his generals are there. It is a monumental history of his life. Within are recorded the names of battles and victories. You can ascend the monument, and then the imperial city lies beneath you. And towering aloft one hundred and thirty-five feet, in the Place Vendome, is seen the Trajan-like column, covered with bas-reliefs in bronze, made from twelve hundred cannon taken from the Russians and Austrians, and representing that series of victories which culminated in the battle of Austerlitz. The palaces of kings and emperors—the monuments of war and victory—the richness and magnificence, and elaborate finish of every thing—the amplitude of the space occupied, and yet the unity of design running through the whole—public, yet private—free of access, and yet guarded by soldiers—belonging to the people, and yet belonging to some one higher than the people—the sense of an imperial prestige—of what has been, leaving its memories behind—of what may be again, where all stand ready to receive it—what has all this to do with a republic? The Louvre is, indeed, appropriated to the arts, and Greek architecture and Greek sculpture are not the natural symbols of despotism; the Chamber of Deputies is no longer occupied, and a rude building has been temporarily erected for the National Assembly; there is a President of the Republic, and he does not reside in the Tuileries.* But all this does not remove the imperial prestige. The Tuileries appears vacated, deserted, lonely. It claims an occupant. These grand displays—these palaces, gardens, and triumphal columns and arches need the echo of a commanding step, and the glance of an eye of majesty. All that is now going on is but an interlude; you feel that the true drama is yet to appear.

Every part of Paris awakens the same impressions. The Bibliothèque Nationale, the Palais National, are still the Bibliothèque du Roi, the Palais Royal. The change of names

* The author was in Paris in the autumn of 1851.

appears like a farce. The Luxembourg still contains the Chamber of Peers, the Council-room with the throne, rooms of paintings and statuary, among which are the forms of princes and princesses, and the magnificent gardens adorned with beautiful statues of the queens of France.

The Pantheon is consecrated to the memory of the great men of France. But in its dome is a painting containing nearly four thousand square feet, where are represented the forms of kings and queens in a sort of apotheosis.

The Palace of Versailles, with its two dependent palaces, *Le Grand Trianon* and *Le Petit Trianon*, forms a royal town —so immense are the buildings—so extensive and adorned are the grounds. The statue of Louis XIV. first meets the eye. Every where are the forms and symbols of royalty. The vast interior is filled with paintings and statues of kings and queens, and of the great emperor, of princes and heroes; paintings of battles ancient and modern, where royalty and nobility fill the eye. The almost interminable apartments are gorgeous with the monarchy of France. Within and without, it breathes only of princely grace and glory. And so it is with all the palaces. Those which are situated in localities removed from Paris, are still so connected with it as to appear a part of it. Indeed, Paris is France.

You go to Notre Dame, and on the Pont Neuf you pass the equestrian statue of Henry IV. And Notre Dame is the place where monarchs were crowned. It is the Westminster Abbey of France.

In the church of the Hotel des Invalides they are building the tomb of Napoleon. It has already cost more than five millions of francs. It is the tomb of the man in whom culminated all the royal power and dignity of France.

In Paris, how can the people escape from the symbols and the pervading presence of monarchy? Whatever they see and converse with, seems to predestine them to a monarchy.

The establishment of our republic was a widely different affair from creating a republic out of a monarchy. Although under the monarchy of England, here were no ancient signs and symbols of monarchy. We were on the virgin soil of nature, with the unchartered privileges of forests and prairies and rivers. All objects around us called us back to natural rights, instead of making us feel the weight of prescription. We received direct from the hand of God what in the Old World is received by inheritance, through forms of law, and under the protection of ancient authorities. There, government appeared omnipotent: in the wild woods of America God alone appeared omnipotent. There, government was the work of former generations, and had its roots in the mysteries of the venerable Past: here nothing was old but nature, and government had to be planted by our own hands, to grow up in our own sight, and to be perfected by our own labors. There, society like the cities, the roads and bridges, and the works of art, was already made and fashioned, had its grades, its moulds of thought, its forms of expression, its manners, its laws, all established—all absolute: here society, like cities, roads, and bridges, had yet to be made and fashioned; and we went to work with the wild and joyous freedom of men felling trees and setting the woods on fire, to make way for green meadows and harvest fields.

In the Old World, to create a republic is to make war upon what the men before us have been doing for a thousand years. To create our republic in the New World, was to make war upon nothing, but to begin a happy existence under the calm sunshine, and in the free air of heaven.

We are often unjust upon the men of the Old World; we do not sufficiently consider their peculiar situation and difficulties. And when they rush into a revolution, and violence and atrocity succeed, and the whole fabric of society is shaken and falling to pieces, we do not always stop to reflect that society in its old forms is like a superincumbent mass of rocks, where the power which alone is adequate to remove them is a power that will shatter them, and make for a time a scene of desolation.

The condition of England is quite different from that of France. England has never attempted a republican form of government. Besides, her limited monarchy—her present Constitution is a growth from seeds sown in the time of her Saxon kings, in her Saxon Witana-gemot. These seeds sprang up under the Norman kings. They put forth when the Magna Charta was wrested from King John, and in the succeeding reign, when an assembly of knights and burgesses was called. They struggled into the light from age to age; they grew more and more; planted in the English soil, they were nourished by the sympathies and blood of English hearts, until the day of their maturity arrived. There were convulsions, and yet the work went on with the steadiness of a law of nature.

France had no such blessed seeds sown in her early times.

From the time of Hugh Capet down, she swelled out more and more into a huge, ponderous, unrelenting despotism, until she attained her grand climacteric, when Louis XIV. proclaimed, "I am the State." The church in England had much that was national in its spirit. The church in France was Rome transplanted. The growth of the church kept pace with the growth of the state, and they interwreathed their branches, like two enormous gnarled oaks, supporting each other. France had no people. She had kings and princes, nobles, prelates and priests. The masses were hewers of wood and drawers of water. Her national growth could only be a ranker despotism in Church and State.

There indeed grew up a middle class of manufacturers, artisans, and traders, and they went to constitute a people. Then, when the Reformation sent its breezes of freedom over France, this middle class was quickened; and not only this class, but there were nobles and men of high character who received the inspiration also. The old twofold despotism of the Church and State now accomplished a deed perfectly in character. It could not join in the new movement, nor could it live in connection with it; it therefore determined to crush it. This could be effected only by murder and expatriation. The massacre of St. Bartholomew's, and the revocation of the Edict of Nantes, were no half-way measures,—they were effectual. The element of freedom was destroyed or expelled, the growth of a people was checked, and all was again reduced to the dead level of despotism.

It is impossible to estimate adequately the dread consequences of such measures upon the national vitality, character and prosperity. France was at once deprived of her most intelligent, enterprising and skilful population. The consequences were not confined to that generation. Principles, forms of character, and habits are propagated as well as features, complexion, and temperament. The virtuous and thrifty families that would have welled out the streams of life through succeeding centuries, were destroyed, or given over to other countries—to England, to Holland, to the wilds of America. France has never made good this loss; she is suffering from it at this moment.

Had the Huguenots been retained and religious toleration granted, the whole national character, and the character of the government, would have undergone a change by a gradual and benignant action; and the atrocities of the Revolution would never have appeared in history. But as the old despotism could not but be determined in its measures, so it turned out that there was power to accomplish them.

And then, again, the despotism went on growing more and more rank. The Church and the State became still more absolute, and still more grossly corrupt. Ambitious prelates, and gay and artful women—the royal mistresses—now governed the State. Pride and luxury and extravagance increased. We are amazed when we read the Court Memoirs of these periods. It is difficult to conceive of such men and women. We hardly know to what order of beings to assign them. They evidently conceived themselves to belong to a very superior order. They were not creatures exempt from ordinary human frailties; on the contrary, they had frailties above measure. But frailties in them ceased to be such, according to a new code of morals: for they were creatures made solely for splendor and pleasure, and whatever contributed to their ends became lawful. For them art, grace, and magnificence were wedded to sensuality. The former elevated and hallowed the latter: the latter inspired the former. They lived in a world which they had created for themselves—a world of palaces and gardens. It had its own manners, modes of life, and laws. It was the magic Paradise of Aloadin, described in Thalaba. It seemed, too, to have the sanction of heaven, for the cardinal's hat and the bishop's mitre were seen among them. The common world was made but for their grosser uses. It contained their butchers' stalls, their kitchen gardens, and their stables; and furnished the slaves who served them, the husbandmen who tilled the ground for them, the manufacturers and artisans who wrought for them all precious jewels and stuffs, the seamen who brought in all the rich commodities of other climes, and the soldiers who fought in their defence, and made conquests to increase their wealth and glory. The king was the magician who created and governed the whole; the god whom all worshipped; whatever he took he had a right to; those whom he smiled upon were great and happy; his frown was despair and death; the virtue of the fairest and noblest women was then most honored when sacrificed to him.

It is a very curious thing to try to imagine what such a man as Louis XIV. thought of himself. He had lived in this splendid and obsequious world from the beginning. He had always been treated as a god. All things had been possible to him. What was it to him to lavish a thousand millions of francs upon the palace and gardens of Versailles? The whole kingdom was at his command; and other kingdoms were his vassals. He never had had one experience of ordinary humanity, how then could he have any sympathy with it? Did not all praise and glorify him, and tremble before him? Was not his will law? Did not all live and move and have their being through him? Was not all concentred in him? How could he come to any other conviction than what he uttered, "I am the State?" With what a consciousness of power must he have walked through his royal rooms, amid the host of gay and highborn attendants! What a perfect self-complacency he must have had! What a scorn and ineffable indignation at any person, or nation even, who would dare to think or act contrary to his will and pleasure! Could such a man ever descend to regret, or penitence, or prayer? Was not the language of his heart, I will take my seat among the gods?

The king is the state, the state is Paris, Paris is France, and France aims to be Europe. How is this immense centralization to be broken up? It will not commit suicide. The destroying force must come from without. Or it must lie somewhere in the lower strata of society, to tear up the smiling plains above by a dread convulsion. The masses have been wronged and crushed for centuries; it will be a rude, mighty and convulsive effort that will heave off the accumulated load. The young Thalaba will tear up a sapling by the roots, dash out the brains of the Enchanter, and the gorgeous vision will depart in thunder and lightning and earthquake. The French Revolution was this unavoidable convulsion and violence. The king and the court, the very centre and mystery of the whole enchantment, will be dashed to atoms. The palaces and gardens where the spells were formed will be desolated. All the forms of royalty and ancient grandeur will become objects of intense disgust. Religion which had allied itself to despotism will be repudiated. In the taste of deliverance and freedom, thought and action will run wild. A thousand theories will be broached, and a thousand experiments tried. In the fierce war upon old authority, sacred principles and laws will be confounded with kingly and priestly abuses.

The English Revolution was the maturity of civil and religious liberty under a limited monarchy, which had been preparing and growing up for ages. The American Revolution was the creation of a republic untrammelled by prescription, and on the basis of natural rights. The French Revolution was the terrible and ungovernable reaction of outraged humanity against tyranny.

The French people first of all aimed to establish a republic, for this was the farthest removed from the old state of things, which they abhorred and had destroyed. This was natural. They failed in the experiment. They were going through a process of education. How could they be ripened at once for the highest destiny of a nation, self-government?

Now the nation was fast becoming the prey of demagogues and factions. Then arose a man of stupendous genius and indomitable will. He scattered the demagogues and factions, and collected the disjointed and warring elements into a mighty empire. The majesty of France had never before been so august and powerful. And now it was represented by a man of the people. He accomplished their will; for he swept away almost the very memory of the old monarchy and nobility; he held the church within his grasp, and made it but the instrument of his policy, while he proclaimed religious toleration; he dashed to pieces the old stolid despotisms, and exploded the principle of legitimacy by setting up new kings, and meting out new kingdoms. The people, indeed, returned to a monarchy, but it appeared to them a monarchy made by their own hands, the concentration of their own energy, and the instrument of their revenge for the wrongs of centuries. The French Revolution is not to be regarded as a hostile movement against monarchy as such. It was an attempt to obtain redress:—it was, too, an act of revenge. It was directed against the government, and, consequently, against the king, nobles, and priests who constituted that government. In its unbounded madness, it perhaps entertained the fanatical purpose of overthrowing all government, and returning to the freedom of nature; and when it talked of a democracy, it was not under any just conception of it as a rational and efficient government, but simply as popular emancipation, and an agrarian overthrow of ancient privileges. And when after passing through the Reign of Terror, and plunging into the whirlpool of the Directory, it became apparent that a strong government was needed, it was natural for the nation to look to the monarchical form as embodying to them the ideas of order and power.

Napoleon, therefore, was called to become the head of

the state by the necessity of events, and by the voice of the people. He fulfilled the fixed idea of government, but relieved it of all the odious associations of the past. His elevation was the triumph of the people over their oppressors. It was a new monarchy which their own hands had constructed. In accordance with this sentiment, Napoleon raised to the highest places in the army and in the state men taken from the ranks of the people. He created a new nobility from the people. Legitimacy was gone, the old regime was gone, talent and energy every where might now indulge in lofty aspirations. The common soldier, if destined to remain always in the ranks, might hope to be enrolled in the Legion of Honor.

France, then, did not become republican, but imperial. Under Napoleon the whole country was a vast military camp. The Leader of the Armies, and involved in perpetual wars, his government had all the absoluteness belonging to such a state of things. But there was, nevertheless, a popular element interfused in its constitution, of which the nation had continually a sense, and which was destined to make itself felt. Hence, when the Bourbons were restored, they did not bring back the old absolutism, but really a constitutional monarchy: and the reappearance of the old spirit in the administration of Charles X. led to his expulsion. In the government of Louis Philippe, the popular element was still more fully developed; and an attempt to restrain it led to his expulsion. The Republic of Louis Napoleon is a momentary triumph of this element.

But who does not see in the whole history of the French

people since the battle of Waterloo, their strong and deep-laid attachment to the memory of their great Emperor? It was a remarkable acknowledgment of this fact, that the shrewd policy of Louis Philippe sought to strengthen his hold upon the throne of France, by bringing home the ashes of Napoleon, celebrating his obsequies, and building his splendid monument upon the banks of the Seine. It was a striking demonstration of the same fact, that a man who, as yet, had acquired no distinction, was elected the president of the new republic, because he had the imperial blood in his veins, and bore the imperial name. Who will be surprised if under him the Empire shall be restored?

The party of the Legitimists, in its worst influences, can only serve to excite the activity and increase the energy of the opposite pole of Red Republicanism; and in its best influence it can be only a conservative power. Red Republicanism is the unextinguished spirit of the first revolution, which can never be laid until the rights of the people are properly vindicated and secured; and even long after this, may remain an instinctive and habitual restlessness. The imperial element lies between the two. It can inhabit the palaces, and preserve the monuments; it can satisfy the taste of the people for display and glory; it can make itself strong enough to control the warring elements: and still it is capable of taking the mould of a limited and constitutional monarchy. Against it there are no national prejudices. On the contrary, the French glory in the memories and monuments of the Empire.

And is Louis Napoleon the man who is to restore the Empire, under the form of a constitutional monarchy? Who knows? I have nothing to say in justification of the measures by which he has virtually assumed imperial power. It will now be but a small advance to exchange the title of President for Emperor. It is, perhaps, his best policy to make this advance. If he should do so, he may in part amend the obliquity of the past, and make himself a benefactor of France, by establishing a government which shall combine imperial strength and dignity with a proper guaranty of popular rights. Neither a mock republic nor an imperial tyranny can stand.

The imperial prestige about Paris certainly increases its interest to a visitor; and in walking through the Tuilleries, he feels that the actual presence of royalty is necessary to the completeness of the scene.

The French have many striking and attractive points of character. One of these, which every one feels at once, is their exceeding polish and grace. The educated and well-bred French are perfectly agreeable in the ordinary and daily intercourse of life. Their manners are easy and natural, and equally removed from hauteur and affectation. You feel entirely at home with them, and receive from them a thousand little attentions, which are paid without the least approach to condescension, and, indeed, in a way that would seem to say that they are obliged to you for permitting them. This may all be very superficial, but, then, what is ordinary intercourse but a superficial exchange of civilities? To speak pleasantly, to bow courteously, to oblige you with some necessary information, to accompany you to a public place, to converse with you in a free and sprightly manner in a drawing-room, to notice some disorder in your dress in the street, and politely to call your attention to it,—all these are not to be despised, for they throw a constant cheerfulness and sunshine around you. They cost but little, it is true, and yet where they are omitted society becomes coarse and boorish.

But this courteous disposition prevails among all classes. It is found among shop-keepers, operatives of all kinds, and the *blouses* in the street. The whole people are pervaded by a spirit of politeness. It is not servility, it is a touch of good-breeding. I happened one morning to step out into the ante-room just as the little char-woman was delivering a basket of coals to my servant; she was quite sooty from her employment, but, instead of slinking away, she turned to me with a native ease, and as if wholly unconscious of her appearance, made a graceful courtesy, and bade me good morning respectfully and properly.

They understand, also, how to turn their politeness to account. I was one day sauntering along the Seine in a careless, absent mood, when I was surprised by a *blouse* suddenly stepping before me, and gently laying hold of the lappet of my coat, saying, with the most courteous air, "Permit me, sir, permit me." He immediately applied a sponge and soap to remove certain spots, which he observed as I was passing by. The thing was done before I could say yes or no, and done so neatly and kindly that I could not be offended. Indeed, I was amused, and could not help laughing at my queer position. Then he offered to sell me some of the soap, extolling its qualities. I could not dispute the good qualities, for he had given me a demonstration of it on my own garment. And then he had done me a kindness, too.

And there he was, a poor blouse who got his living by selling the soap. And so I went away with five francs worth of it stuffed in my pockets. I was conscious that he was *soaping* me in a double sense, but as I could not get angry, I was compelled to reward his friendly offices.

These people, too, always contrive to have a certain air of neatness, when their employment does not absolutely forbid it. They pay attention to dress under the consciousness that their appearance is marked by others. The French certainly live more for show than other people. Hence, when they are walking or sitting in the gardens, they seem to enjoy both the sunshine and their clothes. I was at the railway depôt, getting my luggage weighed, when I happened to fix my eyes rather steadily upon the man who was weighing it. He immediately turned to me and said, with quite an apologetic air, "O, sir, you are looking at my clothes; I know I am dressed very poorly, but I cannot afford to dress better, for I get but little wages." I tried to comfort him, by assuring him that I had not observed how he was dressed: but I doubt whether he believed me, for he continued his apologies.

Paris is the great Emporium of Fashion. Here the world resorts for modes and shapes. Hats, boots, shoes, coats, pantaloons, vests, overalls, cravats—every thing that goes to fit out the outer man of the man; bonnets, shoes, dresses, shawls—the numberless and unnameable articles which go to furnish and adorn beauty, in spite of the poet who says, that beauty when unadorned is most adorned; household furniture, equipages—whatever makes up the splendor and style of life—all are invented, and made to undergo a thousand changes from season to season—now discarded, and now renewed, in this gay and lively city. What is here determined and adopted at once becomes proper and graceful every where. A new style from this grand centre flies through the world, and myriads of hands are set at work copying and reproducing, until the whole generation of old and young, of grave and gay, receive a new appearance with more or less extravagance. No one is independent of it; all in some degree obey it. And it is a proud distinction when some more watchful and enterprising devotee to modes and shapes in some distant capital in Europe or America, gets the start of all others, and appears, for at least one summer day, in the lone novelty of the last Parisian fashion.

Parisian—What a charm there is in that word, how much it expresses, what authority it carries with it, what grace, beauty and propriety it at once conveys!

And what has made Paris thus the centre of fashion? Unquestionably much is to be attributed to the influence of Louis XIV., when the unsurpassed elegance and splendor of his court united with the glory of his arms to give France a predominance in Europe. French became the language of courts, French writers the models of literary composition, and French etiquette and fashions the standards of manners and taste.

But independently of this there is something in the natural genius of the French people which must make them the arbiters of fashion. It is not because they excel all other nations in imagination and artistic capacity generally. The Italians and Germans both surpass them here. The truth is, fashion does not arise from the artistic power, although it cannot exist without it. If fashion were governed simply by æsthetical principles, costume would soon become fixed, as among the ancient Greeks; for the idea of costume, beyond mere utility, is to give effect to the proportions, symmetry, and grace of the human person.

Fashion has its origin in three elements of human nature; the desire of outward and palpable distinction, the love of novelty, and the wish to conceal personal defects. The frequent introduction of new modes, and constant variations of costume, for ever enable a particular class to maintain a distinction in outward appearance. Their position affords them the opportunity to watch the changes of fashion, and even to invite them, while they have the means, to meet the cost which is involved. The love of novelty exerts its power over all classes, and this together with the ambition of imitating the upper ranks of society, serves sooner or later to diffuse a fashion, and to create the necessity of new changes.

The wish to conceal personal defects can lead to new fashions only under the authority of the great. Thackeray has given an amusing representation of Louis XIV. as *Rex*, *Ludovicus* and *Ludovicus Rex*, in which the little rotund figure of five feet two inches is transformed, by means of high-heeled shoes and a towering wig, into a majestic person of six feet. Thus high-heeled shoes and towering wigs were made the fashion. The mode must become general in the court that the king may not appear singular. What the king and his court adopt, becomes, by association, elegant and graceful. The most grotesque costumes have thus come into vogue.

The power which creates these diversities is a lively and

inventive fancy—a power which does not bind itself by æsthetical principles, but which produces its effects by departing from them to a certain extent. To do this happily, æsthetical principles must be understood, and must be allowed to prevail as far as possible; but the endless diversity is gained by a felicitous violation of them. Now herein lies the art of producing fashions. The Parisians have taste, are artistical in their education and habitudes; but, in addition to this, they have beyond all other people a lively and inventive fancy. With them it appears to amount to an idiocrasy, and fostered from generation to generation, under the presence of a gay and splendid court, it has reached a kind of perfection, and given birth to a new and peculiar form of art.

How the changes are started is a sort of mystery which it is difficult to penetrate. There is no formally constituted board of fashion, and no solemn convocation of the fashion-mongers. A common understanding springs up somehow among the members of the several trades, and the new fashion makes its appearance like a new comet in the heavens.

When a new fashion reaches us it is stereotyped; it has one absolute form which all run after. In Paris it is not so. The new fashion appears distinctly enough; but it appears with a graceful freedom, and admits of a variety of styles, where the differences are very nice and yet palpable. This peculiarity seems capable of existing only on the soil where the fashion is born, and prevents the Parisian elegance from ever being fully transplanted.

The influence of fashion upon manners and character, upon manufactures and commerce, is a curious speculation which demands the attention both of the moralist and the political economist. How much of human thought is employed, how much of human passion aroused, how much of human industry and skill exercised by mere fashion! Does it advance civilization, or does it produce a deterioration of the social and national character? is it the parent of good or of evil? or, is it of such a mixed nature, that while we deprecate its follies and evils, we are still compelled to admit it as an element in the order of society which the imperfection of man renders necessary?

An opinion generally prevails in England and America that the French are a fickle and uncertain nation, driven on by impulse, and governed by whim. The same lively fancy which makes them the arbiters of fashion must exert an influence over their whole character, and over public events. Two other facts are to be viewed in connection with this;—that they have never recovered from the terrible reaction which produced the French Revolution, and that their religious and spiritual development is defective.

I usually attended Divine service in the Wesleyan Chapel, in the Rue de la Concorde. It is a small humble place. The service is in English. I there heard holy hymns, devout prayers, and gospel preaching.

The entrance to the Wesleyan Chapel is under the shadow of the Madeleine. The Madeleine is a glorious thing to look at. It is in form and proportions a Grecian Temple of the Corinthian order, and of larger dimensions than the Parthenon. It was begun in 1764, and finished during the reign of Louis Philippe. Napoleon, at one time, during the height of his triumphs, contemplated consecrating it as a Temple of Glory. Here, on Sunday, one may witness solemn and imposing ceremonies, and listen to delicious music. Altogether it is a religious intoxication of the senses.

On the same Sunday I went into the Madeleine and the Wesleyan Chapel. I remained in the former until the hour of service began in the latter. All the shops in Paris were open, and the out-door world was going on as usual. In the afternoon some of the shops are closed. This is after the hours for religious worship. Then the Sabbath is made a day of recreation, and the gardens of the Tuilleries, and the Champs Elysée, are crowded with people sitting, standing, or walking about.

What then is the Sunday in Paris, and what is religious worship? The Madeleine, in connection with the open shops, and the thronged places of amusement, represents the religion of the Parisians—ceremonial, elegant, magnificent, mingled with business, gayety and pleasure. The humble Wesleyan Chapel represents that worship which Christ spoke of when he said, "Where two or three are gathered together in my name, there am I in the midst of them."

The infidelity which prevailed in France during the Revolution was a rebellion of awakened intellect, unacquainted with the true gospel, against the monstrous superstitions, united with priestly ambition and sensuality, which were palmed upon men as Christianity. That infidelity has never been eradicated; nor can it be, until the minds of the people are brought in contact with the simple Christianity of the gospel. The religious and moral condition of France is a compound of Romish superstition and sentimentalism, with the remains of the frivolity and sensuality which existed before the Revolution, and the remains of the infidelity which characterized the Revolution itself.

If the ancient Huguenots could be restored, France would be healed. She will be healed when a race like the Huguenots reappears in the church and the state. The impulsiveness of the French, their taste, fancy, and refinement, when invigorated and controlled by religious principles, serve, in connection with their keen intellect, to mould the finest and most attractive forms of character. France has now many men of the noblest stamp, but they are not in the ascendency.

There is one thing which at once strikes an American in walking about Paris;—young women of rank—I mean unmarried young women—are not met with in the streets, or on the promenades. He will find, too, that they are not introduced into society. The period of education is one of seclusion. The tendency of this is to produce a higher refinement of manners, and a more perfect education.

The intense activity which characterizes Americans appears in every relation of society, and causes us to jump to our conclusions and results. We are in a hurry to do every thing. We are in a hurry to be men and women, in a hurry to complete our education, in a hurry to get married, in a hurry to get rich, in a hurry to set up an establishment, and plunge into the dissipation of society. Boys and girls are disappearing from among us, the beautiful modesty and innocent pleasures of youth are fast becoming a mere legend of the past, and our children go out from the nursery full-grown men and women. Nothing can correct this but a higher culture, creating a higher standard of manners and accomplishments.

I was invited by a friend to visit an educational establishment of the ladies of the Sacred Heart. They have the palace, with its extensive and beautiful grounds, once belonging to one of the old nobility. The inmates of this establishment are high-bred and elegant women, who devote themselves with great fidelity to the education of the young ladies committed to them. All the arrangements are exceedingly neat, tasteful, and comfortable, without any approach to tawdriness and display. The large rooms of the palace, stripped of their mirrors and ancient finery, form airy and pleasant school and lodging rooms. The grounds planted with trees, shrubbery, and flowers, make a rural scene in the midst of the city. They have also a country establishment, to which the pupils are frequently taken for recreation. The system of education, I believe, is thorough, and the discipline mild and kindly, as well as efficient. As a Protestant I would not be guilty of the inconsistency of exposing a daughter to the unavoidable influences of a religion of which I disapprove; but to members of the Roman Catholic Church it must afford, in many instances, a desirable opportunity of removing daughters from scenes of frivolity and temptation, and of enabling them to prosecute their education under very favorable auspices.

It would be well for us could our schools be modelled after a similar plan, so that girlhood might be cherished in a retirement affording the best opportunities for intellectual culture and rational accomplishments. Nothing, however, can com pensate for a proper home education, where parental affection is the sunshine in which young minds and hearts are cherished and unfolded by the pleasant influence of a natural law, without that tyranny, misnamed discipline, which makes war upon the happy spontaneity of childhood and youth, and transforms the most innocent period of human life into a purgatory fit only for ripened criminals.

XVII.

Books and Works of Art—The Bibliothèque Nationale—The Louvre.

BESIDES the Bibliothèque Nationale, the principal libraries of Paris contain not less than twelve hundred thousand volumes. Many of these are accessible to the public. Among them may be named the Bibliothèque de Ste. Genevieve, containing two hundred thousand volumes, and the Bibliothèque de l'Arsenal, containing about the same number. There are, also, libraries of literary societies which are numerous.

The great library—called, successively, the Bibliothèque du Roi, Nationale, Imperiale, then du Roi again, and now, once more, Nationale, and destined, perhaps, to become again Imperiale—is a wonderful and magnificent collection. The department of printed books contains nearly a million and a half of volumes, including duplicates and pamphlets. The arrangement is admirable, so that any volume may be obtained without delay. Nothing is necessary but to hand one of the librarians a slip of paper with the title of the volume written upon it.

This great library is open to students of both sexes during the whole year—with the exception of the month of September, and a vacation of two weeks at Easter—and on every day of the week except Sundays and holidays. There are two days of the week appropriated to promiscuous visitors.

I visited it, for the first time, on the first day it was opened after the September vacation. The long reading-gallery was filled with the studious, who were seated at a table extending from end to end. No whispering is allowed. The same scene was repeated every day I visited it. Among those who were reading I observed a *blouse*, and a woman beside him, who appeared to be his wife.

There are four other departments of the Bibliothèque Nationale: The Cabinet of Medals and Antiques, which contains one hundred and fifty thousand specimens; the Collection of Manuscripts, which contains one hundred and twenty-five thousand volumes; the Collection of Engravings, which contains nine or ten thousand volumes and portfolios, comprising one million three hundred thousand plates, and fills six rooms; and the Gallery of Ancient Sculpture, or the Salle du Zodiaque, so called from the Egyptian Zodiac of Denderah, which is the most remarkable piece in the collection.

The building which contains these collections was once the princely palace of the Cardinal Mazarin. It is a huge structure, five hundred and forty feet long, and one hundred and thirty broad, and is built around a court three hundred feet long and ninety broad.

The Cardinal also has given his name to a noble library in the Palais de l'Institut, which originally was the library of the college which he founded. This library now contains one hundred and fifty thousand printed volumes, and nearly four thousand manuscripts. It is open to the public daily with the exception of a short vacation, and Sundays and holidays.

The library of the Institute in the same building, which contains one hundred thousand volumes, is designed particularly for the members, but others are introduced through courtesy. Indeed, a student in Paris really has access, in some way, to all the immense collections of learning which are found here, and that without incurring any expense.

Side by side stand the collections of books and the collections of art. When I look at Paris in this point of view, the city appears almost built for the sole purpose of accommodating and promoting learning and art. Paris is itself every where adorned with works of art; and the churches, the palaces, the gardens, and public institutions, such as the Palais et Ecole des Beaux Arts, contain innumerable pieces of various degrees of merit. But as the Bibliothèque Nationale is the great collection of books, so the Louvre is the great collection of paintings and statuary. The palace of the great cardinal is consecrated to books: the palace of kings is consecrated to art.

The Louvre is in itself a magnificent piece of architecture, forming a perfect square around an open court, the length of each side being four hundred and eight feet. The staircases, halls, rooms, ceilings, and walls of the interior, are finished in a style of great splendor and richness. But the building is forgotten in what it contains. The first time I entered it, I visited only the *Musée des Tableaux des Ecoles Italiennes, Flamandes, et Française.* I stood here several hours gazing at paintings without weariness, for I really became absorbed like a child looking at wonders.

There is first a large room filled with paintings of the old masters—paintings by Titian, Raphael, Corregio, Poussin, and others of the same stamp. This room opens into an immense gallery—the *Grand Salon*, thirteen hundred and thirty-two feet long, stretching between the Louvre and the Tuilleries. I doubt whether a more magnificent and better lighted gallery can be found in the world for the exhibition of pictures. Here are four hundred and eighty paintings of the Italian school; eight copies of ancient pictures; five hundred and forty paintings of the German and Flemish, among which are many of Rubens; and three hundred and eighty of the French. I might well stand several hours gazing here, for here were objects enough to hold the attention and form a study for an indefinite period. Now I had all the great masters under my eye in one of the finest collections of paintings in the world. There were many artists of both sexes in the gallery making copies. There were many visitors walking about, but there was perfect order and silence, and plenty of room for all.

Many paintings of great merit, and which would have charmed me in any other place, I soon learned to pass by, confining my attention to those great works, the like of which I had never seen before. Upon entering the first room, I was long held by a sleeping Venus of Corregio. In the Grand Salon, I came upon the same subject by Titian, and then I perceived the superiority of the latter in coloring. There were several portraits by Titian which strikingly illustrated his grand excellence. His faces are alive, the eyes look out upon you, the glow of animation is upon the cheek, the lips are speaking, or about to speak.

Titian, Raphael, and Rubens, were artists whom I particularly compared. My mind was full of Rubens from what I had seen at Antwerp. Here was the same style of painting but in inferior subjects. I got at a certain theory of my own, and I made my criticisms from my own instinct. Shall I give out my thoughts? Perhaps artists and connoisseurs will smile at me. Nevertheless I will be simple-hearted, and speak out.

The *Ideal* does not violate or contradict nature, but it carries out the *principles* of nature to a perfection beyond the bare reality. God has made nature after the conceptions of his own mind. He has made man after his own likeness, and endowed him with ideas and conceptions like his own. As God has submitted nature to be improved by man—the agriculturist and mechanician, as his own instrument; so also he has committed to man—the artist, to improve upon the beauty of nature. God has not developed in nature all the possible perfection of beauty contained in the idea of beauty, but he has inspired artists, in different degrees, to make advances beyond the actual nature, and to make indefinite approximations towards that perfection which perhaps no created skill can ever reach. But by these efforts, more or less successful, the artist becomes the great Teacher of the Beautiful, and leads on humanity to those loftier and purer tastes and conceptions, which besides adorning and elevating the present life, may be a preparation for mingling with more perfect forms of beauty in a future state.

Now, the artist produces his effects by lines and colors. He follows the laws of proportion, symmetry, grace, and harmony. In statuary and bare drawing, lines alone are employed. In painting, there is added all the effect which arises from gradation and harmony of colors.

In respect to color, no artist has ever reached, and probably never can reach, what Nature has done. No artist can ever express fully the colors of the rising or setting sun, for the gradations of color are constantly moving, while his work must be stationary. Nor can any artist paint flowers and foliage like Nature, for here the colors of Nature are developed through the agency of the ever-active power of life, while he uses dead paints: just as no art can compound the fragrance of flowers, the sweets of the honey-bee, nor crystallize the diamond, notwithstanding the analysis of the chemist.

In respect to form, the artist has more scope. Having gained the laws of proportion, symmetry, and grace, he may express them more perfectly than he finds them in any natural subject. Hence the genius of a Phidias or a Thorwaldsen may make a more perfect human form than the eye has ever looked upon. There are many influences which go to prevent the full development of human beauty, and to pervert the tendencies of nature: these the artist may avoid, and make man as he conceives of him fresh from the hand of the Creator. The ideal of art, therefore, belongs to form rather than to color.

The most that an artist can do in coloring is to make approximations to nature; and he that approaches nearest is the greatest master of coloring. In some departments of art there is, however, an idealizing of colors. This appears in producing certain effects by a peculiar combination of colors, beyond what we ordinarily or ever see in nature. Thus it appears to me a certain magical sunlight is sometimes thrown over a landscape which goes beyond ordinary nature. Is there not, too, an idealized wildness and grandeur in the light and shadow of Claude Lorraine? Now Titian when he paints human flesh in some way idealizes color. There are faces which he could not idealize, where he could only approach nature. The fresh beauty of the face of a child is as difficult to reach, as impossible to surpass, as an opening rosebud. But it is not so with the rough faces of men. Here a perfection of coloring may be imagined, in keeping with the form and expression of the features, which might exist, but which is marred and faded by the wear and tear of human life. Sometimes the great aim of the artist will be to represent the effects of toil and suffering, and then he can idealize the face, not by coloring, but by lines which give it intense expressions.

According to the spirit of art, there are only certain countenances that ought to be painted. It is as absurd to paint any and every face as it would be to paint natural objects indiscriminately. A true subject of art is a face capable of some striking expression. Such a face is capable of being idealized, while common faces are capable only of being flattered. The grand intellect, the noble soul, the great hero, does not always look the same in the expressions of the countenance and the attitudes of the form. The true artist will seize upon the character, and make the face express it.

Now it is upon these principles that I compare Titian, Raphael, and Rubens. I have already spoken of Rubens as giving the expression of reality. When his subject is great, like the Crucifixion, and he makes it real before you, can you be otherwise than overpowered? Here lies his great power. He gives you form and color as it is.

Titian and Raphael are idealists. This is their distinction. But wherein do they differ from each other? In comparing them, I felt that in something Titian was superior to Raphael; and, also, that in something Raphael was superior to Titian. I soon yielded to the common judgment that Titian is the great master of coloring. I saw that Raphael did not equal him here. But then, what forms of beauty, and what divine expressions there were in Raphael's paintings! And so, I said to myself, Raphael idealizes form, Titian idealizes color, while Rubens paints form and color as it is. Rubens has been condemned for the grossness of his representations: thus, the figure of his Christ in the Elevation of the Cross has been objected to as clumsy and inelegant. The criticism is just. He did not idealize. Rubens, therefore, is inferior to the other two.

There are many small pieces in this gallery of the Dutch artists which are perfect gems in their way. Their elaborate and elegant finish surprised me. It were in vain to attempt any thing like a description of this glorious gallery. There can be only a very crude conception formed of it from the best description that could be given. I visited it frequently, and it alone convinced me how much time it was necessary to spend in Paris to form any tolerable acquaintance with the treasures which this metropolis contains. As I returned from it, I felt a strong sentiment of gratitude to the French nation, to the kings, to the Emperor, to all who had contributed to open this collection to the world, and that, too, gratuitously; and I was constrained to acknowledge that the people who had done this must be great and noble. And the great artists who had produced these works, were not they, beyond the nation, the kings, and the Emperor, the benefactors of mankind? Immortal men! ye were often poor yourselves, but ye have enriched generations of men.

The entrance to the Grand Salon is made through the *Salle des Bijoux*, which contains a rare collection of cups, vases, porcelain, jewels, and other curious and precious objects of the middle ages. The works of Benvenuto Cellini particularly interested me, both on account of the remarkable workmanship, and the character of the artist himself, which is drawn with so much naïveté in his autobiography.

My next visit was paid to the *Musée des Antiques*, which occupies a series of apartments on the ground floor of the

Louvre. This was called the *Musée Napoléon* when it was opened in 1803, and contained all the spoils of Italian galleries of art. At the same time, the Louvre was filled with all the great paintings of Europe. One could wish that, for the sake of convenience, the grand collection could have remained undisturbed in Paris. It was, however, an act of justice on the part of the Allies to restore them to the nations from whom they had been taken. Napoleon probably thought that the magnificent capital of his vast empire claimed this tribute from the subjugated cities. Conquerors have always had their own code of morals. Rome once collected within herself all the riches and glory of the world. Napoleon aimed to make Paris the capital of a modern Western Empire.

But the *Musée des Antiques* is still a rich and remarkable collection. Here are two hundred and forty statues; two hundred and thirty busts and heads; two hundred and fifteen bas-reliefs; and two hundred and thirty-five vases, candelabras, altars, &c. Marred and mutilated as these antiques are by the accidents of time, they nevertheless afford a very clear idea of the perfection and glory of ancient art. What can we moderns do beyond copying them? Are not all the qualities of proportion, symmetry and grace here fully developed?

In giving a representation of natural scenery, coloring, or, at least, light and shade, are necessary; but, in form and expression, what more is required than lines? The marble statue conveys not only the form, but the expressions of life, thought, and passion. The solid material passes out of our thoughts, and pure form and expression seem floating in the air before us. It is a wonderful art! After my first visit to the Louvre, I never entered it without taking a turn through the Musée des Antiques. And there is one statue in particular before which I always paused and gazed long and earnestly. It is a Venus partly robed, of more than natural size, the arms broken off, and the whole figure marred. It was found in Asia Minor about thirty years ago. The perfection of the form, the grace of the attitude, the beauty of the countenance, are still there. There is nothing sensual about it; it is a pure and divine loveliness. To my eye there is nothing in the collection superior to it. If I ever see the Venus at Florence, I shall then have a standard with which to compare it.

So vast is the extent of the Louvre that to walk through it is like walking through a city of the fine arts. There are nine rooms appropriated to the *Galerie Française*, the ceilings of which are painted with historical subjects, and the walls covered with the works of the French artists. The *Musée des Dessins* contains an immense collection of drawings. There are more than seven hundred of the Italian school alone. Then there is the *Musée Grec et Romain*, comprising three rooms filled with Etrurian and Greek antiquities; the *Musée Egyptien*, containing most of the antiquities collected by the French researches in Egypt. The *Galerie Assyrienne* is not as rich as the collection made by Layard, in the British Museum; but the two winged sphinxes, or winged bulls with human heads, dug up at Nineveh by M. Botta, are of far greater magnitude, and more remarkable than the similar figures of Layard, placed in the vestibule of the Museum.

The Louvre, in addition to all its other treasures, contains a library—the *Bibliothèque du Louvre*—once the private library of Louis Philippe. It consists of fourteen rooms, in which are collected eighty-five thousand volumes. A mere enumeration of the different departments of the Louvre would occupy a considerable space. Indeed, this vast building is filled with works of art and antiquities.

All the rooms, with a few exceptions, are thrown open to strangers every day, who are admitted upon showing their passports and entering their names in a book. On Sundays the Louvre is thrown open to the population.

In noticing works of art in Paris, I cannot well avoid adverting to the Gobeline tapestry and carpet manufactory. This, as well as all other works of art, is shown gratuitously. In London, and, indeed, every where in England, the shilling is perpetually demanded. In Paris there is a noble generosity in this respect. Those who attend upon public places in England have the air of men who are watching for an opportunity. In Paris they have an uncalculating, easy, and polite air. In one country you feel that you are continually under the screw; in the other, you visit the exhibitions of art, and enjoy yourself, with freedom.

The Gobeline manufactory, named after Jean Gobeline, a celebrated wool-dyer of the fifteenth century, belongs to the government. The tapestries and carpets are manufactured only for the royal palaces, and for royal presents. The process is very slow. It sometimes takes from five to ten years to make a single carpet. The texture and designs are perfect.

The tapestries hanging up in the exhibition rooms might be mistaken for paintings. Indeed, in several instances I was for some moments at a stand to determine whether the piece before me was the painting which served as a model, or the tapestry wrought after it.

It is very curious to notice the workmen engaged on pieces where portions of a figure are finished, while the rest is an entire blank. In a painting, the whole outline is drawn upon the canvas, and the artist goes over the whole, and brings it forward by gradations. But in the tapestry, every part is completed as the work advances, and you see a beautiful arm without the hand, or an angel with only one wing fledged. Slowly does the workman proceed, adding thread to thread with the nicest adjustment of the shades of color, until he weaves out the whole picture.

Among the monuments of Paris there will, at no distant day, be offered to the public view, in the Church of the Hotel des Invalides, the tomb of Napoleon, which is now in progress. We gained admission through the card of M. de Tocqueville. Under the dome of the church an immense circular crypt is dug, in which the sarcophagus containing the remains is to be placed. The platform for the sarcophagus was not yet completed. There is a gallery running around the crypt, which is to be paved with rich mosaic, and to be adorned with bas-reliefs, representing the principal events of the Emperor's life. One of these was in progress, in which the figure of Napoleon was conspicuous, but it was not sufficiently advanced to enable me to decipher the design.

The twelve colossal caryatides in white marble, and which support an upper gallery, were finished. They are noble figures, the work of different artists, and represent War, Legislation, the Arts and Sciences. Before the tomb, is a magnificent altar of black marble with white veins, the canopy of which is supported by columns of the same material. This appeared to be nearly completed.

Thus does France cherish and honor the memory of the man who most truly represented her spirit, and who, if the hearts of the people are to be consulted, was her most legitimate monarch.

I do not believe the French people will ever return to the old doctrine of legitimacy. And nothing will serve more to strengthen Louis Napoleon than any demonstration on the part of Russia, Austria and Prussia against him. An alliance with these powers can bring nothing to him but weakness. A conflict with them will make him at once the hero of the French people, and enlist in his behalf the sympathies of the world. It is by no means impossible, that Louis Napoleon may be driven to stand side by side with Mazzini and Kossuth in the great battle for the liberties of Europe. A conflict between France and the three despotic powers would open an opportunity for Italy and Hungary. Louis Napoleon has, certainly, given indications of extraordinary qualities, showing the presence of the Napoleonic self-reliance and energy. Like Maurice of Saxony, he may come in at last as a main support of the cause which he at first deserted. Whether he consults fame, or the stability of his power, this is the only course which lies open before him.

I visited Versailles twice. It is about three quarters of an hour distant from Paris by railroad. The first time, I went out to breakfast with M. de Tocqueville, who has a pleasant country residence in the suburbs. I spent two or three hours very agreeably with him and his accomplished wife, who is English by birth, although, I believe, she has resided most of her life in France. M. de Tocqueville is well known to Americans by his admirable work upon our country, the result of a visit he made to the United States about twenty years since. He is one of the noblest and purest characters in France, a finished scholar, and a profound statesman. As a writer he holds the highest rank. He is of middle stature, rather slightly made, of a fine intellectual cast of features, with a grave, meditative expression. His manners are very quiet, simple, and refined, and calculated to win respect and confidence. His conversation was easy and discursive. Little was said about the state of France, a subject which delicacy forbade me to introduce; but we talked a good deal about America, and on literary subjects.

I adverted to the fact that so many literary men entered into political life in France, while in our country they are apt to be excluded. He replied, that in France men of literary distinction entered into political life as a natural consequence of their position, if they chose to do so. He said, also, that he had remarked the fact I mentioned that in our country the most distinguished men did not generally occupy offices under the government. On referring to his book I find the same observation recorded there. While exceedingly liberal, and even democratic in his opinions and tendencies, he has an intellect too acute and calm not to perceive the incidental evils of our institutions.

It is to be deprecated that public honors cannot be certainly looked forward to as a reward of great talents and attainments in our country. One stimulus to intellectual exertion is thus removed. Besides, the country must itself suffer when the policy and tact of the demagogue supplant the gifts of mind, and scholarlike preparations. It is an evil which can be remedied only by the creation of those great institutions of learning, which, like the University of Paris, and the French Institute, both multiply the number of scholars and collect them in associations where they can co-work together, sustain each other, and make their legitimate power and influence to be felt.

I subsequently received several very polite and valuable attentions from M. de Tocqueville, among which was an introduction to the Institute, on occasion of a meeting of the *Académie des Sciences Morales et Politiques*, of which he is the president.

After leaving M. de Tocqueville on the morning above alluded to, I walked to the Palace of Versailles, about a mile distant. On the way I was caught in a shower and thoroughly soaked. I entered the palace of kings with that very meek air which one always gains from such an accident, with all my feathers laid and dripping. It occupied me four hours and a half to walk through all the rooms—a walk estimated at seven miles—and I fairly walked myself dry.

The magnificence of this palace is inconceivable without visiting it. It is like the gorgeous descriptions of the Arabian tales. Every spot on the walls and ceilings is adorned with carving, painting, marble, or gilding.

It is filled with statues, portraits, and historical paintings.

The paintings cannot be extolled in general as works of art, but are to be regarded simply as representations of the leading events of French history. Napoleon, unquestionably, holds the most conspicuous place. His portraits abound; and all the grand passages in his life, his victories, coronation, &c., are displayed on immense fields of canvas.

On a second visit, we extended our observations to the *Grand Trianon* and the *Petit Trianon*, walking through the gardens where fountains, and lakes, and trees, and flowers, are contrived to make a scene of formal beauty and magnificence, variegated by artificial wildernesses, where rocks, and grottoes, and waterfalls are fashioned elaborately into an imitation of what nature does so easily and gracefully. It is well done, considered as man's work, but it is plain enough that the hand of God is not there.

And this Versailles was the grand play-house and play-ground of kings and queens. It cost only two hundred millions of dollars! Does not such a thing as this sow the seeds of Red Republicanism and Socialism in the hearts of the people? Agrarianism, Fourierism, Socialism—there are some grains of truth scattered through these theories, after all: they are a wild protest of the people against oppression and starvation. The country, say they, is filled with abundance, the fruit of our hard labors;—must there not be something wrong in the state, something wrong in human society, when a few grasp it all,—grasp more than they can use—grasp to waste—while we are ground down into the dust by poverty and anxiety? Let all work—that is right; but let work have sufficient wages. While horses are luxuriously stabled, and fed to fatness; and dogs are kennelled, and live on butcher's meat; why may not human beings be clothed and fed, and have a comfortable place to sleep in? Is this God's decree, or is it man's abuse? Now when men talk so under the shadow of Versailles, it will not do to laugh at them; and when they become, too, turbulent, to answer them with bullets and bayonets. *Feeling is the naked truth;* hunger and nakedness are something which men feel. Do not expect these rude masses to reason; they can only feel. Oh, ye statesmen and rulers! ye are the men to reason, when the people thus feel.

XVIII.

The University—The Sorbonne—The College of France—The Institute of France.

THE University of France must not be confounded with the University of Paris. The first relates to the great system of Public Instruction established by Napoleon, and is distributed into three grades: *Instruction Supérieure*, comprising the faculties; *Instruction Secondaire*, comprising Lyceums and Communal Colleges; and *Instruction Primaire*, comprising elementary schools. The University of Paris is the ancient University founded in the twelfth century.

The Sorbonne is the title given to a theological school founded by Robert de Sorbonne, an ecclesiastic of the thirteenth century. The Sorbonne and the University are now really one institution, included in the *Académie Universitaire* of Paris. In the buildings of the Sorbonne the three faculties of Theology, Science, and Letters, deliver their lectures.

The Faculty of Law is established at the *Ecole de Droit*, Place de Pantheon. The Faculty of Medicine is established at the Place de l'Ecole de Médicine.

Lectures on Mineralogy are given at the *Ecole des Mines*. Lectures on Botany, Zoology, and Comparative Physiology, at the *Jardin des Plantes*.

The Faculty of Science is composed of eighteen professors; the Faculty of Letters, eighteen professors also; the Faculty of Law, seventeen professors, and eight assistant professors; the Faculty of Medicine twenty-six professors. The exact number of Theological professors I have not ascertained.

There are three thousand students who attend the lectures of the Faculty of Medicine; about the same number attend the lectures of the Faculty of Law; and fifteen hundred attend the lectures of the Faculty of Science. To these are to be added the students under the Faculties of Theology and of Letters.

The *Collége National de France,* founded by Francis I., is in its character a University, also, where twenty-eight professors give public and gratuitous lectures in almost every department of learning. No enumeration can here be attempted of the number of students, for the doors of the lecture-room are thrown open to all who please to attend.

The *Musée National d'Histoire Naturelle* in the Jardin des Plantes, again is, virtually, a University organization, where fifteen professors lecture on the various subjects of Natural History.

The *Ecole des Beaux Arts* consists of two departments;—painting and sculpture, and architcture. .Twenty professors deliver lectures gratuitously on the whole range of subjects connected with the arts. Annual prizes are distributed. The highest prizes confer the privilege of studying at Rome at the expense of the state, and of passing four months at Athens. There is a very extensive collection of works of art connected with the school. To this the public are admitted on certain days. I of course availed myself of the privilege.

The *Conservatoire des Arts et Métiers* is an institution designed for manufacturers, mechanics, agriculturists, and indeed for every branch of industry. Here are fourteen professorships.

The *Ecole Normale* educates young men who propose to become candidates for professorships.

Many other special schools might be named. My object in naming the above is to give to those who have not made themselves acquainted with the system of education in Paris some conception of the preparations here made for every branch of learning.

The *Institut de France* is a society of learned men, who are not associated for the purpose of giving instruction, but for the purpose of advancing every department of learning by original investigations, by the publication of discoveries, and by correspondence with learned societies, and learned men in other countries.

It is distributed into five academies: the *Académie Français*, consisting of forty members; the *Académie des Inscriptions et Belles-Lettres*, consisting of forty members; the

Académie des Sciences, consisting of sixty-five members; the *Académie des Beaux Arts*, consisting of forty-one members; and the *Académie des Sciences Morales et Politiques*, consisting of thirty members.

The members receive a salary of fifteen hundred francs each, and the secretaries of six thousand francs each.

Paris has more than a million of inhabitants. An immense congregation, this, of human beings. To control these there is first, the power of the law executed by a well-organized police. And then there is in human beings a sense of duty—the force of religious obligation which is more powerful than all. Those whom God and the conscience really govern, the state need not govern. But there is a good conduct induced by cultivation simply, appearing in the control which a sound and enlightened judgment, a sense of propriety, a pride of character and position, a conviction of the necessity of obedience to law and the rules of morality in order to secure the common weal, exercise over human beings in all the relations of life. On the one hand, if the police were the sole power to be relied upon, they would be impotent to control such a combination of physical strength, cunning, audacity, and savage ferociousness as the multitudes of Paris would present. On the other hand, if religious and moral principle were relied upon, it would be found to permeate so small a number as to be quite inadequate to secure public order. But this third element—the result of education, of civilization, is the great source of strength and safety in the present imperfect condition of human society. The farther the influence of pure religion extends the more secure and happy a state becomes. A divine government—a moral self-government, go to supersede the necessity of all other government. But even religious and moral culture would direct and appropriate, and by no means dispense with, the power found in education and refinement.

Take the highest forms of education, first, as an illustration of the regulating power found here. All perceive, at once, that men of science and letters, and artists, and mechanicians, as the direct effect of their intellectual cultivation must be men of order and propriety. They can judge of society as an organism, a work of art, or a machinery, and through their most familiar ideas see all the necessities of law and order. Then cultivation necessarily begets a love of order and decency, and society is regulated by a sense of tasteful proprieties. The same faculties and tastes which would pry into the laws and harmonies of nature, which would make discourses upon philosophy, which in art would make statues and build temples, which in letters would write poems, which in the public improvements would open streets, make roads, institute commerce, agriculture, and the useful arts—in fine, the same faculties and tastes which would elevate and improve our human condition, would, evidently, go, on similar principles, to institute and enforce good laws, and be in themselves a power of social order and harmony. The Greeks and Romans had very little in their religion calculated to build up moral and social order. But they had manly judgments of propriety, they had clear perceptions of social necessities, they had artistic tastes which could not but pervade every thing, and thus their society grew up and was sustained.

When great institutions of learning, and learned societies, and schools of art, and large libraries, and collections in natural history, and models and works of art are all brought to exist together as in Paris, there is a public taste and determination necessarily produced in the direction of learning and arts and social refinement. It appears in the number of youth who are drawn to seek intellectual and artistic cultivation; in the rank and influence naturally attained by authors and artists; in the general intelligence, refinement and literary spirit diffused through society, and strongly expressed in the higher circles, so that education becomes a necessary qualification of rank and high-breeding; in the absence of grossness even in folly and vice, so that pleasure and dissipation lose the form of debauch and hide themselves under the aspect of epicurean art; in the dress, equipages, fashions, modes and manners of the higher classes; nay, it appears in all classes—the whole people are cultivated in different degrees, exhibit a certain refinement and elegance, and are brought to observe tasteful proprieties, and come under restraints, which if not moral, still have a moral result by preventing public indecencies and disorders.

That there are rough and fierce degrees of society in Paris, that there are violent elements in Parisian character, is evident enough when a coup d'état or a revolution takes place, and men pile up the barricades. Then what does the power of the police amount to? Even the soldiery have been swept away. But this vast populace, ordinarily, is composed, and Paris is the seat of elegance and pleasure. Religious restraints certainly are, here, very weak. The power which ordinarily holds them, guides them, and thus preserves the public weal, is a law of order springing out of that cultivation which is carried to such high perfection in large numbers of the citizens, and which sends its waves through every grade of society. Paris is governed by an æsthetical conscience.

The people in the public gardens, on the public promenades, in the presence of beautiful buildings and monuments, in the Louvre, in the Bibliothèque Nationale, in the Pantheon, the Madeleine, the Jardin des Plantes, amid all those objects of taste which meet their eyes every day, in all those institutions of a higher cultivation which they may visit at least, and from whose privileges they are not debarred, gain one form of character, a common taste, and come under the control of the same law.

Now, these are important facts, and are not to be neglected by any great city whatever. As a citizen of New-York, I cannot avoid applying them to our condition. We are hastening on to the magnitude of Paris. We bid fair to reach even the magnitude of London. It is not given to us to see where the limits of our growth shall be drawn. We are filling up with a promiscuous population from all nations of the world.

To secure public decency and order, we shall need every appliance possible. It has been sufficiently demonstrated that a police cannot be a sole reliance in any great city; and in our city far less than in any other, since the city magistracy are elected by the people. We are trying the power of common school education, and the restraints of morality and religion. These we cannot press too far. These influences are unquestionably paramount and mighty. But the principle of education, and the laws of religion and morality, all enjoin the multiplication of the means of cultivation, so that man, created after the image of God, may cultivate powers and tastes which were not given to lie dormant, and experience the force of laws lying in every part of his being, and reach a development in which all the lines of his heavenly original may appear. Man was designed to be governed by the laws of the state as well as the laws of God: this all will admit. But on the same principle, he was designed to be governed by the laws of taste, propriety and elegance, as well as by moral laws. A good citizen, he is not the less a good Christian. A man of taste, he is not the less a man of virtue. Indeed, all the various laws of our being go mutually to sustain each other. Hence, a good citizen will be the better Christian; a man of taste, a man of purer virtue; and religion and morality properly carried out will demand all the excellencies which belong to our proper humanity.

But the point which I designed here chiefly to bring under consideration is one of mere necessity and prudence. Men congregated in a large city are exposed to more corrupting influences than when scattered through the country, and are tempted by greater opportunities of crime. They will therefore tend to become more ferocious and ungovernable. Mob power and violence, exhibiting as it does the worst features of human nature, belongs to great cities. Hence we need here more powerful influences of civilization and refinement: we need art and culture like a constant presence—breathing in the air, beaming in the sunlight. New-York will need in a still higher degree than Paris the humanizing, softening, genial, and subduing power which is found in great institutions of learning and art. It is far easier to mould one people, than a congregation of peoples, tongues and languages like that which constitutes our population. New-York must have an æsthetical conscience, also. It will be a great and difficult work to create it.

Among our population may be found three classes: Those who are governed merely by the spirit of gain—the inordinate and insatiable passion for accumulation; those who are straining after splendor and display without being permeated by just ideas of taste, and without having attained to any high cultivation; and that promiscuous multitude where all the elements of humanity are thrown wildly together.

How large a proportion of our population is embraced by these classes I shall not take upon me to estimate, or even conjecture. Let every one judge for himself. Enough, however, will be apparent to every reflecting person to convince him that there is more for us to imitate in Paris than Paris fashions.

There is probably no place in the world where an individual bent on culture would enjoy equal opportunities. A man of principle can as easily avoid temptations in Paris as in any other great city; and the invitations to study in every department of learning are so strong, and are enforced by such splendid examples, that it would appear easy to think of Paris as containing the haunts of Plato, and the studio of Phidias, rather than obscene mysteries and the orgies of Bacchus.

There is an individual in Paris who forms one of these splendid examples whom I felt desirous of seeing. I had on several occasions received friendly messages from him, and I had long felt so strong an admiration for his genius, and so genial a sympathy with the spirit of his writings, that I did not look upon myself as utterly a stranger to him. I refer to M. Victor Cousin. At the season I was in Paris it was vacation in the University, and the literary men were scattered, some travelling, and some in country retreats about Paris. I inquired for M. Cousin, but he too was gone, and I could not find out the place of his retreat. After I had been in Paris a fortnight, I sent a note to his rooms at the Sorbonne at a venture. In a few days he called on me. Unfortunately, I was out; but he left his card, and wrote on it an appointment to meet at the Sorbonne.

M. de Tocqueville had informed me that he conversed only in French. My own powers of French conversation being limited, I took my young daughter with me to act as an interpreter. I drove to the Sorbonne, and sent up my name. M. Cousin received us in the anteroom in a most cordial manner. I told him I had brought my daughter to help us in our conversation. He appeared delighted with the contrivance; seated us in two chairs in his library side by side, and took another in front of us, and, grasping my hands between his, began to talk in that agreeable manner which is native to the French, and which in him has received all the grace of the highest cultivation. I understood his French generally well enough, and he appeared to understand my English, for each talked in his own language, and when any misunderstanding occurred on either side, my daughter made the way smooth again. He has a large and admirably selected library, comprising the choice literature of different languages. The philosophical department is ample. Among the rest, I found here quite a full collection of American authors on philosophical subjects.

M. Cousin may be about sixty years of age, but he has all the vigor and vivacity of middle life. His head is sprinkled with gray, as if his crown of glory were beginning to form: his eye is bright and expressive: the cast of his features exceedingly fine, indicating thought, refinement, and great kindliness of disposition. He is remarkable for his powers of conversation. His habit of lecturing extempore, united to his careful cultivation of style as a writer, has given his conversation a certain loftiness and elegance of diction, while it flows on as easily as if he were talking in the most careless way, and on the most trivial subjects. He conducted us through his library, which fills one large and two smaller rooms.

He appeared to anticipate political difficulties, and spoke playfully, and yet, perhaps, half in earnest, of being compelled to go to America. "But," said he, smiling, "how could I leave my books? These are my wife and daughter."

"Oh," replied my daughter, "my father will share his library with you." At this his eye kindled, and he smiled with a grateful expression; he seemed touched with the enthusiasm of a young heart.

I spent about two hours with him. I saw him once more when he called to bid me good-bye, before I left for America,

Ordinary readers experience a feeling of repulsion, if not of horror, when French philosophers are spoken of. Their thoughts are prone to recur to Voltaire—once the great master of French philosophers—and to his infidel doctrines. When thinking of Voltaire and his associates, we ought always to temper our abhorrence by the recollection that they were really engaged in a conflict with a corrupted and tyrannical church, and that their opposition to Christianity was more incidental than direct, and carried on under an almost total ignorance of the Gospel of Christ, and the writings of his apostles. But it is true that there has been a great deal of false and dangerous philosophy in France.

M. Cousin belongs to a very different school from the old French philosophers. He has arrayed himself on the side of Christianity and morality.

This is not the place for philosophical criticism, a thing that can be well done only when fully and thoroughly done. But the spirit of this man is genial to the system he has cultivated. He is eclectic; he proposes to examine all philosophies, to disintegrate the truths, to eliminate the errors, and to bring together all truth, wherever found, into one harmonious system. He is not, therefore, to be awed by authority, nor to be swayed by bigotry. Of course, he must find some standard of criticism, or he cannot carry on his process of eclecticism. And it is just here that his philosophy puts on a positive aspect. The last authority is the reason itself in its spontaneous, necessary, absolute development. He, therefore, separates himself from the sensual school of the former French philosophers utterly, and takes his resting-place in the region of the spiritual—the Divine,

At the close of the first lecture of his *Introduction to the History of Philosophy*, delivered nearly a quarter of a century ago, there is the following beautiful passage, which expresses very decisively the character of his aims and researches:

"Young men, you who propose to attend these lectures, love every thing that is good, every thing that is beautiful, every thing that is honest; for this is the foundation of all philosophy. Adding itself to every thing, philosophy communicates to every thing its own form; it destroys nothing. Follow the general movement of physical sciences and the arts; contemplate the instructive spectacle of human intelligence and freedom advancing day by day, to the conquest and dominion of the sensible world; study the laws of our great country; drink in, at the source of arts and letters, enthusiasm for all that is beautiful; nourished at the bosom of Christianity, prepared by her noble instructions for philosophy, and having thus reached the full accomplishment of your earlier studies, you will find, in true philosophy, together with the understanding and explanation of all things, a peace elevated and unchangeable."

XIX.

From Paris to Havre—Homeward Bound.

THE route from Paris to Havre—a distance of about one hundred and thirty miles—embraces a very interesting country. Taking it leisurely in a private carriage, a traveller might find great entertainment in examining the remains of old ecclesiastical edifices in Normandy. At Rouen one ought to stop, if it were only for the purpose of examining the cathedral. We had laid our plans to spend two or three days there; but, at the last, circumstances made it necessary for us to hasten on. We, however, caught a very good view of the old city and the cathedral with its beautiful spires.

Many parts of the country through which we passed were very pleasing and even picturesque. Sometimes we were on the bank of the Seine, and then we shot away again, for no railroad will consent to follow its sinuosities.

The night had set in when we arrived at Havre. An omnibus took us up with our luggage. We ordered the coachman to set us down at the Frascati. It appeared an interminable drive. We soon perceived there was a contrivance on foot to divert us from the Frascati. There was an excuse made for stopping at several other hotels, and we were assured again and again that the Frascati was shut up for the season, inasmuch as it was a mere watering-place. The courtesies were overacted, and we persisted in our first determination. Finally we arrived at the Frascati, and the summer visitors being gone we had our choice of rooms.

From the windows we caught a dim view of the Atlantic, and all night we heard the murmurs of its waves, which seemed to us like "sounds from home." There our path lay, and we had only to step on board the steamer, put out from the shore, and endure or enjoy a few days, as the case might be, and then we would be sailing up the harbor of New-York, and see again the old familiar objects. A few months before, we were dreaming of the Old World, now, we were dreaming of the New: we had taken our step one way, now we were about to step back again.

Our emotions were naturally of a mixed character. We had not been long enough absent to grow tired of travelling. On the contrary, we had only increased our taste for it. Many beautiful parts of Europe remained to be seen. And we said to ourselves, When shall we come back again? Then, on the other hand, it was pleasant to anticipate meeting with those from whom we had parted months ago, and sitting down in our own home, to collect our thoughts quietly, and live over again, in happy talk, the scenes we had gone through. We felt deeply grateful, too, to that kind Providence which had protected and blessed us; and we looked forward with hope to a prosperous voyage home.

That we should at this very moment be calculating upon future travels through Europe will not appear strange to those who have been abroad; for Europe embraces the most beautiful parts of the world, is full of every thing to gratify taste, to nourish thought, and to revive one's interest in all that he has been reading about from his first reading years; and, therefore, those who like ourselves have as yet only made a step there and back again, will hardly rest content until they have returned to complete what is both a rational study, and an exquisite enjoyment.

In the morning the town of Havre was revealed to us, our own locality outside of the town upon the sea-shore, and the good steamer Franklin in which we were to sail home. It was Sunday. We attended church in the Americans' Seaman's Chapel, where we heard a good sermon from an American preacher, in tones that sounded like echoes from the hills of New-England.

The two following days were employed in making those little arrangements which all are familiar with who have made a sea voyage, and in seeing what was to be seen in Havre.

In general, not much is to be seen in Havre. There occurred, however, while we were there, an Annual Fair, like those which once were common in Europe, but which now have almost passed away. It appeared to me like a waif of the past, like an old tale acted out, and interested me exceedingly.

It was held in an open space just in the suburbs. The booths were arranged in long lines so as to form streets. It had the appearance of a little town. Every imaginable article was offered for sale. The goods were generally of a coarse description, and evidently intended for the common people. Before some of the booths the trader was standing and holding forth on the excellencies of his commodities, and offering them for sale. Of a man who had prints for sale, I purchased a view of the Staubbach, and of a woman who sold fruit I bought some fine ripe pears. And these were the amount of my purchases.

In the evening a curious scene was presented. On one side of the encampment was a street appropriated to shows of various kinds. Before one sat a stout elderly man with a grizzly beard, who had grown hoarse with his vociferations. His exhibition professed to be of a scientific character, consisting of various wonderful phenomena. Before another, which was labelled a Museum of Natural History, a man was describing the curiosities it contained with a wonderful fluency of diction; but I soon found that his oration uniformly pursued one stream of thought and language, and that he ended where he began, and began where he ended. Before another a stage was erected, on which stood a man with a speaking-trumpet, and surrounded by a dozen boys in grotesque masks. The boys were making strange antics, while he from his trumpet poured forth an oration whose thundering intonations were intended to drown the efforts of all his competitors. Before another, on a similar stage, was a troop of dancing-boys, and a man dressed in petticoats enacting the part of a female clown. Here, too, was an orator.

This outside parade was intended to attract persons to the inside shows and performances. The street was filled with men and women of the lower classes. All was good-humor among them. There was no quarrelling or indecency. No strong drinks were any where offered for sale. But at many places women were sitting frying cakes, which seemed to be in great request.

Finally my friend and I concluded to enter one of the show booths to see what was going on. What the exhibition was to be we could not exactly make out: it professed to be something about Christianity and Heathenism, and therefore offered some extraordinary attraction. We were ushered into a place of considerable extent, where seats were arranged, and a stage with machinery and scenic decorations prepared similar to a theatre. We were seated in a sort of parquette, where there were only a few persons besides ourselves. Behind were ruder seats where the multitude were collected. On the stage there was an exhibition of gymnastics and tumbling going on.

After this, a pantomime was acted. A beautiful boy of about fifteen, and two pretty little girls of ten or twelve years of age came on the stage. There was a heathen altar before which the girls worshipped, and on which they threw votive offerings of flowers.

The boy represented the Christian hero; he interposed: one of the girls became a convert; the altar was thrown down and the cross erected.

Then, borne on the shoulders of four boys, there appeared coming down a wild pass in the mountains, a grim-looking fellow, with a beard and moustache. He represented the

Heathen hero. When he saw the cross, he rushed forward in indignation, and tore it down. Then follows a battle, in which the Heathen is disarmed. But in the confusion, he succeeds in piercing the bosom of the beautiful convert, who falls down and dies, preserving her cheeks as red as roses. The Christian hero, in pantomime, laments over her. Then, suddenly, a lurid light breaks out, devils rush upon the stage, the stage opens, flames burst up, and they drag the Heathen down to the bottomless pit.

The Christian hero now lifts up the dead body, and lays it carefully upon a ledge of rocks, which, however, shake and look very much like pasteboard. Then he plants a cross beside her, which her hand contrives to hold up. Suddenly a heavenly light breaks out, the dead comes to life, the heavens open, Christ and the angels appear above—all looking very much like pasteboard—and the beautiful saint, smiling rapturously, ascends higher and higher, until the curtain falls, and renders any further ascent unnecessary. The crowd were thrown into perfect raptures. The exhibition closed with some very good dissolving views. The manager, before each performance, appeared on the stage and made a speech, setting forth what he was about to exhibit. He was quaintly dressed. His face was very bad, but very expressive. He showed plainly enough that he was master of his trade. But I pitied the poor girls and boys whose master he was also. The pantomime being of a religious character, reminded me of the Mysteries which, in past ages, were exhibited in churches. When we came out into the street, the orators there were still holding forth, the man with the grizzly beard was hoarser than ever, and the women were frying the cakes as fast as they could, to meet the constant applications of the merry crowd.

Tuesday evening we went on board the Franklin. Early on the following morning we got out to sea. Just as we sat down to dinner we entered the harbor of Cowes. The Isle of Wight was still verdant, but instead of the bright sun of June, there was the hazy atmosphere of October fast running into November.

The same evening we got out to sea again. We had a large number of passengers. The voyage was a prosperous one. And, but for losing a poor fellow overboard the day before we arrived, was attended with no unpleasant circumstances. Every effort was made to save him, but in vain.

We arrived at noon, on Sunday. As we drove home, the people were coming out of church. The other day we were in Paris, and here we were in New-York again. Every object looked just as we had left it. We almost doubted whether we had been away. Then, when we drove up to our own door, I touched the bell-handle with a trembling hand. Are all well? Has nothing happened? The door opens—all are well. Here is my library; here is the chair in which I am wont to sit. It is the old, pleasant home still. We have stepped back again.

THE END.

Enlightened and Pleasurable Reading for all Classes of People.

APPLETONS'

POPULAR LIBRARY OF THE BEST AUTHORS.

MESSRS. APPLETON announce to the Public the issue of a new series of books, attractive in form, and of permanent value and entertainment, intended, in subject and convenience, for the widest popular circulation.

They will be cheap in price, some twenty-five per cent. less than books of their class and elegant execution have been generally published at; but, it is to be understood, that while a desirable cheapness will be preserved, it will not be at the expense of the reader, and of his enjoyment of good taste and fine paper, clear type, and accurate proof-reading. The price will be graduated to the size of the book (not cutting down the book to the price), and when it is desirable to reprint a less known work, to a just remuneration for the edition. The design is to establish a *permanent classical series of the best literature in each department.*

It is the aim of the Popular Library to furnish books of various kinds, and the best of each, of an entertaining and profitable character for general reading, to supply for the delight of all the most agreeable and suggestive authors in narrative, adventure, invention, poetry, sentiment, wit, and humor.

Books will be presented, which, in the words of a great author, "quicken the intelligence of youth, delight age, decorate prosperity, shelter and solace us in adversity, bring enjoyment at home, befriend us out of doors, pass the night with us, travel with us, go into the country with us."

The earl est issues of this series will comprise complete and independent works bv the following among other authors—

THACKERAY (the author of "Vanity Fair"), the late ROBERT SOUTHEY, JOHN FORSTER, SIR HUMPHREY DAVY, JOHN WILSON ("Christopher North" of Blackwood), WALTER SAVAGE LANDOR, the Writers for the LONDON TIMES, the leading QUARTERLY REVIEWS, LEIGH HUNT, the late WILLIAM HAZLITT, the authors of the "Rejected Addresses," BARHAM (author of the "Ingoldsby Legends"), SIR FRANCIS HEAD, JAMES MONTGOMERY, &c., &c., comprising generally the most brilliant authors of the Nineteenth Century.

APPLETONS' POPULAR LIBRARY will be printed uniformly in a very elegant and convenient 16mo. form, in volumes of from 250 to 400 pages each, from new type and on superior paper, and will be *bound* in a novel and attractive style for preservation, in fancy cloth, and will be sold at the average price of fifty cents per volume.

The following books, indicating the variety of the series, are preparing for immediate publication; and orders of the Trade are solicited:—

ESSAYS: A SERIES OF PERSONAL AND HISTORICAL SKETCHES FROM THE LONDON TIMES.

LIFE AND MISCELLANIES OF THEODORE HOOK.

JOHN FORSTER'S LIFE OF GOLDSMITH.

THE YELLOWPLUSH PAPERS AND OTHER VOLUMES, BY WILLIAM M. THACKERAY, AUTHOR OF "VANITY FAIR."

JEREMY TAYLOR; A BIOGRAPHY, BY ROBERT ARIS WILLMOTT.

LEIGH HUNT'S BOOK FOR A CORNER.

THE MISCELLANEOUS WRITINGS OF JAMES AND HORACE SMITH, THE AUTHORS OF THE "REJECTED ADDRESSES."

THE INGOLDSBY LEGENDS, BY BARHAM.

LITTLE PEDLINGTON AND THE PEDLINGTONIANS BY JOHN POOLE, AUTHOR OF "PAUL PRY."

&c., &c., &c.

APPLETONS' POPULAR LIBRARY.

ESSAYS FROM THE LONDON TIMES.

Price Fifty Cents.

Containing the following Papers:

LORD NELSON AND LADY HAMILTON.

RAILWAY NOVELS.

LOUIS PHILIPPE AND HIS FAMILY.

DRAMA OF THE FRENCH REVOLUTION.

HOWARD THE PHILANTHROPIST.

ROBERT SOUTHEY.

THE AMOURS OF DEAN SWIFT.

REMINISCENCES OF COLERIDGE AND SOUTHEY BY COTTLE.

JOHN KEATS.

SPORTING IN AFRICA.

FRANCIS CHANTREY.

ANCIENT EGYPT.

Brilliant original Essays, frequently displaying the neat humor of a Sydney Smith, the glowing narrative sweep of a Macaulay. These Essays exhibit a variety of treatment, and are models of their class. The sketch of the French Revolution of 1848, and the paper on the Amours of Dean Swift, are masterpieces in their different ways; the one as a forcibly painted picturesque panorama of startling events, the other as a subtle investigation of character. The story of Lord Nelson's Lady Hamilton is an example of pathos, where the interest grows out of a clear, firmly presented statement. The paper on Egypt is an admirable resumé of the results of Antiquarian study in a style at once learned and popular.

APPLETONS' POPULAR LIBRARY.

THE YELLOWPLUSH PAPERS.

BY W. M. THACKERAY.

Price Fifty Cents.

Contents.

MISS SHUM'S HUSBAND.
THE AMOURS OF MR. DEUCEACE.
SKIMMINGS FROM "THE DAIRY OF GEORGE IV."
FORING PARTS.
MR. DEUCEACE AT PARIS.
MR. YELLOWPLUSH'S AJEW.
EPISTLES TO THE LITERATI.

The Yellowplush Papers, a work at the foundation of Mr. Thackeray s fame as a writer, appeared in a London edition in 1841, collected from the pages of *Fraser's Magazine.* An imperfect collection, long since out of print, had previously been published in Philadelphia.

It is now revived, in connection with a number of the author's miscellaneous Writings, which will appear in due succession, for its speciality of thought and character, and its exhibition of those fruitful germs of sentiment and observation which have expanded into the pictures of modern society, read throughout the world, in the pages of "Vanity Fair" and "Pendennis." In its peculiar line the Yellowplush Papers have never been surpassed. The character is well preserved and unique as the spelling, which shows that there is a genius even for cacography, and a sentiment as well as a hearty laugh in a wrong combination of letters. It is impossible to resist the infelicity of Mr. Yellowplush. His humor, too, is a pretty serious test of the ways of the world, and profit, as well as amusement, may be got from his epistles, justifying the remark of an English critic, that "notwithstanding the bad spelling and mustard-colored unmentionables of Mr. Yellowplush, he is fifty times more of a gentleman than most of his masters."

www.ingramcontent.com/pod-product-compliance
Lightning Source LLC
LaVergne TN
LVHW020231110826
845151LV00003B/891